HEARTS' GREATEST
EVER SEASON
1957–58

To mark another great
50th Anniversary!

Happy Birthday, Colin
on your big 5-0!

All the best

Mike

HEARTS' GREATEST EVER SEASON 1957–58

The Fiftieth Anniversary Celebration

MIKE BUCKLE

BLACK & WHITE PUBLISHING

First published 2007
This revised and updated edition published 2008
by Black & White Publishing Ltd
29 Ocean Drive, Edinburgh EH6 6JL

1 3 5 7 9 10 8 6 4 2   08 09 10 11 12

ISBN: 978 1 84502 217 4

A CIP catalogue record for this book is available from the British Library.

Typeset by Ellipsis Books Limited, Glasgow
Printed and bound by MPG Books Limited, Bodmin, Cornwall

DEDICATION

This book is dedicated to all those who, since 1874, have been fortunate enough to have pulled on the famous maroon jersey of Heart of Midlothian Football Club.

ACKNOWLEDGEMENTS

Although I can claim that the championship-winning season was achieved during my lifetime, I cannot say that I was old enough to witness the event. However, with the help of others I have been able to produce this record of the season which I hope will give an insight to some younger supporters and bring back very happy memories for those fortunate enough to have seen the greatest Hearts team – ever.

Without wanting to sound like Gwyneth Paltrow on Oscar night, I would like to acknowledge the following for their help and support while I have been writing this book . . .

Firstly, all at Black & White Publishing, particularly Campbell, Patricia, Alison, Janne, Eddie and John.

For sourcing some of the illustrations I would like to thank Bill McLoughlin at D. C. Thomson, Hearts memorabilia collector extraordinaire Gary Cowan, the extremely talented Doug Ensom, Bill Geddes, Alan Davidson, Norrie Rush and John Kerr. Brian Johnstone at Almondvale Programmes for his help in sourcing programmes (at a reasonable price, of course). David Speed and Derek Brown for their help with hard-to-find 'reserve' team details. Similarly, both Tommy Foley Jnr and Gerry Quigley for helping with hard-to-find Billy Higgins in South Africa!

There are some people who never fail to amaze me with their encyclopaedic knowledge of football and their particular clubs, so I am indebted to John Davie (just about every club there is!), Peter Gilham (Brentford), John Northcutt (West Ham United) and Ralph Morris (Ipswich Town).

For agreeing to write the foreword I owe a great debt of gratitude to one of the few players I have seen play at Tynecastle who would not have been out of place in the great team of '57–58: Hearts legend John Robertson.

No acknowledgement in this book would be complete without mentioning all twenty-two players who took part in that marvellous season. I would, however, like to give special mention to Dave Mackay, Jimmy Murray, Gordon Marshall, Freddie Glidden, Alex Young, Danny Paton and Willie Lindores, plus the aforementioned Billy Higgins, all of whom have been very helpful and are true gentlemen in every sense of the word.

Finally, just like Gwyneth, I would like to thank my family, Ann and Bob, for ensuring that I had the proper upbringing as a Hearts supporter; and Kim for her encouragement and contacts within the media (who, by the way, are not as bad as some might make out).

CONTENTS

FOREWORD

by JOHN ROBERTSON

How do you start a foreword to a book about the most successful team that has ever worn a maroon jersey? A team that smashed every known record in Hearts' great history, on their way to securing the club's first title in sixty-one long years. Do we talk about the record number of goals scored (132)? Or maybe the fact that they only lost one league game during the season? Or the fact that they finished thirteen points ahead of their nearest rivals, Rangers?

This was a season of many stories of many players who etched their place not only in the history of Heart of Midlothian but in Scottish football itself. Every one a hero, every one a legend in the true meaning of the word.

It is this team that by adding the title to the League Cup win in 1954, and the Scottish Cup triumph of 1956, gave Hearts the proud history it has. Further League Cup wins and another championship ensured that Heart of Midlothian was entrenched as one of Scotland's great clubs.

The '57–58 championship team became the standard bearers for all those players who in future pulled on the maroon jersey. It was they who were part of the magical era that all Hearts fans yearn for once more and whose feats all players strive to emulate.

It would be wrong to single out names, as this was truly a unique team that swept all before them with a style and swagger that is unlikely to be seen again. I make no apology for my admiration and respect for every member of this team and, along with thousands of supporters, I salute their outstanding and incomparable contribution to the history of Heart of Midlothian FC.

INTRODUCTION

by DAVE MACKAY

Before the start of the 1957–58 season I had already experienced many landmark dates in my then short footballing career: 26 April 1952, the day I signed professional terms for the club; my debut in the famous maroon jersey for the senior side against Clyde on 7 November 1953; 23 October 1954 when I was part of the Hearts side that lifted the club's first trophy in many a year with a convincing 4–2 defeat of Motherwell in the League Cup final. Next, of course, came 21 April 1956 when Celtic were beaten and the Scottish Cup returned to Tynecastle after too long a gap. Away from Gorgie there was 26 May 1957 when I gained my first full international honour against Spain in the world-famous Bernabéu stadium.

All proud moments – but nothing to how I felt when Tommy Walker called me into his office on 8 August 1957 to tell me that I was to be captain of the club I had supported as a boy. It was a dream come true. I was to lead one of the finest sides in Scottish football, containing the legendary 'Terrible Trio' and Tynecastle stalwarts Tommy Mackenzie and Freddie Glidden. Plus, in Alex Young, Ian Crawford and Johnny Hamilton we had three of the finest exponents of 'wing play' in the game.

Despite the riches of talent, the previous season had ended trophy-less so the team started the 1957–58 season in determined mood – none more so than yours truly. However, little did I know when I led the side off at Rugby Park after losing to Kilmarnock on the opening day of the season that almost a year to the day later it would lead to my finest moment yet.

The date was Wednesday, 13 August 1958, the time 7.15 p.m. prior to a League Cup tie against Third Lanark. It was then that I had the great privilege to participate in the ceremony to unfurl the Scottish League Championship flag at Tynecastle for the first time in sixty-one years. It had been won in record-breaking style, playing a brand of football rarely seen before or, dare I say it, since.

This account of that remarkable season has brought back many happy memories for me. For those who stood on the Tynecastle terraces during those heady days, I hope that they also enjoy reliving the moments. For those less fortunate who were not around at the time, this book may only document one season in the long glorious history of the Heart of Midlothian Football Club but it is probably the finest season ever.

PROLOGUE

THE GENESIS OF THE GREATEST TEAM EVER

Though some say the Celtic and Rangers are grand,
The boys in Maroon are the best in the land.

So the song goes – and, according to the 'Glorious' DVD I have recently watched, 2005–06 was the 'best season ever in the history of Heart of Midlothian Football Club'. Mike Smith's eloquent description of the season in his book *Hearts: The Diary of an Incredible Season* confirms that I have indeed been privileged to see what was perhaps better described as an extraordinary season. However, it just cannot live up to what happened over fifty years earlier when the boys in maroon were indeed *the* best in the land.

Probably Hearts qualifying for the Champions League for the first time and then winning the Scottish Cup in the same season does add up to success for Hearts fans of a certain age, and I cannot deny that I am certainly one of them. I also had the good fortune to be in the company of my father at Celtic Park on that glorious day in May 1998, at the time I never thought that this could be eclipsed. Since then it has without doubt been something of a roller-coaster ride for everyone of a maroon persuasion, but as far as I am concerned nothing has.

I was born a Hearts supporter, thanks to the influence of both my dad, Bob, and grandfather, Jim. However, I am sure my mum, Ann, would claim some credit for being part of the process as well. Since then I have taken great pride in my heritage and because of both these men (and you, Mum) I have had what some (my bank manager for one) might consider an unhealthy interest in the teams of the past.

1

My grandfather was the first to take me to Tynecastle. As a good friend of Hearts legends John White and Tommy Walker, plus being one of the first agents for the Hearts Lottery, Jim Thallon did not find complimentary tickets hard to come by. I was the lucky recipient and was able to join him standing in the enclosure every second Saturday.

During that time grandad Thallon and his pal, whom I was only allowed to call 'Mr Carruthers' (who turned out to be Eric's dad), kept telling me what I was watching was a hopeless approximation to what had gone on only a couple of years before. I couldn't believe it. Here I was, watching a team that for the most part of the year were top of the league, and I was convinced that I would see the league flag at Tynecastle for the first time in my young life. Somehow I had come to believe that success was my right as a Hearts supporter, all thanks to the stories of past triumphs I was told by my dad and grandad.

I must admit my confidence did take a knock that season when at the end of February 1965 Dundee hit seven past my hero at the time, Jim Cruickshank. Even when that year's Scottish Cup campaign ended the next again week through in Motherwell, I convinced myself that Hearts would now be able to 'concentrate on the league'. I watched them go on an undefeated run from then until 24 April, until the last game of the season at home against Kilmarnock. The rest, as they say, is history.

Standing in the enclosure at 4.45 p.m. that day and watching Willie Waddell skip across the pitch, I was naturally disappointed but not despondent. After all, I had been brought up on the stories of two recent league successes, so surely it would be Hearts' time again soon? More importantly, surely I would never have the heartache of seeing the team I love lose the title on the last day of the season . . . would I?

Much has been written about the Russian Revolution at Chelsea and how success there is due in the main to the investment of Mr Abramovich. Similar comparison has been made with the arrival of Mr Romanov to Tynecastle, although the investment is not quite on the same scale. Despite the successes of his first season in charge, seeing Hearts wrestle the league title from the Old Firm is his prime aim, allegedly. This was last achieved over forty-six years ago and here again comparison can be made with Chelsea, as there was a gap of fifty years between their league championship wins.

It is perhaps best to reflect on what are quite rightly considered to be the 'golden days' of the club during the '50s. After standing in the enclosure back in 1964–65, when I went home at night I heard of the exploits of Conn, Bauld and Wardhaugh and how the likes of Wallace, Gordon and Traynor could never match them. I didn't understand. I was watching Willie, Alan and Tommy help Hearts bring the league title to Tynecastle wasn't I, so what made the old school better than them? Oh, the innocence of youth, because since then I have read every book available about the history of this great club and I now concede my dad and granddad might have had a point.

However, they never really spoke much about the championship-winning side of 1957–58, nor gave the achievement any real credit. Strangely, neither have any of the books I have read since. Even Albert Mackie's famous book *The Hearts*, published a year later in 1959 and described as 'a book for perfervid Scots and lovers of football everywhere' (no, I had no idea what perfervid meant either!), only devotes two pages to what was a truly remarkable season. The excellent *Gritty, Gallant, Glorious* by Norrie Price gives a more respectable four-page report, but to me neither provides an insight into how the title was achieved for the first time in sixty-one years.

This was 1957 and the Hearts had started winning trophies on a regular basis three years earlier when they won the League Cup, beating Motherwell on 23 October 1954. The Scottish Cup followed in 1956, but despite the team being runners-up in both the 1953–54 and 1956–57 seasons, the league flag had not been seen at Tynecastle since 1897.

The man at the helm for these triumphs was Hearts legend Tommy Walker, but we have to start the story with the architect of these successes, Davie McLean. It was McLean who was responsible for signing most of the team, including of course the 'Terrible Trio'. Perhaps, though, his shrewdest piece of business was to bring Tommy Walker back to Tynecastle in December 1948.

Walker had been a leading light with Hearts for fourteen years (354 appearances, 190 goals) before the temptation of £8,000 was enough to see him being allowed to leave Gorgie for Chelsea (that Stamford Bridge connection again). Tommy spent two years at the Bridge, where in that short time he became a firm favourite. Some readers may be familiar with the 'Farewell Souvenir' brochure that was issued by Chelsea when Mr McLean persuaded him to return north. A remarkable tribute for any player, let alone one who had only spent two seasons at a club. There again, Tommy was a remarkable man.

When he came back, his primary role was to be assistant to manager McLean although he did manage to make one final appearance at Tynecastle on 8 January 1949. Surprisingly he turned out at right-half, which probably contributed to his rather poor performance in a 1–0 defeat by Dundee.

After that, Tommy concentrated on learning the managerial game from McLean but he would have hoped for a longer apprenticeship before Edinburgh was stunned by the news of McLean's premature death on 14 February 1950. Walker was then appointed both club manager and secretary as Hearts were about to embark on the most successful period of their long and colourful history. So from the early '50s, a very good Hearts side entertained all of Scotland. Why, then, do I maintain that the class of '57–58 was by far the best?

I think it is generally agreed that winning the league is the greatest achievement for any. My dad would disagree. To this day he maintains the greatest moment for Hearts in his time was when they brought the League Cup back in 1954. His argument is that, because it was the first triumph after so many barren years, it set the marker for what was to follow. A good argument – but for the purposes of this book let's pretend he is wrong for once!

It was therefore magnificent that Hearts were at last able to fly the league flag again but for me what makes it more remarkable was the manner in which they did it. Bear in mind that stalwarts of the side were playing on a part-time basis. Jimmy Wardhaugh (journalist), Freddie Glidden (West Lothian Council), Alex Young (mining engineer at Burghlee colliery), Johnny Hamilton (miner at Woolmet colliery) and Gordon Marshall (apprentice joiner) were just a few of the players who worked nine to five and then trained in the evening.

Then there is the age of some of the team. I know that Alan Hansen would disagree, but the '57–58 side proved long before Manchester United that you can win things with youngsters. Gordon Marshall, for instance, was doing it long before Craig Gordon, having made his first-team debut at the tender age of seventeen in a friendly against Newcastle United.

Gordon had joined the club from junior side Dalkeith Thistle in August 1956, after Tommy Walker had spotted him playing for Balgreen Rovers against Edina Hearts at Saughton enclosure a month earlier. Back then Scottish football operated at juvenile, junior and senior levels. If Gordon had signed straight from his juvenile side and things had not worked out at Hearts, he would have been barred from playing junior football. A crazy rule indeed, but no stranger than the one that prevented him representing Scotland.

With his father in the Army and stationed in England, Gordon was born in Farnham, Surrey, but after only a few months the family headed back to Scotland. So despite spending his formative years in Edinburgh, where he attended Craiglockhart and Tynecastle schools, he was ineligible to represent Scotland. All the same, Gordon does claim to have been a Scottish international, for *five minutes*. After having played golf at Kilspindie one day, he returned to the clubhouse to be congratulated on being picked for a Scotland Under-23 squad. He was more aware of the rules than the SFA and had to get Tommy Walker to phone Park Gardens to inform them of his place of birth.

When he joined up at Tynecastle in 1956, Hearts only had one goalkeeper, Thomas Wilson Brown, on their books: veteran Jimmy Watters had left the club for East Fife and Willie Duff had been called up to do his national service with the King's Troop of the Royal Horse

Artillery in St John's Wood, London. After an injury to Wilson Brown, Gordon was to make his first-team debut against Kilmarnock at Tynecastle on 17 November that year. He stayed in the team for a further four games but, after losing five goals to a Rangers side that were eventually to go on and pip Hearts for the title, he was replaced by Wilson Brown for the next game.

Hearts remained in the hunt for the league with Brown between the sticks, until they came up against Kilmarnock at Rugby Park. Tragically for their title challenge, they went down 4–1 and Wilson Brown paid the price. Gordon took over for the remaining six games of the season but despite being on the losing side only once – but perhaps crucially the most important game of the season at home against Rangers – he could not help Hearts raise the league flag at Tynecastle.

Before the new season had even begun it looked like Gordon might be out of the picture at Tynecastle. He did not even rate a write-up in the 1957 handbook published by the club prior to the start of the new campaign. Willie Duff was still away on national service and turning out for Charlton at the time, but was still thought worthy of a pen picture, as was Wilson Brown. However, despite his tender years, Gordon started as the no. 1, only missing three games through injury during the season.

Another 'youngster' who stood out during the season was Alex Young who, despite playing in the Scottish Cup triumph two years earlier, was still a mere twenty-year-old. His first-team opportunities were obviously hampered by the 'King of Gorgie' – Willie Bauld – but a couple of troublesome injuries to Willie, plus Alex's ability to play in most forward positions, led to him being the only 'ever-present' of the league campaign.

Then there were guys like George Thomson, Jimmy Milne, Jimmy Murray and Andy Bowman who, despite limited first-team appearances in previous seasons, came in for more renowned stalwarts such as Tam McKenzie, Bobby Parker, Freddie Glidden and Alfie Conn. Throw in Bobby Blackwood, who only arrived back at Tynecastle mid season after serving his national service with the King's Own

Scottish Borderers in Malaya, and you are now starting to get an idea of how special the team and the achievement was.

Let's not forget that the wages then were nothing like the amounts being paid to the 'stars' of today. In fact it was still the age of 'wage capping' and £18 was as much as a footballer could aspire to. To supplement this meagre income, some of the first-team men also held down a job Monday to Friday.

Dave Mackay, in his book *The Real Mackay*, devotes only page 70 to the achievement, although he can be forgiven as he has so many other highlights to cover in his glittering career. I once mentioned this to Davie and his response was perhaps the most revealing thing I have heard said about the season. 'Son,' he said, 'we won so many things in those days it was just expected.' This sentiment has been echoed in conversations I have had with both Jimmy Murray and Gordon Marshall: the team feared no one, they had the mentality that they were just not going to lose, and for the most part they didn't.

The maroons won the league by a margin of thirteen points (when a win was only worth two), scoring a record number of goals (132) and losing only one game. The team only failed to find the net on one occasion, a disappointing 0–0 draw with Third Lanark in Glasgow.

With so many goals, I – like many others who are not old enough to have witnessed this great side in action – might have expected the 'Terrible Trio' to have bagged the lion's share. But no, only Jimmy Wardhaugh made a telling contribution with both Bauld and Conn missing many games through injury. In fact the trio never even played a league game together that season. Of the nine games Bauld played, he managed to score five goals and Conn notched four in his five games – still an impressive contribution by both. Alex Young and Jimmy Murray were the men who ended up as nos 2 and 3 in the scoring charts and, remarkably, both had started the season in the reserve side.

Everyone at the club contributed to the effort. Even the groundsmen should get special mention and the game against Queen of the South played at Tynecastle on 10 March highlights this perfectly. The match only went ahead after Mattie Chalmers and Willie Montgomerie had cleared the lines after a heavy snowfall at teatime. The pitch and terracing were still covered in snow when Hearts kicked off at 7.30 p.m. Unimaginable these days.

Another departure from today was that the team did not bother playing any pre-season friendlies. No, they played friendlies *during* the season. Midweek games against the likes of Bolton Wanderers, Norwich City, Manchester City and Newcastle United were played during the first half of the season. Nothing, though, was too great a challenge for this Hearts side. Even Scotland and the British Army were beaten in 1958.

While I am at it, I will add that while the first team were winning their league, the reserves were showing there was strength in depth by winning their league in impressive style and only losing narrowly to Aberdeen in the Reserve League Cup final.

This book attempts to describe just what it was like for players and fans alike when the league flag once again flew over Tynecastle. So let's look back over a season when the players were earning under £20 a week, you could read their autographs and there really was a 'flair' team in Edinburgh.

1

PRE-SEASON AND THE LEAGUE CUP

When the Hearts players reported back to Tynecastle for pre-season training on 14 July, a week after city rivals Hibs, trainer Johnny Harvey and his assistant Donald McLeod were there to greet the players. Both had attended Football Association courses in Wales during the summer and there they learned the latest techniques in coaching and training, something that Johnny Harvey was particularly interested in. So as well as viewing the construction work of the new concept of floodlights for the first time, the players were introduced to some interesting new limbering-up exercises. The whole squad (with the notable exceptions of Dave Mackay, Ian Crawford and Bobby Blackwood, who were still on national service duty, plus Jimmy Wardhaugh who had taken up a job in 'civvy street' during the summer) were put through their paces at Tynecastle.

Tommy Walker and Johnny Harvey both realised that fitness was the key to a good challenge for the honours. Had it not been for a few injuries the previous season, the league flag would almost certainly have been flying at Tynecastle for the first time since 1896–97. They had narrowly lost out on the title to Rangers, with only two points separating the sides. In fact Hearts had led the way from mid October until the end of April, but the injuries to Bauld and Conn in particular proved too much of a handicap. Poor results against teams that were to finish in the lower half of the league followed, as did disappointment.

On 19 January 1957 at Tynecastle they drew 2–2 against Ayr United, who went on to finish bottom of the league with only nineteen points from their thirty-four games. Two 1–1 draws against a Falkirk side that finished fifth-bottom did not help the cause. Perhaps the most damaging result to the title challenge was the 5–2 reverse at Tynecastle on 13 October 1956 against East Fife, who finished the season one place below Falkirk.

Failure against eventual winners Rangers also cost the side in both the league and the Scottish Cup. Despite a historic win against Celtic the previous season, the Jam Tarts' defence of the trophy only lasted one round. They were unlucky to get drawn against the 'Gers in their first game in the cup, but at least the game was to be played at Tynecastle. Home advantage did not count for much that day, however, as Hearts were well beaten 4–0, their worst reverse of the season.

Even the League Cup, the trophy that had ended the honours drought two years earlier, did not provide any comfort for the Gorgie faithful. Hearts had been drawn in the same section as Hibs and the first game of the season took place at Tynecastle on 11 August. Imagine the atmosphere in Gorgie Road at 4.45 p.m. that day after a crowd of 42,000 had witnessed a rampant Hearts side demolish the Hibees 6–1. Only four days later the euphoria had worn off slightly as a 2–1 reverse at Firhill saw the team come down to earth with a bump.

A 5–0 thumping of Falkirk in the next game raised the spirits and this was quickly followed by yet another comfortable win over Hibs at Easter Road. So when Partick Thistle visited Gorgie, hopes were high for a victory that would take the team into the knockout stages. The Jags, however, had other ideas and headed back to Glasgow with a point after securing a 2–2 draw. A 1–1 draw with Falkirk in the final fixture ensured that there would be no Jambo joy in the League Cup that season.

Johnny Harvey must have been happy with their fitness levels, as on Tuesday, 15 July he took the squad down to Gullane. Not, as you might imagine, to pound up and down the dunes (which would become a feature of pre-season in the Jock Wallace era), but for a round of golf. This was the first of many unusual 'outings' that the Hearts embarked upon before the season kicked off, obviously a product of the thinking brought back from Wales.

The following day, twelve of the squad got the chance to show off their skills in the annual Musselburgh Gala five-a-sides. Hearts fielded two teams in the event: Raith Rovers, mistaking the day of the event, had not sent a team. These days that would probably have incurred the wrath of the suits in Park Gardens but in 1957 it only took a few phone calls from manager Walker to raise the extra players required to enter Hearts 'B'.

Unfortunately the boys selected must have been a bit put out to have their evening interrupted at such short notice, as they made an early exit from the competition to rivals Hibs. Hearts 'A' fared better and made it all the way to the final, only to fall at the last hurdle to the same Hibs side that had accounted for the 'B' team.

The following day there was a chance to avenge the defeat when both teams took part in the annual Press Charities five-a-side tournament at Powderhall. Dave Mackay, Bobby Kirk, Jimmy Wardhaugh, Jimmy Murray and Johnny Hamilton represented Hearts – an attack-minded team indeed, especially when you consider there was no goalkeeper in the side! It was Dave Mackay who donned the yellow jersey and he performed well enough to see Hearts reach the final where they met old rivals Hibs. With the rain lashing down, Hearts took the lead through Johnny Hamilton. Hammy had been in great scoring form the whole night and had scored a hat-trick in the semi-final when the team saw off Dundee 5–0. Just before half time Hibs managed to hit back when Willie Ormond equalised. Ormond struck again midway through the second period when his neat lob beat Mackay. Beaten again by the Easter Road outfit.

A full week went by before normal training was interrupted – this time by a cricket match. On Thursday, 25 July a Hearts XI headed down to Stockbridge to take on the Grange. Unfortunately the crowd did not get to see opening bat Jimmy Wardhaugh strut his stuff, as the usual Edinburgh July weather prevented any play.

However, the whites were looked out once again on Monday, 29 July when the boys went to the Meadows to take on the mighty Edinburgh Public Parks XI. A large crowd turned out to watch the game and the princely sum of £10.12s was collected for charity. Perhaps not surprisingly, the game ended in a tie, each side scoring eighty-one runs. Hearts might have won it, but a promising last-wicket partnership between Tam Mackenzie and chairman (and cricket captain) Nicol Kilgour was ended when 'big Tam', going for the 'big hit', only succeeded in lobbing the ball back to Jimmy Morrison to be caught and bowled. Jimmy Wardhaugh gave a taste of what was to happen in the months to follow and finished Hearts' top scorer. His total of thirty-three runs was to eclipse his eventual goals tally by five. Even 'King Willie' was of no help with the bat and it was reported that 'he signed more autographs than scored runs'. He didn't do too badly as a wicket-keeper, though. For the Richie Benauds amongst us, the scorecard was:

Wardhaugh	b Scott	33
Murray	c and b Morrison	2
Milne	b Morrison	2
Higgins	b Lawrie	0
Howieson	b Morrison	8
McLeod	b Scott	0
Bauld	c Orde b Kennedy	7
Cumming	c Scott b Kennedy	6
J. Thomson	b Morrison	1
Mackenzie	c and b Morrison	11
Kilgour	not out	5
Extras		6
Total		**81**

The next day you would have thought that trainer Harvey would have had the team put in a hard session at Tynecastle. Far from it: the 30th had been chosen as the day of the Grace Allison Trophy, an annual golf match played along with the players and staff of Hibernian. It had been donated by Mrs Grace Allison to 'foster friendly rivalry between the clubs'. Mrs Allison was the wife of Mr W. S. Allison, the chairman of the Charities Day committee, who had also donated the eponymous trophy that was played for by an Edinburgh 'select' against English opposition.

This year the competition for Mrs Allison's trophy was played over the links at Longniddry and the Jam Tarts produced the winner in George Campbell. George was a reserve team forward who was in the middle of studying for a chemistry degree at Edinburgh University, so his brains were not entirely in his feet. A member at Dunbar Golf Club, George played off a handicap of ten and shot a net sixty-nine. This was good enough to pip Hibs' Eddie Turnbull and Hearts' Nicol Kilgour by a shot. However, the most remarkable scoring feat went to Hibs' left-half John Baxter, who managed to take 151 for seventeen holes. Totally demoralised, John did not hole-out at the eighteenth; it was not recorded how many strokes he had taken before he 'picked up'.

Thursday, 1 August saw the fifty-second Annual General Meeting of the shareholders take place in the Brown Gymnasium (now the players' lounge in the main stand) at Tynecastle. Despite the lack of success, the end-of-year accounts showed that at least the club had been able to make a profit. After deductions, such as £19 bank charges and a shareholders' dividend (*less* income tax) of £498, the club went into the new season with a healthy balance of £6,735 – a great financial starting-point for mounting a serious title challenge, at least – and although there was money to fund a few new faces, and even after the setbacks of the previous season, Tommy Walker was reported in the *Evening News* as being 'happy with the players available'.

After working on their fitness for the rest of the week, some of the players got the opportunity to take part in another annual event that took place on the Saturday. This time it was actually football related and was the Edinburgh Select charity match for the Allison Trophy. The English opposition to accept the challenge this year was Preston North End, whose side included one Tommy Docherty and England legend Tom Finney. Bobby Kirk, Dave Mackay, Alex Young, Willie Bauld, Ian Crawford along with 'reserve' John Cumming, all made the short journey across town to Easter Road to take on the Lancashire side in the charity game.

EDINBURGH SELECT v PRESTON NORTH END

Before the game started there was some fine entertainment lined up for the large crowd that had turned out. They were regally entertained by the 4th Battalion of the Ugandan Rifles and the Corps of Drums of the 6th Battalion King's African Rifles. No sooner had the bands concluded their programme of music than more of the King's African Rifles took to the field in native costume. There then commenced a mock battle that, had Michael Caine witnessed it, his performance in *Zulu* some years later might have improved. After performing some tribal dances the real warriors made way for their footballing counterparts.

'Gay' Gordon Smith (no, it didn't have the same connotations then) and the 'Prince of Preston', Tom Finney, led out the teams. Preston got the game going and were soon into their stride with Jimmy Baxter and Tom Finney posing the biggest threat to the home defence. But after fifteen minutes it was Edinburgh who came the closest to opening the scoring, with a Hearts combination creating the chance. Ian Crawford crossed for Willie Bauld whose trademark head-flick found Gordon Smith. The shot looked net-bound until Tommy Docherty seemed to appear from nowhere to head clear.

It was developing into a fine game and five minutes later the Englishmen went one up. Former Falkirk man Sammy Taylor beat Dave Mackay out on the left, then passed inside to Tommy Thompson who supplied the ball that allowed Les Dagger to (dare I say it) stab a low shot into the net past Leslie. There was worse to come for the 'Select' when, seven minutes later, Preston went two up. Tom Finney swept the ball out to Dagger on the wing and from his cross there was Jimmy Baxter to head home. After he had got his head to the ball, the ex-Dunfermline player's momentum carried him into Leslie who then needed attention. With Leslie off the park, his place between the posts was taken by Hibs full-back George Muir and John Cumming came on as his replacement. After a couple of minutes Leslie was back in the fray and Muir returned to his left-back role. Trouble was, no one told John Cumming and for over a minute Edinburgh played with twelve men. They probably could have done with that number for longer, as they were finding it difficult to contain Preston. The eleven did, however, manage to hold out for the rest of the half but they had to survive a scare six minutes before the end when Tommy Thompson headed into the net, only to see his effort ruled out for offside.

The start of the second half saw John Cumming come back onto the field, this time as replacement for the concussed Leslie, and it only took two minute before he was picking the ball out of the net. John Plenderleith misjudged a long through-ball from Baxter and Thomson beat the substitute keeper easily.

The 'Select' were playing just like that, a disjointed select, while Preston were playing as a team. But there was a chance for Edinburgh to pull one back seven minutes into the half when an all-Hearts move saw Crawford supply the ball to Bauld who set up Alex Young only eight yards out. Unmarked and with only Fred Else to beat, his shot sailed well over. The move seemed to rejuvenate the 'Select' and they should have had a penalty on the hour mark when an Ian Crawford cross clearly struck Joe Walton on the hand. Referee Bowman thought otherwise and only awarded a corner. From the kick, Willie Bauld sent in a tremendous overhead kick only for Else to match his agility and bring off a magnificent one-handed save.

Two minutes later and there was yet another lucky escape from a corner for Preston. This time Walton used his head to clear the danger after Jimmy Harrower had sent in a flying header. The pressure eventually told in seventy-eight minutes when Dave Mackay got a consolation goal, hitting a splendid free kick into the top corner of the net.

Edinburgh Select: Leslie (Cumming), Kirk, Mair, Mackay, Plenderleith, Preston, Smith, Young, Bauld, Harrower and Crawford
Preston North End: Else, Cunningham, Walton, Docherty, Dunn, O'Farrell, Dagger, Thompson, Finney, Baxter and Taylor

While the charity game was taking place, Hearts had sent Jim McFadzean, Freddie Glidden, Johnny Hamilton, George Thomson and Jimmy Murray to Glasgow to take part in the annual Ibrox Sports Day. This time the Hearts emerged victorious in a five-a-side competition with Jim McFadzean grabbing a hat-trick and Freddie Glidden, who played in goals, the other goal after dribbling the length of the pitch. The 4–0 win in the final against the hosts brought the season's first trophy for the Tynecastle cabinet and it would be joined by a few others by the end of that season.

Another full week of training and the boys must have been yearning for a break, so on Monday a side was selected to play golf against the Earl of Roseberry's Estate at Dalmeny, played over the earl's private nine-hole course. His team got off to a winning start when he and his partner Dr G. Hughes, defeated chairman Kilgour and manager Walker. Not having any 'political' motives to worry about, Davie Mackay and Willie Bauld levelled things in the next match when they beat estate factor Simon Carruthers and ex-Hearts and now 'head forester' Sandy Brown. In the end a moral boosting victory of five matches to four was achieved by the Hearts and, after the match, as the *Evening News* reported, 'a fine outdoor meal was enjoyed by all'.

That put an end to all the pre-season special outings and things started to get slightly more serious. With the first game of the season looming, speculation was rife as to what the starting line-up was going to be.

In the League Cup section the Maroons had been drawn against Kilmarnock, Dundee and the amateurs of Queen's Park. Killie had finished in third place in the league only four months earlier so it was anticipated they would pose the strongest threat to winning the section. With the fixtures having thrown up an away tie at Rugby Park as the first game, it was vital that Hearts got off to a good start.

All week articles were written in the *Evening News* and *Evening Dispatch* debating the best line up for the game. Hard as it is to imagine now but there was talk that the 'Terrible Trio' had lost some of their sparkle and maybe it was time for a change. Alex Young was the main contender to force his way into the side. In the previous season he had deputised for Conn, Bauld and Wardhaugh at various times, he had also shared the no. 7 jersey with Johnny Hamilton throughout the season. In total he played in thirty-four games scoring seven goals but it was not just Alex who was causing Tommy Walker the headaches.

There were choices to be made further back as well: for instance, who should start in goal? Gordon Marshall had finished last season but had only just turned eighteen. Could he handle the pressure or was Thomas Wilson Brown a safer option? There were options in the back line too: Freddie Glidden was not free from the back and stomach trouble that had kept him out the side for the last few weeks of the previous season, but Jimmy Milne had done well as his deputy. However, another injury victim, Johnny Cumming, was ready for a return having fully recovered from being injured at Tynecastle against Falkirk on 23 February.

Finally on Thursday, 8 August the manager told the press that Marshall had got the nod in goals, Mackenzie and Cumming were back and Conn, Bauld and Wardhaugh would spearhead the attack with Hammy pulling on the no. 7 shirt. Wilson Brown, Jimmy Milne and Alex Young were to turn out for the reserves at Tynecastle. Finally, it was announced that Dave Mackay would be the new club captain.

KILMARNOCK v HEARTS

On 10 August a sizeable contingent paid ten shillings to travel on the football special that British Rail ran from Edinburgh. As it turned out, their ten bob would have been better spent on a few bottles of Jeffrey's Lager, 'the beer of quality', as they witnessed a poor start to the new season.

Things started well as Dave Mackay won the toss and Hearts got the new season under way but it was Kilmarnock who took the game to the visitors in the early stages. Dave Burns got the better of Bobby Kirk, then squared to the unmarked Gerry Mays who somehow contrived to put the ball wide. An early let-off, but Hearts did not heed the warning. Tom Mackenzie had to be at his best to thwart

Bertie Black and then Billy Muir in quick succession as Killie kept pressing.

Against the run of play Hearts got the first corner of the game but Ian Crawford's kick went behind before it could reach the middle – not a good start. He did better a few minutes later as he sent in a precision cross that allowed Alfie Conn to warm Jimmy Brown's fingers. Another corner resulted in Jimmy Wardhaugh incurring the wrath of the crowd when he was adjudged to have been too 'robust' in his challenge on the home keeper after Brown had dropped the high ball. The surprising thing was that it was not just the home support that took exception to Jimmy's challenge. After that moment Jimmy could do nothing right in the eyes of some who had made the trip from the capital. It clearly unsettled 'Twinkletoes', as his game suffered from then on.

Kilmarnock were giving as good as they got and Bill Harvey passed up a decent chance following a free kick from Mays. With twenty-two minutes gone the hosts should have taken the lead when Black found his way through the Tynecastle defence. Gordon Marshall came out to block the danger but the inside-left took the ball round the keeper, only to put his shot wide. The breakthrough did eventually arrive in the twenty-eighth minute when Mays flicked on a Willie Muir corner and there was Harvey to slip it beyond Marshall.

It was as if the goal had angered the footballing gods, for thunder and lightning began to roll and flash around Rugby Park. Sure enough the rain followed, coming down the moment Mr Wilson blew for the start of the second half. It didn't distract Hearts in their search for the equaliser as they went straight on the offensive. First Bauld and then Conn threatened Jimmy Brown's goalmouth but the goal just wouldn't come. Ian Crawford was next to try his luck but his pile driver was high, wide and not particularly handsome. Despite having applied all the second-half pressure, it was Hearts who fell further behind: in the sixty-third minute a simple move saw Davie Burns pass to Mays and the centre hit a perfectly placed shot that gave Gordon Marshall little chance.

Hearts were up against it if they were to salvage anything from the game, but try as they might they could not breach the Killie defence for the goal that would get them back into things. With only a minute left, Ian Crawford swung in yet another corner, perhaps mindful of what had happened earlier in the game, and with Wardhaugh in close attendance ex-Jam Tart Brown seemed to take his eye off the ball. It fell straight to the much-maligned Jimmy, an opportunity he did not waste. It was nothing more than a consolation, though, as no sooner had Kilmarnock restarted the game than referee Wilson blew the final whistle. Hearts could have no complaints about the defeat.

Hearts: *Marshall, Kirk, McKenzie, Mackay, Glidden, Cumming, Hamilton, Conn, Bauld, Wardhaugh and Crawford*

This was not the start to the season that Hearts had wanted, but back in Edinburgh the reserve team had done better and beaten their Kilmarnock counterparts 1–0. It took only six minutes for Alex Young to open the scoring when he took a neat pass from Jim McFadzean and former Hearts favourite Bobby Dougan couldn't prevent his crisp, low strike entering the net. Always on top, Hearts wasted a few good chances to increase their lead with Jimmy Murray being unlucky when he might have done better with a header when handily placed. Hugh Goldie was showing some neat touches and twice he tested Billy Neill in the Kilmarnock goal; but still the second goal remained elusive.

In the second half, the game continued in the same manner and a piece of magic from Goldie on the wing allowed Foley a free header, but once again Neill was equal to the task. Jim McFadzean and Andy Bowman both spurned opportunities to wrap up the game and in the end Alex's goal proved decisive – at least one Hearts side had got off to a winning start.

Hearts 'A': *Brown, J. Thomson, Lindores, Bowman, Milne, G. Thomson, Foley, Murray, Young, McFadzean and Goldie*

HEARTS v QUEEN'S PARK

For the next few days the Hearts were castigated in the press for their performance. Ian Thomas in the *Evening Dispatch* advocated wholesale changes with Kirk, Mackay, Cumming, Wardhaugh and Conn all for the chop. Despite the criticism and Mr Thomas's advice, Tommy Walker decided to name an unchanged team against Queen's Park on Wednesday, 14 August.

In his programme notes he wrote: 'The "Curtain" has been raised for yet another Season and on to the "stage" have come many teams all with but one thing in mind – to win an "Oscar". Obviously the Prizes are few being only Four in all, therefore, with thirty-seven Clubs praying and playing for just one of those coveted awards, you can well imagine that the "performances" should be keen and good.' He went on with further theatrical references until concluding: 'So, your favourite "actors" are on the "stage" not as individuals but as a team. You too are invited to become part of the team and who knows we may have cause for rejoicing two or eight months from now.' Unfortunately, only a few weeks later his hopes for success in the first competition of the season were 'Gone with the Wind' – but by the end of the season Hearts were definitely 'The Invincibles'.

A good crowd of just over 20,000 turned out to watch what 'Tron Kirk' in the *Evening News* was to describe as 'a magnificent display by the Terrible Trio'. A six-goal haul by the three had the correspondent telling his readers that Conn, Bauld and Wardhaugh were far from finished as a unit. He did, however, allude to the fact that the amateurs did not provide very good opposition: only James Ferguson in goal got pass marks and had it not been for his intervention on two notable occasions, the score would have reached double figures.

It was Queen's Park who had started the brighter, with a strike from Andrew McEwan testing Gordon Marshall (who took two attempts to gather the ball). The amateurs' good start did not last long and, from a pass by Alfie Conn, Willie Bauld opened the scoring after nine minutes. That seemed to settle the Jam Tarts as they proceeded to go to town and almost had the game won in the first twenty minutes, by which time they were three up. Jimmy Wardhaugh netted number two in the fifteenth minute, then was on the spot again five minutes later.

Surprisingly, despite Hearts' obvious superiority, the scoreline stayed that way until a minute from the break. That's when Queen's got themselves onto the scoresheet, if not exactly back into the game. They were awarded a penalty after John Cumming was adjudged to have handled the ball in the box and James Robb made an easy job of beating Gordon Marshall from the spot.

However, after the restart Hearts had doubled their tally in a four-minute spell. Alfie Conn got the first in the forty-ninth minute with a well-placed header and the cheers had hardly subsided before Johnny Hamilton went on a mazy run that ended with him slotting home number five. Two long minutes went by before it was 6–1, with Jimmy Wardhaugh completing his hat-trick after good work by Willie Bauld.

Now every home side forward had scored with the exception of Ian Crawford. That was the sign for Ian to stamp his mark on the game. Fine play by Jimmy Wardhaugh set him up in the sixty-ninth minute and it was 7–1. Queen's lost the ball straight from the kick-off and Crawford supplied a magnificent ball for 'King Willie' to bulge the net for a second time. It was Ian himself who rounded off the Hearts scoring with his second, thirteen minutes from time.

Andrew McEwan managed to nick another one for the amateurs before the end to complete the scoring for the night. But despite this hiccup, as the crowd streamed out onto McLeod Street they were understandably happy with the result. The pleasure was tempered slightly by the news that, up at Dens Park, Kilmarnock had defeated Dundee 3–0. So despite their scoring spree, Hearts were left second in the table.

Hearts: *Marshall, Kirk, Mackenzie, Mackay, Glidden, Cumming, Hamilton, Conn, Bauld, Wardhaugh and Crawford*

The 'A' team had also won but not just as handsomely as the firsts. The only change to the side was George Dobbie taking over from Jim Foley, who had not recovered from the knock he had taken against Kilmarnock. In the end they were far too good for the 'Strollers' and ran out comfortable 3–1 winners at Lesser Hampden.

The reserves had gone ahead in the first half when Alex Young supplied the ball that Jim McFadzean couldn't fail to put away. Although they were by far the better side in every department, Hearts allowed Queen's Park to snatch an equaliser when Wilson Brown was beaten by a Campbell free kick. In the second half there was no such slip-up and they regained the lead when McFadzean got his second after beating the home side's offside trap. George Dobbie rounded off a good all-round performance when he blasted the ball beyond William Pinkerton in the Queen's goal.

Hearts 'A': *Brown, J. Thomson, Lindores, Bowman, Milne, G. Thomson, Dobbie, Murray, Young, McFadzean and Goldie*

DUNDEE v HEARTS

To keep in the hunt, Hearts had obviously to win on their trip to Dens Park, so after their free-scoring display the previous Wednesday, Tommy Walker had no hesitation in naming an unchanged side once again. It was not an automatic decision, as Johnny Hamilton had given the manager a scare after picking up an ankle injury against the Spiders. Good work by Johnny Harvey on the Thursday and Friday ensured that the winger was able to pull on the no. 7 jersey, leaving Alex Young in the reserves once again.

Dundee had been basking in sunshine all day, until five minutes before the game's 3 p.m. kick-off, when the heavens opened. It soon became clear that the conditions would make it impossible for either side to play a passing game. Too often the ball would get stuck in the puddles of water that had formed on the pitch. Hearts did not find it easy and it took an unorthodox headed clearance by Tam

Mackenzie, when on his knees, to stop George Christie putting the dark blues in front.

Hearts created their first opportunity after seventeen minutes when Bill Brown dived to his right to keep out a shot from Alfie Conn. They had an even better chance seven minutes later when Johnny Hamilton sent in a tremendous delivery, only to see Ian Crawford balloon the ball over.

The rain continued to fall and for the last twenty minutes of the half it soaked the blue and maroon jerseys to such a state that it was almost impossible for the crowd to distinguish which side was which. Some players complained to referee McClintock that they were finding it difficult even to see the ball in these conditions. After the ref blew for the end of the half, he immediately went with his linesmen to inspect an area of the park near a corner flag that had become flooded with the rain.

After a twenty-minute interval and with it still raining cats and dogs (and they walking about in twos), no one was surprised when the referee decided that further play was impossible. The game was abandoned and a replay scheduled for the following Tuesday.

The 'drookit' Hearts were: Marshall, Kirk, Mackenzie, Mackay, Glidden, Thomson, Hamilton, Conn, Bauld, Wardhaugh and Crawford

The weather back in Edinburgh was not as bad as that endured by the first team, as the colts continued their winning start to the season. Straight from the kick-off they worked their way up the park and when Andy Bowman found Alex Young unmarked in the box there was only one outcome. Hearts were all over their opponents and might have gone two ahead when a clever Jimmy Murray overhead kick just skimmed the bar. Next to try his luck was Hugh Goldie, when he fired in an angular shot that hit the side netting.

It was one-way traffic and Dundee keeper Jim Ferguson did well when he managed to tip a rocket from Jim McFadzean over the bar. The Dens Park custodian then denied McFadzean (again) and Young in quick succession. But he could do nothing two minutes after the break, when Alex Young once again found a way past him. Alex then became goal provider when he passed to Jimmy Murray. With his back to goal, Jimmy put through a cheeky back heeler which caught the Dundee defence napping and Hearts were three up.

Dundee did show signs of resistance and Wilson Brown had to look lively to deal with a rasping shot from Clive Wallace. Despite this, it was Hearts who got the next goal, through who else but Alex Young. In sixty-three minutes Hugh Goldie sent one in from the wing and there was Alex to complete his hat-trick. He was not finished there and rounded off a great afternoon when he grabbed his fourth and Hearts' fifth, shortly before the end.

Hearts 'A': Brown, J. Thomson, Lindores, Bowman, Milne, Higgins, Dobbie, Murray, Young, McFadzean and Goldie

DUNDEE v HEARTS (REPLAY)

Thankfully the weather had improved by the time an unchanged Hearts side kicked off on 20 August. After a couple of early chances for both teams, it was Dundee who took the lead after only seven minutes when a shot from Jimmy Chalmers beat Gordon Marshall in the Hearts goal.

Although a setback, it did not deter the visitors who were showing a lot more endeavour than they had done during the abandoned game. Dundee's lead only lasted three minutes: Willie Bauld got Hearts back on level terms after Dens keeper Bill Brown spilled the ball right at Willie's feet. The game raged from end to end with the Hearts defence looking a little shaky. Perhaps it was just as well that Ian Crawford was giving Dundee defender Hugh Reid a torrid evening and Willie Bauld was benefiting from the wing man's service. It was Ian's tussle with Reid that led to the Dundee man handling the ball to concede a penalty midway through the half. Much to the surprise of the travelling support, Willie Bauld placed the ball on the spot. Strange as it may seem, this was Willie's first-ever attempt from the penalty spot but everyone in the crowd fully expected to see Hearts take the lead. It did not work out that way. Willie was too deliberate with the shot and Brown made an easy save. In all his time at Tynecastle Willie scored many goals but never one from a penalty; perhaps this weak effort explains why!

As the half drew to a close, Jimmy Wardhaugh was next to miss a golden opportunity to put Hearts in front when he shot over an unguarded net from only five yards out. An unbelievable miss, but Jimmy did manage to make amends almost on the half-time whistle when he stooped to nod the ball past Bill Brown after Dave Mackay had floated in a free kick.

Six minutes into the second half, Dundee scored an unusual equaliser although the goal scorer was not aware that he had done so until a few minutes after the event. As a through-ball came towards the Hearts goal, big Tam Mackenzie, who had not been at his best so far, attempted to clear the ball ten yards from goal. The on-rushing Alan Cousin had little opportunity to avoid the ball and it caught him full on the face. It was hard to determine who had the biggest look of shock on their face between Cousin and Gordon Marshall as the ball ricocheted into the net. Cousin needed lengthy attention from trainer Sammy Keane before he could continue.

Although the defence continued to struggle, the forwards created many good chances and only the fine work of Bill Brown kept the scores level. One save from Alfie Conn was straight out of the top drawer as the Hearts man had looked odds-on to put the Maroons back in front. Despite their best attempts, the winner would just not come and both sides had to settle for the draw that only suited Kilmarnock. Now Hearts had won one, drawn one and lost one while Kilmarnock were still unbeaten. It was beginning to look as though qualification was slipping away.

Hearts: Marshall, Kirk, Mackenzie, Mackay, Glidden, Cumming, Hamilton, Conn, Bauld, Wardhaugh and Crawford

All the talk down Gorgie way was about the form of Davie Mackay after a particularly poor display at Dundee. Questions were being asked if the captaincy of the side had maybe come too early: was the responsibility just too much for the youngster?

On Thursday, 22 August Tommy Walker announced that his side for the all-important game against Kilmarnock at Tynecastle would be chosen from fourteen. Along with the eleven that played at Dens Park, George Thomson, Jim McFadzean and (not surprisingly) Alex Young were brought into the reckoning.

Despite the shaky performance in the last game, the defence remained the same and on the day the only new face in the side was that of Alex Young. It was Alex's first start of the season and, like his debut for Hearts against Partick Thistle almost exactly two years earlier, it was to replace one of the 'Terrible Trio' – this time, Alfie Conn, who had an ankle injury.

Born in Loanhead, Alex always dreamed of playing for Hearts and, at the age of fifteen while he was playing for Broughton Star in the Edinburgh Juvenile League, he got the opportunity. Former player Duncan McClure was working for Hearts as a scout and, recognising Alex's outstanding talent, invited him to Tynecastle for a meeting with Tommy Walker. He agreed to sign provisional forms with the Gorgie club, but then he had already done that with Newtongrange Star!

When he turned sixteen, Alex stepped up from the Under-17 league to play for Musselburgh Union Under-21s. After a season in the Honest Toon, Alex found Newtongrange exercising their option and calling him up to the juniors. A move from outside-right to centre-forward saw his name on the scoresheet regularly, but even so it was a surprise to Alex when he got the call from Tynecastle to report for pre-season training in July 1955.

After three outings with the reserves and still only eighteen years old, he was selected to replace the injured Willie Bauld. Like Bauld before him, Alex scored on his debut, hitting the winner in a 2–1 victory at Tynecastle. He then scored in the next four games, including – again like the great Willie – a hat-trick against East Fife. When Willie recovered Alex moved to outside-right and then inside-right, covering for the injured Johnny Hamilton and Alfie Conn respectively. In his debut season he scored twenty-seven times (only Jimmy

Wardhaugh bettered that), he was part of the side that brought the Scottish Cup back to Tynecastle and he gained his first international cap at Under-23 level. Not a bad start to a professional career.

The following season, Alex's versatility saw him play in every position in the forward line except outside-left; that is perhaps why he found it harder to score, only managing to do so seven times. However, he was still performing well and received a further six Scottish Under-23 call-ups. And now with Conn being out, Alex again stepped up to the Hearts first team in a move that would make one of the biggest impacts on the club's season.

HEARTS v KILMARNOCK

Knowing that only a win would do, the forwards took the game to Killie giving the defence a relatively easy afternoon. It took some superb defending by the away side and yet another failure from the penalty spot, this time by Ian Crawford, to deny Hearts the victory their play so richly deserved. It often happens that a player returns to play against his former club and has the sort of game that makes fans wonder why he was ever allowed to leave. So it was that day, when ex-Hearts keeper Jimmy Brown gave a superb display in the Kilmarnock goal.

Kilmarnock got the game started and could have taken the lead after a mere thirty seconds when Freddie Glidden was caught out by a through-ball from George Taggart. Gordon Marshall was alert and did well to get to the ball before the in-rushing Beattie, but it only went as far as Davie Burns who, with the Hearts keeper on the ground, hit it straight back into the goalie's arms.

After the early scare Hearts took command with Mackay, Hamilton and Wardhaugh all threatening the Kilmarnock goal. Alex Young had the chance to mark his debut with a goal in twenty-eight minutes when he ran on to a header from Willie Bauld but a rush of blood to the head saw Alex fire the ball well wide. In an almost identical move, Bauld set up Johnny Hamilton who provided an almost identical finish.

Jimmy Brown was leading a charmed life in goal: in quick succession, shots by Young and then Wardhaugh were cleared from the line. Everyone was having a go and even Tom Mackenzie tried his luck with a free kick that shaved a post. The Rugby Park side could not hold out forever and, five minutes before half time, Jimmy Wardhaugh latched onto a pass from Willie Bauld and scored easily. It should have been two a couple of minutes later when Brown couldn't get to a goal-bound header from Jimmy Wardhaugh. Right-back Ralph Collins, who had earlier headed an Ian Crawford effort off the line, could only use his hand to stop the ball this time. It was Crawford who stepped up to take the kick – but for the second game in a row Hearts failed to convert from the spot, Ian putting the ball well wide. As the referee blew for the end of the half, Collins came in for sustained abuse because the 15,000 crowd knew just how important his illegal intervention might turn out to be.

The thought was not lost on the team, either, and right from the restart they went about trying to get the vital second goal. Jimmy Wardhaugh had a good chance early on but saw his attempt blocked by Brown once again. The Killie keeper knew nothing about a trademark header from Willie Bauld but unfortunately for the centre the ball hit the crossbar and went over.

Right on the hour mark the inevitable happened. With the hosts having been so much on top, Kilmarnock went up the park and scored in their first attack of the half. Freddie Glidden conceded a corner when he tackled Dave Burns. The winger took the kick himself and Gerry Mays was first to his cross and sent a powerful header behind an astonished Gordon Marshall.

Hearts went all out to get back on top but Brown did well again when he turned a Jimmy Wardhaugh shot over for a corner that came to nothing. Eight minutes after drawing level, Kilmarnock should have gone into the lead. Tom Mackenzie was the man of the moment when he got his head to the ball just before Davie Curlett looked likely to score. In the ensuing stramash it was Big Tam to the rescue again when he made a goal-line clearance from a shot by Mays. He was not done there and, in a sweeping move to the other end of the park, he saw his effort come thumping back off the crossbar.

With eight minutes to go Alex Young thought he had won it for Hearts but Jimmy Brown somehow saved his close-range shot. Alex could only stare in disbelief. With one last throw of the dice Alex made a great run down the right but, with the goal gaping, Jimmy Wardhaugh could just not get on the end of his low cross.

Hearts' play deserved better but the draw all but ensured that it would be Kilmarnock and not Hearts who qualified from Section 4.

Hearts: *Marshall, Kirk, Mackenzie, Mackay, Glidden, Cumming, Hamilton, Young, Bauld, Wardhaugh and Crawford*

The 'A' team were not faltering in their League Cup challenge and once again gained both points, but they met stiff resistance and had to fight hard against Kilmarnock 'A' at Rugby Park. They went a goal down inside five minutes when former Penicuik Athletic player John Caven beat Jimmy Milne to a long through-ball. Wilson Brown came rushing out of his goal but the Killie forward managed to beat him to it and prodded the ball home.

Hearts didn't take long to hit back and five minutes after going behind they were back on level terms when Alan Finlay scored from a couple of yards out. The game was being played in driving wind and rain, which was making for a very tricky surface, but it did not prevent Hearts playing some clever passing football and their lead was well merited when Jimmy Murray found the net in the thirty-fourth minute.

After the restart the colts continued to dominate the play and Jim Howieson increased their advantage when he scored after being set up by Finlay in fifty-five minutes. Hearts were now comfortably in control and the win was confirmed when Jimmy Murray capped a splendid game by scoring his second of the day. Although Killie did grab a goal back before the end, it was Hearts' day as they remained unbeaten in the section.

Hearts 'A': Brown, Parker, Lindores, Bowman, Milne, G. Thomson, Murray, Howieson, Campbell, Finlay and Goldie

With a couple of players out injured, manager Walker decided on Tuesday, 27 August to make a couple of positional changes for the following day's trip to Hampden. In defence George Thomson came in for John Cumming, who had taken a knock to his right hip the previous Saturday. Young took over from Hamilton, who had not recovered from the badly swollen ankle sustained against Kilmarnock. Wardhaugh then moved to the no. 8 slot to allow Jim McFadzean to come in at inside-left.

On the day of the game, the Board of Directors confirmed that at the conclusion of the season Hearts would tour Canada. Details were still sparse, but Hearts would play a minimum of eight and a maximum of ten games between May and June.

QUEEN'S PARK v HEARTS

Unfortunately the changes, forced or otherwise, did not pay off as Hearts drew a blank against a side they had knocked nine past in their previous meeting. There was no doubt that the forwards had numerous chances and 'Preston' in the *Evening News* reported that Queen's Park could easily have atoned for the 'embarrassing defeat'.

After ten minutes Willie Lindsay just missed connecting with a Ron McKinven cross. Then not long afterwards, Junior Omand had a claim for a penalty when he was impeded on his way through on goal. However, Hearts also had their chances and Jimmy Wardhaugh almost claimed a goal similar to the one scored by Cousins for Dundee at Dens Park; a hefty clearance cannoned off his body, but on this occasion Jim Ferguson in the Queen's goal was on the spot to clutch the ball.

The worst miss of the night was kept to near the end and it fell to the usually reliable Willie Bauld. With twenty minutes remaining, great work from Alex Young gave him an opportunity – but from only two yards out Willie contrived to put the ball wide of the target.

It was certainly one of those games to draw a veil over and it ended any chance of Hearts' qualification to the knockout stages. Certainly the display gave Mr Walker more questions than answers, with only the performance by Alex Young being a plus.

Hearts: Marshall, Kirk, Mackenzie, Mackay, Glidden, Thomson, Young, Wardhaugh, Bauld, McFadzean and Crawford

The reserves were also involved in a dour game at Tynecastle, although they did manage to grab both points. With the Queen's Park colts intent on stifling the Hearts attack, it was poor entertainment for the majority of the first half. When Danny Paton managed to break the deadlock with a thunderous volley, it should have been the signal for the Glasgow side to open out their play. However, they continued to defend in dogged fashion, restricting the opportunities of the home side. Hearts continued to struggle but made sure of the points when Hugh Goldie finished off a slick move involving Andy Bowman and Jimmy Murray.

Hearts 'A': Brown, J. Thomson, Lindores, Bowman, Milne, Higgins, Paton, Murray, Campbell, Finlay and Goldie

On Friday, 30 August, there was a new face at training as Bobby Blackwood reported at Tynecastle, back from service with the King's Own Scottish Borderers in Malaya. Although it would be a few weeks before he could be considered for first-team duty, this was a piece of good news for the manager.

HEARTS v DUNDEE

For the last League Cup tie, Alfie Conn had recovered from his ankle injury and took his usual place in the side, while Jimmy Wardhaugh moved back to inside-left at the expense of McFadzean. This seemed to inspire the team and the forwards returned to something like their imperial best – although if they had taken all the chances they created, there was no doubt they would have run out more handsome winners that the 4–2 scoreline suggested. Once again, though, the away team had in Bill Brown what 'Restalrig' of the *Evening News* was to call 'the personality of the game'. I would consider that to be what we would now call man of the match!

Willie Bauld was first to test Brown and the Dundee man did well to get to Willie's left-foot drive. A positive start and it was Jimmy Wardhaugh who opened the scoring with a blistering strike that Brown could do nothing about after only eight minutes. From that moment on, Hearts always looked more dangerous than their opponents. Bauld in particular was causing all sorts of problems for the dark blues' defence and once again he brought out the best in Brown when the goalie pulled off a wonderful save from a headed effort. He was soon at it again when he got his fingers to a glorious shot from Alfie Conn that looked destined for the top corner of the net.

The second goal was not far away and in twenty-one minutes Alex Young looked certain to get it as he broke through the Dundee back line. Just as he was about to shoot, he was bundled to the ground by Bobby Cox. The referee had no hesitation in pointing to the spot and Bobby Kirk became the third penalty-taker of the season. With the sound of ironic cheers coming from the terracing, unlike Bauld and Crawford before him, he made no mistake.

Dave Mackay played with far more assurance than had been seen in the previous games and he was unlucky not to score when his left-foot attempt from twenty-five yards saw Brown a beaten man for once – but Bobby Cox popped up out of nowhere to clear on the line. Dundee continued to battle away and were rewarded after thirty-two minutes when Alan Cousin got his head to a George McGeachie cross and gave Gordon Marshall no chance; but the goal didn't knock Hearts out of their stride, as they continued to pound Brown's goal. Alex Young and Jimmy Wardhaugh were left shaking their heads as the keeper denied both men in quick succession.

Nine minutes after the break, the Gorgie side held a two-goal lead once again. The ball was moved neatly from Young to Thomson to Crawford, who delivered the perfect ball for the 'King' to finish with aplomb. Then Jimmy Brown denied Alfie Conn for a second time with a save that even brought an ovation from the home support. Just when it seemed he would not be beaten by another Hearts man, Brown was let down by his own defence. He looked to have an effort by Willie Bauld well covered until Cox stuck out a foot that diverted the ball behind the stranded keeper. Willie did what every good striker does and claimed the goal.

Hearts were now so far on top that it looked like they were only trying to create a hat-trick for Willie Bauld. They tried so hard, in fact, that with only four minutes left on the clock they fashioned an incredible miss. The centre received a pass from Alex Young and then played a one-two with Jimmy Wardhaugh. Although well placed to score, he saw that 'Twinkletoes' was in an even better position. However, Jimmy was so taken aback that he skied the ball over the bar from close range.

Two minutes later and Gordon Marshall was caught out from a pass back by Tom Mackenzie which allowed Cousin in for his and Dundee's second of the game. It was too little too late for the Dens Park men as Hearts ran out worthy winners.

Hearts: *Marshall, Kirk, Mackenzie, Mackay, Glidden, Thomson, Young, Conn, Bauld, Wardhaugh and Crawford*

For the record, the League Cup table finished as follows:

	Played	Won	Lost	Drawn	For	Against	Points
Kilmarnock	6	3	0	3	12	6	9
Hearts	6	2	1	3	17	9	7
Dundee	6	1	2	3	11	13	5
Queen's Park	6	0	3	3	8	20	3

So although they did not qualify, the Hearts team at least rounded off their League Cup campaign in style. With the first game of the league the following Saturday being against the same opposition, there were high hopes that the men in maroon would start off on the right foot with another victory. As it transpired, they certainly got their wish.

The reserves, on the other hand, had gone one better. Although they dropped their first point in their final game against Dundee, they topped their section quite comfortably. They started the game on the back foot with Wilson Brown being by far the busier keeper – his early save from George O'Hara was the pick of the bunch – but he had to take some of the blame when the colts went behind after thirty-seven minutes. Home forward Hugh Robertson made the most of a mix-up between the goalie and Bobby Parker and nudged the ball home despite Brown's frantic efforts to make up for his mistake.

It was another goalkeeping error, at the other end, that brought the youngsters level. A minute before the interval Billy Higgins sent in a free kick and Dundee's keeper, Jim Ferguson, came off his line to make the catch. Unfortunately for him he let the ball slip from his grasp; with three Hearts men waiting to pounce, it hit off centre-half Ralph Mackenzie and into the net.

Hearts should have capitalised in the second half when the unlucky Dundee keeper had to leave the field after taking a knock to the head, with right-back Jack Stewart taking over in goal. Remarkably, after ten minutes of treatment Ferguson returned to the field and played out the remainder of the game on the right wing.

Hearts 'A': Brown, Parker, Lindores, Bowman, Milne, Higgins, Finlay, Smith, Foley, McFadzean and Goldie

The final Reserve League Cup table read like this:

	Played	Won	Lost	Drawn	For	Against	Points
Hearts	**6**	**5**	**0**	**1**	**16**	**4**	**11**
Dundee	6	3	2	1	11	12	7
Kilmarnock	6	2	3	1	12	14	5
Queen's Park	6	0	5	1	5	14	1

2

A WINNING START (SEPTEMBER)

Before the league season kicked off, Rangers, Scotland's representatives in the European Cup, began their campaign with a home game against French champions St Etienne. On Wednesday, 4 September a good performance saw them win 3–1 and most of Scotland were genuinely pleased for the Ibrox outfit.

An ankle knock picked up by Alfie Conn in the last game enforced manager Walker to make a change to the side and Jimmy Murray became the fourth player in seven and a half games to occupy the position.

As a schoolboy at Tynecastle, Jimmy had shown great potential and was a regular choice for his school and also at district level. On leaving 'Tynie' he joined a successful Shaftsbury Park side before moving to Merchiston Thistle, and it was at Merchiston that he first caught the eye of the Gorgie talent scouts. His performances led to Hearts offering him professional terms but the club wanted him to be farmed out to Dunbar United. Jimmy's dad, Jimmy senior, had played for Dunbar in the past and knew that the 'robust' nature of the division would not be of benefit to Jimmy's development. Rangers had also been tracking Jimmy and soon became aware of the breakdown in negotiations between the two parties, so they called him through to Ibrox for talks about his future. When Davie McLean got wind that he might lose Jimmy, he told Tommy Walker to get his signature immediately. On 27 September 1950 Jimmy signed on the dotted line to fulfil his boyhood dream.

Although he did not go to Dunbar, he did spend the next eighteen months playing in the 'C' Division and the reserves. Jimmy showed up well and his name appeared regularly on the scoresheet. His performances certainly caught the eye of 'Tolbooth' of the *Evening News*. In his report for the 'C' League Cup tie against Falkirk at Tynecastle in February 1952, he wrote that the game 'produced no thrills but the answer to Hearts' problems, lack of incisive thrust on the wings'. The First XI had just scraped past Raith Rovers 1–0 in a Scottish Cup tie at Tynecastle on 9 February but they had not impressed and two players in particular drew the harshest criticism from the *Evening News* man. 'I witnessed the weakness on the wings in the Raith cup tie and in the League games before it,' he wrote. 'No two players could contribute less. Rutherford admittedly has football but lacks vim: Urquhart has only one football foot and lacks alacrity.' But he had the solution: 'The answer is Cumming and Murray. Both carry football, skill, vigour, tenacity and marksmanship.'

Three weeks later, John Cumming got his chance when he took over the left-wing slot from Johnny Urquhart but Jimmy remained in the reserves. With his ability never in doubt, it was still a surprise when three weeks later he made his debut against Stirling Albion at Tynecastle on 15 March 1952. The 'shock' was that he replaced Willie Bauld in the side and not Eddie Rutherford as 'Tolbooth' had advocated.

Willie had been an ever-present in the side that season and only three days earlier had been part of the team that defeated Airdrie 6–4 in a memorable Scottish Cup replay at Tynecastle. Willie had scored a hat-trick and 'Cockburn' of the *Evening News* described 'The King's' performance as having 'touched the very peak of his form', adding: 'The centre has been superlative in every phase of his play in recent weeks, but here, well he was right above the class of every other forward on the field.' So there was a lot for Jimmy to live up to.

As Hearts were out of the running in the league but had a cup semi-final looming, the manager decided to rest four players for the Stirling game. Out went Tam Mackenzie, Davie Laing, Willie Bauld and Jimmy Wardhaugh and in came Tom McSpadyen, Jock Adie, Jimmy Murray and John Cumming respectively. With the spotlight firmly on Jimmy, he did not disappoint and scored in a comfortable

5–2 victory. The *Evening News* was back to its normal ways, though, when 'Lauriston' wrote: 'Chief interest was centred on the display of Murray, leading the senior side for the first time. Murray tried hard and showed many clever touches, but the fatal "C" Division slowness was evident in many of his moves.' Perhaps not surprisingly then, Willie Bauld came back from his 'holiday' – as the newspapers had described it – for the next game and Jimmy had to wait nearly three seasons before he got another game in the first team.

He eventually returned on 16 April 1955, against Motherwell, and then played in the last four games of the season. Although he didn't get his name on the scoresheet he showed up well, but with Alfie Conn and Willie Bauld still ruling the roost plus a versatile youngster called Alex Young coming on the scene, Jimmy was limited to only another four appearances the following season. It was perhaps an example of the strength in depth that was at Tynecastle at the time, and also Jimmy's versatility, that for three of those appearances he played in the unfamiliar right-half role.

Things began to improve in the '56–57 season when Jimmy turned out on twelve occasions. His strike rate was tremendous and he found the net no fewer than seven times in his dozen outings. So when he was selected for the first home league game of the season, the Hearts support could be assured that the team would not be weakened in any way.

After seven years, this was to be the opportunity Jimmy had been waiting for and he grabbed it with both hands. After starting off in the reserves, by the end of the season he would go on to be an integral part of the championship-winning side and also gain his first Scotland 'cap' against England. He would also be chosen to represent his country at the World Cup finals in Sweden and gain the distinction of being the first Scot to score in the final stages. Incidentally, to date Jimmy has never received any recognition from the SFA for this, nor even for the fact that he was part of the side in Sweden, as 'caps' were not awarded for games outwith the home internationals. Perhaps this is not surprising given the SFA's track record but it is a disgrace nonetheless; let's hope they see the error of their ways soon.

John Cumming was welcomed back to the side to face Dundee after recovering from a series of knocks and he took over from George Thomson at left-half.

HEARTS v DUNDEE

On Saturday a crowd of 19,700 – some of whom had taken advantage of the football special trains that ran from Musselburgh, Duddingston and Leith North in those days – paid two shillings for adults and ninepence for OAPs, HM Forces and children (that's ten and four new pence for those of you born after decimalisation) to witness a five-star display by the Hearts. The Scotland selectors who were in attendance that day must have left with a lot more questions than answers, though. There to run the rule over Freddie Glidden as a replacement for Rangers' George Young, they never got to see what Freddie could do as he was rarely troubled throughout. On the other hand, Dundee's Doug Cowie, another contender for the position, had one of his worst games for a long time. The displays of both John Cumming and Willie Bauld had to have caught their eye to bring them into contention, but it was Alex Young who was the architect of the easy win.

Our old friend 'Edina' in the *Evening News* wrote that 'long before the game was over the main task was to get Young the goal his play had deserved'. In fact, Alex was the only forward not to get his name on the scoresheet. It was as complete a team performance as had been seen at Tynecastle so far, even eclipsing the 9–2 victory over Queen's Park because Dundee provided a slightly better quality of opposition.

Both Dave Mackay and John Cumming were on top of their game and provided many good balls out to either wing which Young and Crawford used to great effect. Even Willie Bauld found time to use the left wing as often as he played in the middle. This allowed Jimmy Wardhaugh to act as a second centre-forward which was shown to great effect when Hearts scored their sixth. A pass from Cumming found Bauld on the left, Willie swung over a bullet of a cross and Jimmy rose majestically to nod the ball beyond the helpless Bill Brown.

Before that, though, Hearts had been rampant from the moment they went ahead in the eighth minute when 'debut boy' Jimmy Murray headed them in front. Three minutes later Willie Bauld added number two after Brown could only push a Jimmy Wardhaugh shot into his path. Hearts pressurised the Dundee defence throughout the half and it was no surprise when, after good work by John Cumming, Ian Crawford nodded in the third after thirty-eight minutes.

There was no let-up in Hearts' play after the restart as Willie Thornton's men struggled to cope with Hearts' free-flowing football. In the fifty-fourth minute, for the second week in a row, Bobby Cox fouled Alex Young in the box and Bobby Kirk once again made no mistake from the penalty spot. Sixty-two minutes gone and it was 5–0, Ian Crawford getting his second after a sublime pass from Jimmy Wardhaugh. Jimmy rounded off the scoring with Hearts' sixth in the seventieth minute after John Cumming and Willie Bauld had combined well to set up the chance.

Despite losing six goals, the crowd gave Bill Brown a rousing cheer as he left the pitch, for without his intervention the home side could easily have reached double figures. It was the kind of form that would eventually see him make his international debut at the end of the season in the World Cup finals in Sweden.

For Hearts it was a vintage performance to start off the league campaign and an early indication of what the Gorgie faithful were to witness in the coming months.

The Hearts team for the first League game of the season was:
Marshall, Kirk, Mackenzie, Mackay, Glidden, Cumming, Young, Murray, Bauld, Wardhaugh and Crawford

On the same day, the second string took on Dundee at Dens Park – not in the league, but in a Second XI Cup tie. Although they scraped through 2–1 after scoring all the goals (Dundee's counter came from an own goal by Bobby Parker), the game was notable for the fact that Bobby Blackwood made his comeback after finishing his national service.

The 'A' side were quick off the mark and it only took them four minutes to open the scoring when Hugh Goldie headed home. Hearts made good use of having the wind behind them but were caught out when Clive Wallace broke through: with only Wilson Brown to beat, he made a mess of his attempt and the keeper collected easily. Jim Howieson nearly increased the lead but his well-struck drive came thudding back from the upright. Despite Hearts' superiority, Dundee were making a game of it and a young lad called Alan Gilzean missed a glorious chance just before the break.

After the restart and now playing against a strong wind, Hearts found it a bit more difficult and it was the wind that played a major part as the hosts grabbed an equaliser. Standing five yards from goal, Bobby Parker made an attempted clearance which flew high in the air and blew back under the crossbar past a startled Wilson Brown. Undeterred, Hearts fought back and regained the lead in sixty-seven minutes when Danny Paton got what turned out to be the winner.

Hearts 'A': *Brown, Parker, Lindores, Bowman, Milne, Thomson, Blackwood, Howieson, Goldie, McFadzean and Paton*

Despite not getting on the scoresheet, Bobby Blackwood put in a good performance and on Monday, 9 September he was included in a strong team that was sent to Countess Park to take on Dunbar United. The game had been arranged as a 'thank you' from Hearts, as in recent years they had used the juniors side as a 'feeder' club for up-and-coming players. Sadly, none of the six ex-Dunbar men, David Kidd, Willie Lindores, Jim Howieson, Alan Finlay, Jim Foley or George Campbell ever became a leading light in Gorgie.

A big crowd turned out to watch the visitors start well. As the game wore on, the juniors started to take the game to Hearts. Bobby Parker playing at right-back was the star man as he marshalled the defence to keep United out. It was 0–0 at half time, but after fifteen minutes of the second half the home side took the lead when Fraser flicked the ball over 'Newman' in the Hearts goal. Many locals in the crowd recognised the Hearts trialist keeper to be Keenan from Ormiston.

Blackwood, Finlay and Murray all passed up chances to equalise but it was Dunbar who went further ahead after a shot from Stevens beat Newman. This seemed to act as a wake-up call as Hearts then had their best spell of the match which led to Bobby Blackwood pulling one back. Despite Hearts' constant pressure and forcing numerous corners, their equaliser would just not come and the juniors ran out worthy winners.

Not a very encouraging performance and perhaps some of the team would have thought they had done themselves no good in trying to force their way into the first team. As it turned out, however, nothing could be further from the truth: six of them went on to play their part during the season.

The team that lined up was: Newman, Parker, Newman, Bowman, Smith, Thomson, Blackwood, Murray, Foley, Finlay and Paton

Perhaps with the result in mind when Tommy Walker announced the team to play Airdrie, there was only one possible change from the side that easily saw off Dundee. Johnny Hamilton came back in contention after he had recovered from a leg knock, but Alfie Conn was still out with his troublesome ankle injury.

AIRDRIE v HEARTS

Airdrie were in good form. They had beaten Hibs 4–1 in the League Cup and only two weeks earlier had knocked nine goals past East Fife. In the corresponding fixture the previous season, Hearts had been 3–1 down early in the second half and it needed goals from Dave Mackay and John Cumming to equalise before Johnny Hamilton popped up with the winner moments from time. Already this season Hearts' away form was in stark contrast to their excellent home displays, so they were a cautious lot as they ran out at Broomfield.

Any doubts anyone might have had were blown away by half time as Hearts went in five goals to the good. The scoring started as early as the fourth minute when Willie Bauld – who had been operating on the left wing – picked out Ian Crawford. Ian's volley was going wide of the mark until the unlucky John Quinn got in the way and deflected it past Dave Walker in the home goal. Quinn almost got his second a minute later when he got in the way of a clearance by Doug Baillie. The ball struck him full in the face and deflected inches wide.

Dave Mackay was out of luck when his rasping twenty-five-yarder rattled the crossbar just after Michael Quigley had been on hand to clear a drive from Jimmy Murray off the line. Only ten minutes gone and what a whirlwind start, but nothing compared to the devastating thirteen-minute spell which saw Jimmy Wardhaugh score in the fourteenth, fifteenth and twenty-seventh minutes. Despite a lot of research, including many an hour on the wonderful Londonhearts.com, I am unable to confirm if this is the fastest-ever hat-trick by a Hearts player. It would surely be hard to beat.

His first came when he caught Dave Walker napping and back-heeled a pass from Willie Bauld into the net. The keeper was at fault a minute later, failing to hold a cross from Willie Bauld, and when the ball dropped Jimmy pounced to tap home. He completed his hat-trick twelve minutes later by heading in a pinpoint delivery from Alex Young.

Alex, running the Airdrie defence ragged, was unlucky not to score when he headed inches wide from yet another cross from Willie Bauld. In the forty-first minute, Alex was again denied when Walker got down well to stop his left-foot attempt. Then a minute later he turned provider when he slipped a pass to Jimmy Murray, who duly scored the fifth goal of the half.

More Alex Young magic early in the second period saw his cross met by Ian Crawford, who bulleted a header into the net. Ian was in the thick of things again when, after fifty-eight minutes, he was brought down by Baillie and for the third game in a row Bobby Kirk blasted home.

Although Airdrie countered with two goals by Tommy Duncan and Joe Caven in the sixty-third and seventy-third minutes respectively, there was never any danger of Hearts losing the game. The only question that remained was how, after such a good performance, Willie Bauld and Alex Young did not get their names on the scoresheet. Alex did have one last glorious opportunity near the end, when a defence-splitting pass from Ian Crawford put him through, but somehow he managed to put the ball wide when an open goal was beckoning.

Hearts: Marshall, Kirk, Mackenzie, Mackay, Glidden, Cumming, Young, Murray, Bauld, Wardhaugh and Crawford

Back in Edinburgh there were five names on the scoresheet as the reserves matched the first team by scoring seven as well. The scoring started as early as the second minute when a clever lob by Bobby Blackwood found Danny Paton in space and he took his chance with aplomb. It was Blackwood who doubled the score in fifteen minutes when he beat Airdrie keeper Willie Goldie from close range. Airdrie did hit back, through John McGill, when he managed to poke the ball home after a melee in the goalmouth. After that, it's fair to say the roof caved in for Airdrie. Hearts went in at the break 3–1 up after Blackwood notched another when his fierce drive went in via the underside of the bar.

After the restart, Airdrie tried to get back in the game and Ian McMillan was out of luck when Newman pulled off a decent save. Hearts' reply was swift and George Campbell got number four when he knocked the ball home at the second attempt. He was on hand once again, minutes later, to make it five. Not long afterwards Bobby Blackwood got number six.

Hugh Goldie rounded off a fine individual performance by getting number seven. Hugh had been prominent throughout and it looked as though he had a point to prove against his hometown side. He was born and bred in Airdrie and after he had been 'capped' for Scotland schoolboys it was a surprise when no local side took him on. Hugh travelled through to Edinburgh every week to turn out for Slateford Athletic. And it was there that Tommy Walker signed him on an amateur form and then on his seventeenth birthday offered him a professional contract. Although he had not yet made his first-team debut, on this kind of form surely it would not be long before he took the step up.

Hearts 'A': Newman, J. Thomson, Parker, Bowman, Milne, G. Thomson, Paton, Blackwood, Campbell, McFadzean and Goldie

Willie Bauld was in fine spirits when he met up with the rest of the Scottish League side on Monday afternoon before they sailed (yes sailed; there was no Ryanair then) to Dublin to take on the League of Ireland. Strange perhaps that, despite Hearts' start to the season, Willie was the only representative from Gorgie. Surely there was no Old Firm bias back then as well?

However, with the World Cup in Sweden coming up, it was an opportunity for Willie to enhance his chances of replacing Jackie Mudie in the Scotland attack. How well he took it. He swept delightful passes out to both wings and his head flicks constantly split the Irish defence. He was instrumental in the Scots recording a flattering 5–1 victory. Bauld himself might have had more to show for his perform-ance than one goal, had any of the other forwards provided him with the service he gave to them. In the first half, Irish keeper Kelly managed to push a drive from Willie onto the post but could do nothing in the seventy-fourth minute to prevent the Hearts man capping a great display when he scored Scotland's fifth.

When he returned to Edinburgh, Willie had certainly enhanced his reputation and would surely now be at the head of the queue for full international honours when Scotland faced Ireland the following month. His first priority, though, was to continue his fine form against a Hibs side that had also started the season with two wins, against Aberdeen away and Motherwell at home. They sat just behind Hearts at the top of the league and the clash between the two sides the following Saturday was the talk of pubs (and no doubt a good few

steamies) throughout Edinburgh all week. So much was the anticipation, in fact, that a long queue had formed outside Thornton's
sports shop on Princes Street (now Ernest Jones the jeweller) well
before they opened at 8.30 a.m. to sell stand tickets for the match.
Hardly surprising, then, when the available briefs were snapped up
in only half an hour.

Before the kick-off, the League stood as follows:

	Played	Won	Lost	Drawn	For	Against	Points
Hearts	2	2	0	0	13	2	4
Hibs	2	2	0	0	8	2	4
Raith Rovers	2	2	0	0	6	2	4

HEARTS v HIBS

Even with a full squad to choose from, it was still an easy decision
for Tommy Walker to announce that he would keep an unchanged
side, as there was no thought of a 'rotation policy' in 1957.

Hearts swamped the visitors from the start and for the third week
in a row they managed to get off to the best possible start. The game
was only seconds old when Pat Hughes fouled Jimmy Wardhaugh.
Bobby Kirk floated in the resultant free kick but Lawrie Leslie did
well to hold Jimmy Murray's header. A minute later he was left with
little chance when another free kick was flicked on by Willie Bauld
to Jimmy Wardhaugh, who put the home side into the lead despite
the attention of three Hibs defenders.

The onslaught was non-stop and it took only another five minutes
before Ian Crawford had doubled the lead. Alex Young swung in a
corner and Ian was on hand to slam the ball home.

Hibs had no answer to the devastating play of the hosts, their only
effort seeing outside-left Andy Aitken blast the ball well over from
twenty yards. Hearts, on the other hand, were creating all sorts of
problems for Leslie. The goalie pulled off a magnificent save from a
Willie Bauld header in the twenty-third minute, but he could do
nothing a minute later when he was beaten for the third time. From

another corner, Ian Crawford sent the ball into the middle, Alex Young headed towards goal and it looked as though the Hibs keeper had it covered until Jimmy Murray nipped in to get his head to it and Hearts were three up.

Leslie was Hibs' hero again when, in quick succession, he prevented Hearts going further ahead through Crawford, Bauld and then Mackay. When a rocket from Dave Mackay did eventually beat him, he was fortunate to see George Muir on the line to head clear. The half-time whistle could not come soon enough for the beleaguered Easter Road outfit.

The Maroons had played some scintillating football in the first forty-five minutes and if they had kept it going in the second forty-five they could easily have doubled their final tally. Another goal-line clearance, this time by Hughes, prevented Jimmy Murray getting number four a minute after the restart; and then Willie Bauld also went close, but once again Leslie managed a superb save.

Midway through the half, Hearts appeared to drop down a gear but Hibs still found it difficult to take advantage. Eventually they did manage to snatch one back through Eddie Turnbull after Gordon Marshall was caught out by a cross from the left by Aitken. This slightly took the shine of a polished Hearts performance, but as referee Mr Brittle blew the final whistle no one in the 34,000 crowd was left in any doubt who could claim the right to be Edinburgh's number-one team. The question was, could this Hearts side finally go on and claim to be Scotland's number-one side?

Elsewhere Rangers had lost 3–2 in the first Old Firm encounter at Ibrox and Clyde had banged six past Partick Thistle in the 'other Glasgow derby'. So Hearts were on top of the league, followed by Clyde and Celtic. Despite this – some people are never happy! – in his report of the game for the *Evening News* the following Monday, 'Restalrig' was highly critical of the tendency of the home team to 'free wheel' throughout the second forty-five. Although neither Gordon Smith nor Andy Aitken on the Hibs wings got much change from the Hearts backs, once again the performance of both Dave Mackay and John Cumming came in for criticism. Maybe the reporter's nom de plume reveals where his allegiances lay, so perhaps his comments are not that surprising. The forwards did manage to catch the scribe's eye although he chose to praise the display of the visiting goalkeeper, Leslie, for keeping the score down. All the same, he did concede that Alex Young turned in an inspired performance and had given Boyle in the Hibs defence a very uncomfortable afternoon.

Kings of the Capital: Marshall, Kirk, Mackenzie, Mackay, Glidden, Cumming, Young, Murray, Bauld, Wardhaugh, and Crawford
Not even the Kings of Leith: Leslie, Muir, Boyle, Hughes, Plenderleith, Baxter, Smith, Turnbull, Harrower, Preston and Aitken

Of course it was not just the first string who were doing well. The reserves had also got off to a 100 per cent start to the season. Taking the opportunity to view the strength in depth on the books, Tommy Walker took his place amongst the 9,000 crowd at Easter Road on Monday, 23 September to watch the 'wee derby'.

After achieving the same scoring feat as the senior side the previous week, the reserves emulated them again by scoring only a few minutes after kick-off. Johnny Hamilton gained possession just inside Hibs' half and, after a sparkling run, let fly. Although Jackie Wren in the Hibs goal got his hand to the ball he could not stop the Tynecastle winger putting his side one up.

With plenty of possession, Hearts were on top throughout, but the closest they came to increasing their lead was when Bobby Parker fired in a free kick from just outside the box. Wren redeemed himself from his earlier mistake and managed to push the ball onto the post and away to safety. Before the end of the half, the Hibs keeper also did well to deny both Bobby Blackwood and George Thomson as the 'wee' Hearts continued to dominate.

The start of the second half saw Hibs come a bit more into the game through good work from Jim Thomson in particular. Despite this, it was the men from Gorgie who went further ahead when George Thomson netted after a throw-in by Billy Higgins was left by the Hibs defence. Hearts were content to see out the remainder of the game, but were fortunate when Johnny Frye managed to escape the attentions of Jimmy Milne: his shot hit a post and rebounded clear.

Hearts 'A': *Brown, Parker, Lindores, Bowman, Milne, Higgins, Paton, Blackwood, Campbell, G. Thomson and Hamilton*

During September an Asian flu epidemic had been sweeping the country. In England, Everton applied to the FA to have their game against Blackpool, scheduled for Saturday, called off as they had eight first-team players suffering from the bug. In Edinburgh it was reported that 13,000 children were missing from school. Remember, back then there were no shopping centres for the little darlings to hang around during the day, so they were all genuine influenza sufferers.

It didn't take long before Tynecastle became affected and on Wednesday, 25 September the headline on the front page of the *Evening Dispatch* read: 'FIVE HEARTS PLAYERS STRUCK DOWN BY FLU.' It was reported that Kirk, Bauld, Mackay, Young and Wardhaugh had all caught the virus. They were joined on the sick list by reserve-team players George Dobbie, Hugh Goldie and Jim Foley.

Tommy Walker had no option but to assume his role as club secretary and contact the Scottish League to ask for the game against Partick to be called off.

Despite the fact that a large number of SFA representatives had made the journey to France to see Rangers draw 1–1 in the second leg of their European Cup tie, there was somebody at Park Gardens to grant permission, and so the game became the first in Scotland to be affected by the epidemic. You wonder if those in charge these days would either have been as sympathetic to Hearts' plea or even been able to make such an immediate decision without calling a committee meeting.

There was some good news for Messrs Bauld and Mackay that day: along with Ian Crawford, they were named in the Scotland squad to meet Ireland on Saturday, 5 October. Willie was also pencilled in for the Scottish League side along with John Cumming to play the Irish League under lights at Ibrox on 9 October. Another flu sufferer, Jimmy Wardhaugh, was named as 'travelling reserve' for the match.

It turned out that the Partick–Hearts game was not the only one called off that weekend. The scheduled game between Dundee and Kilmarnock was also postponed due to the Rugby Parkers reporting that four first-team members were laid low. Hibs didn't have any sickness worries and took advantage to pull themselves nearer to Hearts, beating Airdrie 4–0 at Easter Road in a game that saw Hibs legend Lawrie Reilly make a scoring return to the first team after having been out for a lengthy spell through injury. The semi-finals of the League Cup also took place that day and Celtic saw off a spirited Clyde side 4–2 while Rangers accounted for Brechin 4–0 – thus setting up the first Old Firm meeting in a national final for twenty-nine years.

Although Hearts could not field a team at Firhill, and despite the fact that Jim McFadzean and Johnny Hamilton had joined the growing list of players down with flu, there were still enough reserves available to take on Partick at Tynecastle.

As might have been expected, it took the new-look side a while to get in their stride. George Campbell might have broken the deadlock when his fierce strike hit the bar with colourfully named Partick keeper Alfredo Renucci well beaten. Bobby Blackwood was showing up well and was unlucky when, in one incident, he had three attempts at goal and each one blocked by a Partick defender. He then provided an inch-perfect cross for George Thomson but the big man could not direct his header on target and the ball sailed harmlessly over.

Although Hearts could not find a way through in the first forty-five, it took only a minute of the second period for them to take the lead. From a wide position George Campbell sent in a teasing ball that was met by Danny Paton, whose fierce shot from seven yards gave the Partick goalie little chance. The goal lifted the team's confidence and Alan Finlay got his name on the scoresheet when he swept the ball home.

Hearts continued to press and their superiority was rewarded when

Bobby Blackwood was the next to beat Renucci as he first-timed the ball into the corner of the net. George Thomson had been unlucky with his efforts on several occasions throughout the game, but his luck changed ten minutes from time when he rounded off the scoring with a neat finish.

Hearts 'A': Brown, Parker, Lindores, Bowman, Milne, Higgins, Paton, Blackwood, Campbell, Thomson and Finlay

3

HEARTS SEE THE LIGHT (OCTOBER)

By Monday, 1 October there had been sufficient improvement in the sick list for Hearts to be able to carry out a full-scale practice match to test out the newly installed floodlights. Only Kirk, Mackay and Young didn't start for the first team as they took on the reserves testing the conditions under the lights. At 7.15 p.m. the thirty lamps on each of the four pylons were switched on for the first time. The players reported that only the corners of the park were not sufficiently illuminated and the installers promised to remedy this before the scheduled official hanselling the following Monday against city rivals Hibernian.

This was a new era for football with both Hearts and Hibs embracing the latest technology, unlike a certain prominent team from the West of Scotland. Tommy Walker used the occasion to announce that Hearts would join representatives of Hibs, Partick Thistle, Tottenham Hotspur, Newcastle and Manchester City at a meeting on Sunday to discuss a proposed British League Cup. The competition would take the form of the Scottish sides playing the English sides, home and away, under lights throughout the season. It seems that the Old Firm were not as keen then to join the English league as they are now.

The next visitors to Tynecastle were to be East Fife who had been encouraged by their recent results, although their manager Jerry Dawson did recognise the task that his team faced. Little did he know just how big that task would prove to be. The three flu sufferers at Tynecastle had all recovered and on the Friday afternoon it was what was fast becoming the familiar line-up that was announced.

51

HEARTS v EAST FIFE

No one in the 28,000 crowd that flocked to Tynecastle could have quite anticipated just what a fantastic attacking display they would witness. At the end of the game the maroon-clad fans went home ecstatic. As well as seeing their favourites scoring nine times without reply, twice they saw the woodwork prevent further goals, and as seemed to be customary for Hearts, the visiting team keeper produced some great saves to prevent his side further embarrassment.

In the early stages it looked like East Fife might provide the Maroons with a stiff challenge and the Hearts faithful on the terracing began to get slightly restless. Not for the first time, the home defence looked shaky and could have lost two goals early on. Jimmy Bonthrone had watched a spectacular effort go narrowly over before Bobby Kirk was called upon to clear a header from Bobby Gillon off the line. Slowly Hearts began to work their way into the game and Willie Bauld started the goal rush in twenty-four minutes with a neatly placed header following the perfect delivery from Alex Young.

Twenty-six minutes and Hearts had scored number two from a magnificent solo effort from Dave Mackay as he netted from fully twenty-five yards after going on a twisting run from midfield. The Fifers were deflated and soon afterwards they were nearly three down when a tremendous Alex Young effort thumped the back of a post. The third goal was not far away, though, and Jimmy Wardhaugh was the man that got it when, after a clever dummy from Ian Crawford, his shot beat Ron McCluskey in the visitors' goal. Mr Symes' whistle to end the half could not come quick enough for the beleaguered Fife side

The onslaught continued in the second half and the East Fife keeper must have wondered what was happening when he was beaten by yet another thunderbolt, this time a twenty-yard stunner from John Cumming: fifty-three minutes gone and Hearts were already four goals to the good. Five minutes later and the tally was five, Jimmy Murray catching out the visitors' defence when he sent in a well-placed free kick for Jimmy Wardhaugh to run on to. His well-directed shot went in low at McCluskey's right-hand post.

HEARTS SEE THE LIGHT (OCTOBER)

The Fifers managed to stem the tide for the next ten minutes but, despite the combined attempts of Frank Christie, Sammy Cox and former Hearts favourite Jock Adie, they could not stop Jimmy Murray continue his goal-scoring run to make it 6–0. Hearts showed no mercy and only a stunning save by McCluskey prevented Alex Young making it seven. And the stopper could do nothing in the eightieth minute when he failed to hold a shot from Jimmy Wardhaugh, for there was Willie Bauld to make it the 'magnificent seven'.

Now both Willie and Jimmy Wardhaugh were looking for hat-tricks but time was running out. It duly arrived for Jimmy in the eighty-fifth minute. Ian Crawford was unlucky not to score when his goal-bound effort was blocked on the line, but fortunately for Jimmy the ball broke to him at the back post, where he had the easiest of tasks to add to Hearts' total. With only three minutes remaining, Alex Young was finally rewarded for all his good work throughout the game when he rounded off the scoring for the afternoon.

Hearts: Marshall, Kirk, Mackenzie, Mackay, Glidden, Cumming, Young, Murray, Bauld, Wardhaugh and Crawford

So for the second time this season, Hearts had found the net nine times and Jimmy Wardhaugh had notched another hat-trick. Could anyone stop the Maroons? They would soon get the chance to show off their talents further afield. In a groundbreaking move, the board agreed to have discussions along with other Scottish clubs and their English counterparts about an inter-league competition.

After the meeting of the 'Big Six' in Newcastle the next day, it was announced that the new tournament would go ahead under the auspices of the Scottish Football Association – not the Scottish League. Unusually for Scottish football, neither organisation could agree as to the merits of the competition. Particularly outspoken on the matter were Celtic, who claimed that it would detract from the value of Scottish competitions and that 'only certain clubs would be able to play glamorous games'. Changed days indeed, but I suspect their decision had more to do with the fact that they steadfastly refused to install the floodlights that would allow them to take part in the competition. Finally it was agreed that the games were to be played weekly from mid October to the beginning of December, with a trophy being awarded to the winners.

HEARTS v HIBS (FLOODLIGHT FRIENDLY)

First on the 'friendly' agenda was the visit of Hibernian on Monday, 7 October in a game to mark the official switch-on of the Tynecastle floodlighting system. Such an auspicious occasion was recognised by the presentation of writing sets (Parker pen, biro and pencil, no less) to the players and trainers of both clubs. Imagine what the likes of Barry Ferguson and Derek Riordan would have made of that. Hearts gifted Hibs a silver quaich and a suitably inscribed tankard went to each director. Honorary President the Earl of Rosebery saw fit to mark the occasion by presenting the club with a photograph of himself and I am sure the board were suitably grateful for such a generous gift. The presentations were concluded when the electrical contractors Miller and Stables, who had installed the system, presented a silver tea set to the club.

Despite the fact that both Cumming and Bauld were to play against the Irish League on Wednesday, they were included in the side. However, the flu bug had struck again with Tam Mackenzie being the victim this time, so Willie Lindores was drafted into the side in his place. It was perhaps ironic that this was Willie's first start of the season, as it might have been that he was lining up for the visitors.

As a schoolboy with Knox Academy, Willie was an outstanding footballer. Not only did he gain six caps at that level, he was also appointed captain of the side. After school, Edinburgh Thistle, who were the recognised juvenile side for Hibs, snapped him up. Willie captained a successful side that included Tommy Preston and both of them then signed provisional forms with the Easter Road club. Before he could play in green and white, Willie was called up for his national service at RAF Leuchars. When he returned to the Lothians he signed for his local club, Dunbar United, a side with close associations with Hearts. His displays came to the attention of Tommy Walker and soon agreed professional terms with Hearts in 1956.

He made his first-team debut against Partick Thistle on 3 November that year. Although Willie Bauld got the goal that won the game, it was the debut boy who got the limelight. His display was outstanding and the *Evening News* ran the headline: 'Lindores is a Hearts find.' However, the next again week, Tam Mackenzie had recovered from injury and was back in the first team. Willie only managed one further game that season, again deputising for the injured Mackenzie.

So with 'Big Tam' out, once again Willie made the step up. Unfortunately, on his debut this season he came up against the mercurial Gordon Smith, although he was not solely to blame for what turned out to be a disappointing defeat since the whole defence paid the price for some slack marking. It was a performance that allowed 'Tron Kirk' to use puns like 'Hearts fused badly [and] they were short circuited by a lively Hibernian side'. Certainly not up to *Sun* reporter standard.

It had started out so well. Slightly against the run of play, Hearts had raced into a two-goal lead through Willie Bauld and Jimmy Wardhaugh but, unlike the league game a couple of weeks earlier, Hibs didn't capitulate. Mackay and Cumming had their work cut out against the fast-moving Hibs forwards. Eddie Turnbull, Joe Baker and Tommy Preston caused all sorts of problems for the Maroons and the only possible cause for complaint the Hearts fans in the 25,000 gate could have had at the final whistle was the performance of match referee Tom Edwards. An Edinburgh man, Mr Edwards made two vital decisions during the game, both of which went against Hearts. Draw your own conclusion!

After eighteen minutes Jimmy Murray forced a corner and Ian Crawford sent the ball into the middle, where Alex Young headed the ball back across goal for Willie Bauld to become the first player to score 'under floodlights' in Gorgie. Minutes later, Tommy Preston missed a good opportunity to equalise, but it was Hearts who increased their lead. From an Ian Crawford throw-in John Cumming stabbed the ball forward to Jimmy Wardhaugh who, from twenty yards, lashed the ball high into the top-right corner of the net past Leslie. On twenty-five minutes the deficit was reduced when Joe Baker, deputising for Lawrie Reilly, fastened onto the ball and cut in from the left. Gordon Marshall could only parry his shot into the path of the in-rushing Tommy Preston, who did the rest.

Hearts began the second half brightly and Lawrie Leslie had to look sharp to save a vicious strike from Jimmy Wardhaugh. Not long after that, he was busy again and did well to tip over a screamer from John Cumming. Then came the referee's first controversial decision, when Willie MacFarlane looked to have handled inside the area. 'Penalty,' shouted the home support; 'no chance,' signalled the whistler.

Gradually Hibs began to take a grip of the game and it was no surprise when they drew level in sixty-five minutes when Preston rose to meet a cross chipped over by Gordon Smith. After leaving five Hearts men trailing in his wake, he looked to have run the ball over the bye-line before sending over his delivery. The ref chose to ignore Hearts' claims and the goal stood.

Willie Bauld tried everything he knew to put Hearts back in front but he was thwarted when Leslie managed to pull off yet another magnificent save from one of his pile drivers. That chance aside, it was all Hibs and it was not long before they took the lead. Following a Smith corner, Preston nodded down to Baker who hooked the ball behind Gordon Marshall. Then, in seventy-two minutes, it was that man Tommy Preston again when he completed his hat-trick and Hearts' misery, scoring from another Gordon Smith corner kick.

The Hearts team on the historic night was: Marshall, Kirk, Lindores, Mackay, Glidden, Cumming, Young, Murray, Bauld, Wardhaugh and Crawford
Hibs' line-up was: Leslie, Muir, McFarlane, Turnbull, Paterson, Nicol, Smith, Preston, Baker, Harrower and Ormond

The following day Willie Bauld and John Cumming travelled through to the west to play for the Scottish League against their Irish counterparts. Jimmy Wardhaugh travelled with them but it was a wasted train fare as he didn't make the team and was left sitting in the stand. If either Bauld or Cumming were feeling the effects of playing three games in five days it didn't show, with Willie in particular having an outstanding game in the 7–0 win.

With the score at 1–0 at half time, it was already apparent that Willie had formed a formidable partnership with Aberdeen's Graham Leggat. Sammy Baird of Rangers, however, did not seem to gel just as well and our friend 'Edina' of the *Evening News* was calling for Jimmy Wardhaugh to replace him and play alongside Bauld and Leggat in the full Scottish side. Although Willie grabbed a brace and helped the Aberdeen man notch a hat-trick, it was widely accepted that if he had Jimmy instead of Baird alongside him his tally would have been far more. It remained to be seen if the Scottish selectors would be able to see past their West Coast bias when they selected the side to take on the Swiss in a World Cup qualifier at Hampden on 6 November.

On Friday, 11 October the team for the trip to Cathkin was announced and, despite a disappointing display against Hibs the previous Monday, Willie Lindores retained his place in the side due to Tam Mackenzie's prolonged illness. There was an enforced change with George Thomson coming in for John Cumming, who had become the latest Tynecastle flu victim.

The talking-point, though, was the fact that the Scottish League had threatened to expel both Hearts and Hibs for their participation in the proposed 'Anglo-Scottish Floodlight League'. In the morning post, both clubs had received a letter from the Scottish League's Fred Denovan which stated that 'should you proceed in taking part in the Anglo-Scottish floodlight competition the management committee will not hesitate to use the Rule 56 of the Scottish Football League'. The rule to which the far-sighted Mr Denovan was alluding stipulated that the League had the power to suspend, fine or expel any club guilty of violating, infringing or failing to observe the rules of the league. This rule had only been drafted a few weeks earlier by the league's committee in an attempt to stop the ground-breaking competition. The trouble was that the rule had yet to be ratified by the Scottish Football Association and they were not due to meet till the following week. The decision to send the letters had been taken at a meeting that had been convened at Ibrox but had not included the participating clubs. It was obvious which two clubs were behind the move; how times have changed.

It transpired that the English teams due to participate had received a similar warning from the Football League. It was a farcical situation, as the first game was due to take place the following Monday when Tottenham were due to play Hibs at Easter Road. The London club had already made travel arrangements and it was thought they were prepared to follow through with their plans.

Neither Hearts nor Hibs offered their comments on the matter. All Tommy Walker would say was that he had received the letter but was only concentrating on the job in hand, beating Third Lanark the next day.

THIRD LANARK v HEARTS

Despite the fact that Third Lanark had upset the odds the previous week by beating Kilmarnock at Rugby Park, thus picking up their first points of the season, it was the Jam Tarts who were firm favourites to come away with both points. As always seems to be the case with Hearts, however, things didn't work out as expected. They got off to a very poor start at the back with Freddie Glidden in particular having difficulty coping with Thirds' centre, John Allan. On this occasion, the play of the forwards could not pull the game round and with SFA President John Park and selector George Brown sitting in the stand, it was not a good day for Messers Bauld and Wardhaugh to draw a blank.

Expected to keep up their high-scoring performances, the team just never got going. The game was played in a high wind, which may have been a factor, but the travelling support had not seen such bad passing and shooting from their favourites all season. Once again Hearts came up against a goalkeeper in inspired form – this time it turned out to be the Jocky Robertson show. What made things worse was that Jocky hailed from Edinburgh and was a self-confessed Hearts fan, but he was the man responsible for ending Hearts' 100 per cent start to the season.

League debutant Willie Lindores was the first to test Robertson when he used the wind advantage to hit one from long range. Although it had the distance, it didn't have the power to unduly trouble Jocky, who made a comfortable save. After ten minutes, he was called into action again and saved well from Willie Bauld after the centre had been let in when a dummy from Jimmy Wardhaugh had baffled the home defence. He denied the 'King' again two minutes later when he dived low to his right to turn a crisp effort round the post. Willie did eventually beat him with a header after twenty minutes but Owen Cosker was on the line to boot the ball clear.

It took twenty-five minutes for the hosts to mount their first raid and Gordon Marshall did well to guide a try from former Hibs defender Jim Brown over the bar. From the resultant corner, Bobby Craig should have done better than head over when he had been left unmarked.

Despite having most of the possession, Hearts were doing nothing with it and it was Thirds who should have taken the lead in the thirty-second minute. Brian Callan made progress down the left and sent in a tremendous ball across goal but unluckily for the home side there were no takers on hand. Hearts responded by galloping upfield, but Willie Bauld was denied once again when his powerful strike was saved by the keeper. Robertson was becoming Willie's nemesis. To prove the point he thwarted Willie again after thirty-eight minutes, sticking out a foot to stop the centre putting Hearts in the lead.

Willie's luck didn't change in the second half and Jocky was at it again when he somehow got his body behind a pile driver from the Hearts no. 9. Thirds steadily worked their way into the game using the wind advantage to good effect. They had a decent penalty claim with sixty-six minutes on the clock, when Freddie Glidden looked to have used an arm to clear the ball. A moment later, Freddie required treatment from the trainer after coming off second-best in a tussle with Johnnie Allan. After a few minutes with the 'magic' sponge Freddie was able to carry on but he was clearly feeling the injury. Allan took advantage of the centre-half's handicap and beat him easily before firing in a ferocious effort but Gordon Marshall flung himself full length to prevent Hearts going behind. It was Gordon's turn to keep his side in the game with 'wonder saves' and, with only eight minutes remaining, his stop from a Geoff Slingsby thunderbolt certainly entered that category.

Thirds were in full cry and had a second penalty claim turned down when Bobby Craig tumbled in the box after an untidy challenge from Willie Lindores. Another decision by the referee came to Hearts' rescue moments later when Brian Callan was pulled up for offside after breaking free of the Hearts defence. The match ended with one last effort from Willie Bauld but once again he was denied, this time by the side netting, as he couldn't quite get his angle right with a vicious shot from the right.

Without doubt the poorest display of the season had seen Hearts lose their 100 per cent start. But to make matters worse, news filtered through that Hibs had beaten Queen's Park 2–0 at Easter Road and had knocked Hearts off the top of the league.

Hearts: Marshall, Kirk, Lindores, Mackay, Glidden, Thomson, Young, Murray, Bauld, Wardhaugh and Crawford

	Played	Won	Lost	Drawn	For	Against	Points
Hibs	6	5	1	0	13	5	10
Hearts	5	4	0	1	25	3	9
Clyde	4	4	0	0	14	3	8

There was better news back at Tynecastle, where the 'A' team had kept up their impressive start to the season by emulating the first-team performance the previous week by scoring nine. Hearts were 7–1 ahead when the half-time whistle went and a further two goals in the second forty-five saw them maintain their perfect start to the season.

Playing in an unfamiliar blue strip, Hearts raced into a three-goal lead after only six minutes. With two minutes on the clock, George

Campbell got his head to a corner from Danny Paton to open the scoring. Two minutes later and a precision pass by Alfie Conn split the Thirds defence that allowed Paton to fire home from twelve yards.

Third Lanark were rattled and their cause was not helped in the sixth minute when centre-half Peter Catterson attempted a clearance that hit left-back Hugh Smith and bounced behind Bill Herd into the net. George Campbell got his second after eleven minutes before Thirds managed to pull one back. A rare attack by the visitors ended with a penalty being awarded when Andy Simpson was impeded in the box. Alex Harley stepped up and drilled his spot-kick beyond Wilson Brown with ease.

However, any hopes of a comeback were thwarted in a remarkable two-minute period just before half time. In forty-three minutes Johnny Hamilton was hauled to the ground in the box and Jimmy Milne had no trouble beating Herd. A minute later and George Campbell completed his hat-trick for goal number six. Hearts gained possession straight from the kick-off and there was still enough time in the half for Alfie Conn to grab another.

Not surprisingly, the second period could not match the first for goal scoring opportunities, but it was Thirds who reduced the leeway when Andy Simpson headed in from a corner. Hearts regained their six-goal advantage in sixty-five minutes when Johnny Hamilton picked out Alan Finlay, who finished with aplomb. The scoring finally came to an end when Alfie Conn got his second ten minutes from time.

Hearts 'A': Brown, J. Thomson, Mackintosh, Smith, Milne, Higgins, Paton, Conn, Campbell, Finlay and Hamilton

Reserve League:

	Played	Won	Lost	Drawn	For	Against	Points
Kilmarnock	6	4	1	1	21	9	9
Hearts	**4**	**4**	**0**	**0**	**22**	**3**	**8**
Hibs	5	4	1	0	14	9	8

BOLTON v HEARTS (FLOODLIGHT FRIENDLY)

There was no time for the senior XI to reflect on their poor performance and the dropped point against Third Lanark as they gathered
at Tynecastle on Sunday to head off to Bolton to take on the Wanderers
at the opening of their floodlighting system.

The display at Burnden Park was infinitely better than at Cathkin,
but for the second time in a couple of days Hearts only came away
with a draw. For the game Bobby Blackwood took the place of Ian
Crawford on the left wing, as Ian had taken a knock against Third
Lanark. In defence, George Thomson was moved to replace Willie
Lindores with seventeen-year-old Billy Higgins earning a call-up from
the reserves.

Hearts supporter Billy had signed from Dalkeith Thistle in June,
but he had nearly become 'the one that got away' after being provi-
sionally signed by Rangers. From his early schooldays at Dalry
Primary he had shown promise and he was a regular in Edinburgh
Select sides. However, a move to non-football-playing Boroughmuir
meant that Billy did not take the recognised schools football route
to a professional career. Instead, he played for Balgreen Rovers in
the juvenile ranks and it was there that he came to the attention of
scouts from several senior sides including Hearts.

But it was Rangers who moved first and offered him a lucrative
£3 a week which he would receive when he signed a professional
contract on his seventeenth birthday. Prior to this, during the 1956–57
season, Rangers farmed him out to Dalkeith Thistle where his performances attracted interest from Hearts again. With Billy 'tied' to Rangers,
it would be difficult to get him to Tynecastle, but the lure of playing
in Gorgie was too great for him and, despite losing out financially (the
£3 a week had by that time added up to a tidy sum), he successfully
negotiated his release from the Ibrox club with Scot Symon. Now in
his first season he found himself lining up with his heroes at Burnden
Park.

The first forty-five minutes was played in a distinctly 'friendly'
manner and neither goalkeeper was called into any serious action.

Jimmy Wardhaugh's neat passing was a feature of Hearts' play throughout, so it came as no surprise that it was Jimmy who eventually put Hearts into a well-deserved lead early in the second half. Willie Bauld began the move and Alex Young carried it on before putting in a cross that Jimmy deflected past eighteen-year-old Joe Dean (a replacement for England international Eddie Hopkinson) in the Bolton goal. It amazed the 22,000 crowd that Hearts didn't manage to add to their tally, so much were they on top. Even the prompting of Nat Lofthouse could not get his side into the game.

However, in seventy-eight minutes George Thomson was adjudged to have pushed Robert Deacon in an off-the-ball incident in the box. A very generous decision by the ref, but Terry Allcock sent Gordon Marshall the wrong way from the spot to make it 1–1. So although Hearts didn't get the win they probably deserved, the polished performances of Thomson (despite the penalty incident), Murray and Wardhaugh gave the team heart for their next league fixture against Aberdeen.

The Hearts team that night was: Marshall, Kirk, Thomson, Mackay, Glidden, Higgins, Young, Murray, Bauld, Wardhaugh and Blackwood

On the same evening, the first of the 'Anglo-Scottish League' fixtures went ahead with Spurs' visit to Easter Road. It had been decided to go on with the game but on a 'friendly' basis. In an entertaining game Hibs ended winning 5–2 in front of an 18,000 crowd, but it was thought this might be the one and only game ever played in the 'League'. Not only was there the thorny question of the League managements' stance: the 'low' turnout did not appear to make it financially viable. The participating clubs had agreed to split the gate, but Spurs' share had not cleared the £1,000-plus-expenses offers they had received from the continent. It was thought that they were now unwilling to fulfil their fixtures up north if the games were to be played on a 'friendly' basis.

The SFA had so far ignored the debate about the new tournament, but the selectors could hardly ignore the form of Hearts so far that season, and again the team were to be represented at yet another level. On Thursday, 17 October Mackay and Young were selected for a Scotland Under-23 XI to meet Holland Under-23 at Tynecastle on the Wednesday of the following week. It didn't end there, as Johnny Hamilton and George Thomson were to be among the reserves for the game and Johnny Harvey was to be trainer. Interestingly, no Rangers or Partick Thistle players were in the squad, as they had an important Glasgow Cup tie arranged for the same evening!

In the same Under-23 side was Norrie Davidson, the Aberdeen forward who, along with Graham Leggat, would provide a dangerous attack for the Hearts defence to deal with. Leggat had proved his worth the previous Saturday when he netted five times against Airdrie. Also in that game, seventeen-year-old Dumfries schoolboy Billy Little wore the no. 9 shirt in place of Davidson who was out through flu. He had played so well that he retained his place in favour of the more experienced man who lined up at inside-right. However, as had already been seen that season, Hearts had their own free-scoring forwards.

With Mackenzie and Cumming not fully recovered from flu, there was only one change to the side that had drawn with Bolton on Monday. Wilson Brown took over from Marshall in goal, as Gordon had also taken a knock in the game.

Wilson had started his career with Lanark United and it was not long before he was attracting the interest of several senior clubs. Chelsea and Motherwell were both keen to get his signature before Celtic took him on trial and he even played for the Parkhead side against Dumbarton in a benefit match for Tommy Donegan. However, the then Hearts keeper Jimmy Brown had already spotted his potential at an SFA coaching session. Jimmy ensured the Tynecastle management were aware of Wilson and on 18 October 1952 he signed for the Hearts.

For the next eighteen months he continued to play for Lanark United before he was called up to Tynecastle. Unfortunately, this coincided with the start of his national service with the Royal Scots, but because they were stationed at Glencorse Barracks, Wilson managed a handful of 'C' Division games during his first season at the club. The next season Wilson made his first-team debut against Raith Rovers in the League Cup after Willie Duff had been injured a few days earlier against Partick Thistle. He stayed between the sticks for a further three League Cup ties and the opening league game of the season against Dundee before Duff recovered from injury and took over in goals.

By the start of the 1956–57 season Wilson's national service had come to an end and, with Willie Duff starting his period in the Forces, Wilson played the majority of the games in goal that season. However, he did miss the last six games when the young Gordon Marshall wore the yellow jersey.

Billy Higgins' good performance at Bolton earlier in the week meant he kept his place in the side, as did Bobby Blackwood who continued in place of Ian Crawford.

HEARTS v ABERDEEN

This game was sure to be a test of Hearts' mettle after the disappointing result against Third Lanark the previous week. Although they did not manage to hit the high standard of the last game at Tynecastle, the Gorgie men were far too good for a lacklustre Dons side. A commanding George Thomson nullified the threat of Graham Leggat and inside-right Norrie Davidson had a match to forget. Jimmy Murray continued his fine scoring form by notching a brace, but it was Alex Young who got the goal of the game with a superb left-foot shot from twenty-five yards out. Bobby Blackwood marked his return to the side by getting the fourth and final goal of the game.

Hearts appeared in an unfamiliar change strip of all white shirts and shorts to avoid a clash with the away side. The outfit might have been different but it was a very familiar start to the game as they roared into attack straight from the off. George Thomson announced his presence to Graham Leggat in the first minute with the Scottish internationalist needing attention from the trainer before he could continue. He had plenty of time to recover as Hearts dominated the play for long spells, with Bauld and Wardhaugh both going close.

When Aberdeen did get a chance, Billy Higgins and George Thomson were there to snuff out the threat of both Davidson and Leggat. George in particular looked as though he was out to make his mark on the game, or Leggat, as he received a long lecture from the referee Mr Phillips for his second 'robust' tackle of the game on the Aberdeen forward.

Despite their domination Hearts did not manage to manufacture a clear-cut chance until, with twenty-six minutes gone, the trusted combination of Wardhaugh and Bauld combined to set up Jimmy Murray who rammed the ball past Fred Martin. Unlike so many other games at Tynecastle so far that season, though, the opening goal was not the sign for the away team to capitulate and Aberdeen were more than a match for the Maroons. It was fair to say that it was the half-back line of Archie Glen, Jim Wallace and Ken Brownlie that were responsible for keeping the Dons in contention. But just as it looked as though Aberdeen might force an equaliser, Hearts broke up the park and doubled their advantage two minutes before the interval. Jimmy Wardhaugh was the architect once more with a defence-splitting ball to Jimmy Murray who finished in style.

After the break Hearts continued in the same mood, Bauld and Young combining well to produce an opportunity for number three, but Martin in the Dons' goal was alert to the danger. It didn't stop Willie putting in a hefty challenge on the keeper, which resulted in a stern word from the ref.

At the other end, all debutant Wilson Brown had to do was watch as Hearts mounted attack after attack but it was not until the seventy-fifth minute when he had something to celebrate. Alex Young made the points safe when he scored Hearts' third. It certainly was a 'twenty-first celebration' to remember, as this was Hearts' twenty-first league goal at home so far. It certainly was in the 'special' category: Alex collected the ball thirty yards out, then proceeded to waltz past three Aberdeen defenders before sending a superb left-foot shot high into the net from twenty-five yards.

Nothing could top that goal, but Bobby Blackwood tried his best when he took a potshot from the edge of the area. Possibly the ruck of players in front of him wrong-footed Fred Martin, for the Aberdeen goalie dived the wrong way as Bobby's attempt hit the back of the net.

Despite what was an easy 4–0 win, the performance didn't seem to satisfy the support and no doubt there was plenty of discussion in the Craigmillar Hearts Supporters' Club's new premises which had opened that day. Obviously the crowds in those days were a lot harder to please. Imagine beating Aberdeen by four goals and still complaining! High standards indeed. The news that Hibs had suffered a 3–0 defeat at Dens Park, allowing Hearts once again to take over at the top, might have lightened the mood.

In the Monday edition of the *Evening News* the report of the game concentrated on the fact that 'the poise and polish of the previous season had gone', this despite the fact that the defence had only conceded three goals in six league games. 'On numerous occasions they had shown a little nervousness that at times verged on panic,' according to 'Restalrig'. However, Edinburgh City product George Thomson had done himself no harm with a solid show against the Dons and his 'challenges' on Leggat had won warm approval amongst the Gorgie faithful. Was he to be the final piece in the jigsaw?

Hearts: *Brown, Kirk, Thomson, Mackay, Glidden, Higgins, Young, Murray, Bauld, Wardhaugh and Blackwood*

Amazingly, on the same day the reserves had once again emulated the first team's result from the previous week. In a dull game the spirited Pittodrie youngsters held them to a no-scoring draw. With Wilson promoted to the first team to replace the injured Marshall, Hearts drafted in a trialist to play in goals.

The stand-in keeper performed well and Hearts had their chances throughout but could not break down a resolute Dons defence. George Campbell should have done better than hit Aberdeen stopper Reg Morrison on the legs after he got a second opportunity when the keeper could not hold his initial attempt. Next, Hugh Goldie hit one from twenty yards, only to see the big keeper get down well to turn the ball round the post.

Some positional changes by Aberdeen after the beak saw an improvement in their play and it was not long before Bobby Bryans gave Newman in the Hearts goal his first real test. At the other end Ian Crawford almost beat Morrison when the keeper failed to deal with the winger's shot. Once again he let the ball squirm from his grasp but unfortunately for Hearts there was no one on hand to take advantage.

Hearts 'A': *Newman, J. Thomson, Lindores, Smith, Milne, Bowman, Paton, Campbell, Goldie, McFadzean and Crawford*

Despite the setback they remained in touch with league leaders Kilmarnock who had now played three games more than the wee Jam Tarts.

	Played	Won	Lost	Drawn	For	Against	Points
Kilmarnock	9	7	1	1	31	12	15
Hearts	**6**	**5**	**0**	**1**	**24**	**4**	**11**
Hibs	7	5	1	1	17	11	11

On Wednesday a Scotland Under-23 side including Alex Young and Dave Mackay took on their Dutch counterparts at Tynecastle. A feature of the match was the appearance on the park of the Dutch team fifteen minutes before kick-off. Dutch coach Elek Schwartz amazed the crowd by sending his men out for a series of limbering-up exercises. This was so unusual that the normally unflappable groundsman Mattie Chalmers was caught out when Schwartz asked for footballs to practise with.

Despite the lack of a pre match warm-up, it was the Scots who took the game to the visitors. An all-round impressive performance was capped off by goals from the Clyde pair George Herd and Dan Currie, plus the Hearts duo, as the Scots cruised to a comfortable 4–1 victory. Indeed, Dave Mackay was the best player on view and his counter from the penalty spot was just reward for his performance. He now looked ready to step up to the full international side once again.

HEARTS SEE THE LIGHT (OCTOBER)

Dave had made his international debut against a strong Spanish side in the Bernabéu stadium back in May that year. He had taken the place of Rangers' Ian McColl, but the Scots went down 4–1 and Davie paid the price as McColl was restored the next game in the team that drew 1–1 with Northern Ireland on 5 October.

Hearts' next game was the usual tough trip to Ibrox to take on a Rangers side that had played three games fewer in the league. They had been impressive so far in their campaign in the European Cup, but had been a slightly less so when they could only manage to draw 1–1 with Partick Thistle in the Glasgow Cup tie played on the same evening as the Scots' Under-23 clash.

The news from the Hearts camp was that John Cumming had recovered from injury and was available to return to the starting line-up. Young Billy Higgins returned to reserve team football to play for the still-undefeated second string that also included Gordon Marshall in goals.

Some 10,000 fans turned out on the Friday evening to see the 'A' team take on the Rangers reserves under the floodlights at Tynecastle. It turned out that there would be another similarity between the first and second string. After taking an early lead, when Hugh Goldie headed home a Danny Paton cross, the second string were rocked when Bobby Morrison equalised in the twenty-fifth minute.

Despite Johnny Hamilton and Hugh Goldie running the 'Gers' defence ragged, Hearts couldn't find a way through. It was a bad-tempered encounter and Rangers' left-half Bill Logie received a long lecture from the referee after a bad foul on Alfie Conn. Alfie got his revenge in the best way possible when, with the game drawing towards a close, Billy Ritchie in the Rangers goal fumbled a high ball and Alfie was on hand to stroke home the winner.

A Rangers keeper making a mistake for a Hearts winner – surely that would never happen again for a long time.

Hearts 'A': *Marshall, J. Thomson, Lindores, Smith, Milne, Higgins, Paton, Conn, Goldie, McFadzean and Hamilton*

RANGERS v HEARTS

Even back then, visits to Ibrox had rarely been fruitful for Hearts. In the previous twelve league games they had only managed three wins. Indeed, in the same period at Tynecastle Hearts had only won once. However this time, in what turned out to be the proverbial game of two halves, the Maroons managed to return to the capital with both points as they fought back from two down to win 3–2 and could even afford the luxury of another penalty miss (this time by Bobby Kirk).

Fresh from a thumping 7–1 defeat in the League Cup final by arch-rivals Celtic the week before, Rangers were in determined mood to get back on track. This was perfectly illustrated in the match programme, where club chairman John F. Wilson wrote about their resolve for the future. You could almost feel the old chap's anger at the result when, in true Winston Churchill style, he wrote: 'Believe me, that in speaking for my Board of Directors and in fact all within the Ibrox Stadium, I assure you we shall go forward confident that from this hour of disappointment will come, as in the past, moments of high endeavour and undoubted worthy achievement.' He went on, 'Fruit does not grow on branches alone. The Ibrox trunk is healthy, and I have no doubt whatever but that we shall return to the summer of production.' Hard to imagine a club chairman rambling on in riddles these days.

Mr Wilson's words of wisdom certainly inspired the players of the day as they went at Hearts straight from the start. Wilson Brown rushed from his goal in the first minute to block a shot from Billy Simpson. The ball spun into the air over the keeper but George Thomson raced back to make the clearance before it could trundle over the line.

Dave Mackay and John Cumming looked decidedly uncomfortable, with the blustery conditions doing nothing to help the back line. The 'Gers took full advantage. Despite a couple of opportunities at the other end, they took the lead in the seventeenth minute. Johnny Hubbard played the ball into the middle and the Hearts defence, watching for the threat of Don Kichenbrand, allowed Simpson to run in and glance the ball into the net. Things did not look good for the Gorgie men – never having been behind in the league this season, the away support began to wonder how the team would react.

They answered by coming back strongly and when Willie Moles failed to clear properly, Jimmy Murray was presented with a golden opportunity. Moles' mistake took Jimmy by surprise, with him ending up shooting weakly straight at George Niven. The 'old heads' then created a chance with Wardhaugh nodding on to Bauld but the 'King's' effort came back off the post and Niven was able to collect the rebound.

Despite Hearts pressing forward, it was Rangers who went further ahead in twenty-eight minutes, in controversial circumstances. Wilson Brown went up to collect an innocuous cross from Hubbard but, as he was in the air, Don Kichenbrand came rushing in. The big South African was not nicked named 'Rhino' for nothing and the goalie took the full force of the centre's challenge, crumpling down in a heap. The ball broke to Billy Simpson; with Brown lying motionless, he lashed the ball into the empty net from fifteen yards. It was a goal that could only be witnessed in two grounds, both in Glasgow.

After treatment the shaken goalie was able to carry on but Hearts found themselves with a mountain to climb. Rangers went in for the kill, knowing that Brown was still groggy. The defence stood firm, protecting their keeper but Dave Mackay put him under a bit of pressure when he was short with a pass back and he had to race from his line to save from Kichenbrand at the second attempt. The incident certainly tested the stopper's powers of recovery.

The team's powers of recovery were evident two minute before the interval, when Jimmy Wardhaugh brought them back into the game. Willie Bauld pounced on another mistake by Willie Moles after the defender missed a through-ball from Alex Young. As the 'King' ran in on goal, he stumbled as he went round George Niven and with the goal gaping the ball broke back to Alex – he rolled it to Jimmy, who fizzed a left-foot drive into the net, via the upright.

Surprisingly, the home support did not share Jimmy's joy and the police had to wade into the crowd to restore order in their own unique fashion.

The goal had inspired Hearts and it took only three minutes after the restart before they drew level. Eric Caldow was guilty of a poor clearance as the ball found its way to Willie Bauld, who made no mistake this time.

It was end-to-end stuff, with both sides having their chances, but Hearts were given the perfect opportunity to beak the deadlock in fifty-six minutes. Wardhaugh won the ball just inside the Rangers box and audaciously chipped it over the advancing Niven. The ball was heading into the back of the net until Eric Caldow managed to get back to punch the ball away. Up stepped Bobby Kirk, but he became the latest member of the 'Hearts Missed Penalty Club' when his fierce strike sailed well over the bar.

Despite the miss, Hearts were in the ascendancy and in the sixty-seventh minute George Thomson went on a storming sixty-yard run. After beating three men, he slipped the ball to Jimmy Wardhaugh. Jimmy found the marauding Alex Young, who made space before firing in a shot. Although it was rising, Alex had hit it straight at George Niven, but the keeper took his eye off the ball and let it slip over his head and into the net. Sammy Baird and Don Kichenbrand did not take kindly to the goal and this time the referee, not the police, dealt out his own brand of punishment.

The game was still far from over and, although stunned, Rangers came roaring back. But they came up against Freddie Glidden, who emerged as the hero of the day. After having what had been a titanic struggle, he had now got the measure of Rangers' main threat, Kichenbrand. It was just the latest episode in what had developed into a fascinating 'match-up' that had started back in the summer of 1955 when Freddie had first come up against Don on Hearts' tour of South Africa.

With 'Kitch' well marked and a goal down, Rangers seemed to run out of ideas and Hearts looked the more likely. Eric Caldow (still on the park despite the deliberate handball) cleared a shot from Willie

Bauld before George Niven had to be at his best to prevent Bobby Blackwood increasing the lead.

The hosts did come close to getting an equaliser with twelve minutes left, when Thomson cleared a header from Sammy Baird with Wilson Brown stranded. The keeper redeemed himself in the dying seconds as he brought off a brilliant save from a sweetly struck free kick from Ian McColl. A great result for Hearts – but one that must have given the Rangers chairman palpitations.

Hearts: Brown, Kirk, Thomson, Mackay, Glidden, Cumming, Young, Murray, Bauld, Wardhaugh and Blackwood
Rangers: Niven, Caldow, Little, McColl, Moles, Miller, Scott, Simpson, Kichenbrand, Baird and Hubbard

By the end of October Hearts led the way by two points but had played a game fewer than their two closest rivals Raith and Hibs.

	Played	Won	Lost	Drawn	For	Against	Points
Hearts	7	6	0	1	32	5	13
Raith Rovers	8	4	1	3	14	9	11
Hibs	8	5	2	1	15	10	11

Immediately after the Rangers game Willie Watters, chairman of St Mirren, contacted the Tynecastle directors to enquire about the possibility of selling Alfie Conn. Hard as it may seem to believe, the board did not immediately turn down the offer. Instead they agreed they would discuss the matter at their next board meeting during the week.

Tuesday, 29 October saw the Scottish selectors fail to recognise the fine form of the league leaders and only Willie Bauld and Jimmy Wardhaugh were named in the 'Reserves in Attendance' for the World Cup qualifier against Switzerland the following Wednesday. Despite Davie Mackay having been in outstanding form during the unbeaten run, he was still left out in the cold. The same day, Hearts continued their two-games-in-a-week pattern when the first team squad caught the train down to Norwich to take on the Canaries in a friendly on the 30th. The only omission from the team that had taken on Rangers was Wilson Brown, who had injured an arm in the clash with 'Rhino' Kichenbrand at Ibrox. Gordon Marshall had recovered from his injury and re-assumed his place between the posts.

NORWICH v HEARTS (FLOODLIGHT FRIENDLY)

It certainly turned out to be a special day for a certain Fraser Macdonald Smith and his proud parents. While serving in the RAF at Turnhouse during his national service, Fraser's father (known only as K. H. Smith, I'm afraid) regularly attended Tynecastle, but after being demobbed he moved home to Norwich. He was so pleased about hearing of Hearts' visit that he wrote to the club wishing them well in their quest for the championship but added that, since the recent birth of Fraser, he would probably not be able to attend the game. In what can only be described as a magnanimous gesture, Tommy Walker took time out from pre-match preparations and, along with directors Alex Irvine and Robert Tait, visited the Smith family home.

Unfortunately Smith senior was at work, but Mrs Smith was the grateful recipient of what was described at the time as 'an appropriate piece of silver' marking the arrival of Fraser and match tickets to enable her husband to see the game with a couple of his friends. It takes some managers all their time to even grunt to supporters these days, but this was just another example of how remarkable both Tommy Walker as a man and Heart of Midlothian as a club were.

For the second game in a row it was a game of two halves, with the Maroons managing to win by the odd goal in seven – six of them coming in the first half of what turned out to be a pulsating ninety minutes. Despite a bright start, Hearts went one down after thirteen minutes when Peter Gordon pounced on a loose ball after Gordon Marshall couldn't hold a shot from John Gavin. However, it only took Jimmy Murray a minute to snatch the equaliser with a fine drive from outside the area.

HEARTS SEE THE LIGHT (OCTOBER)

Following excellent passing play by the forwards, Jimmy Wardhaugh put Hearts ahead with a well-placed drive. Another minute and another goal, this time from Alex Young who took on the home defence and finished off a tremendous solo effort in style.

Comfortably ahead 3–1, Hearts were stunned when Norwich hit back with two quick goals of their own just before the interval. A rare mistake by Gordon Marshall in the fortieth minute saw City pull one back when he allowed a speculative strike from Peter Gordon to slip from his grasp and into the net. He had no chance five minutes later, when Ralph Hunt found the back of the net after he got on the end of a cross from Billy Coxon seconds before the whistle sounded for the end of the half.

The second half could not quite live up to the standard set in the first. Hearts reorganised to snuff out the danger that had been posed by Bobby Brennan. George Thomson effectively marked the Irish international out of the rest of the game. At the other end, Ken Oxford in the home goal kept the Hearts forward line at bay but he was let down by his defensive colleagues with twenty minutes remaining. As they tried to clear the ball, everyone seemed to get in each other's way and Jimmy Wardhaugh pounced to get what turned out to be the winner. I am sure that if Mr Smith had managed to be part of the 17,909 crowd, he wandered home to young Fraser MacDonald having been royally entertained.

Hearts: Marshall, Kirk, Thomson, Mackay, Glidden, Cumming, Young, Murray, Bauld, Wardhaugh and Blackwood
Norwich City: Oxford, J. Wilson, Ashman, R. Wilson, Butler, Crowe, Gordon, Brennan, Gavin, Hunt and Coxon

4

A SHOCK DEFEAT (NOVEMBER)

HEARTS v MOTHERWELL

Back to league business on Saturday, 2 November and the next visitors to Gorgie were a Motherwell side including Gerry Baker, the brother of Hibs' Joe. However, it was another 'Well youngster who stole the headlines when Ian St John bagged a brace that was enough to see Hearts drop only their second point of the season. There were a couple of changes to the team that had beaten Rangers, as Marshall had proved in midweek that he was sufficiently fit again to regain his place from Wilson Brown. On the left, Ian Crawford came back to partner Jimmy Wardhaugh, with Bobby Blackwood being the man to step down after sustaining a cut above his eye against Norwich.

From the start there were question marks posed against the defence, when the loss of an early goal put the Gorgie men on the back foot. Ian St John took advantage to make it 1–0 when Gordon Marshall was deceived by an innocuous ball into the area from Willie McSeveney, the Motherwell centre. Hearts responded strongly with Willie Bauld bringing out the best in Alan Wyllie after eleven minutes, when his powerful free kick beat the defensive wall but the former Penicuik keeper was well positioned to turn the ball round the post. It took another four minutes before the breakthrough came. Jimmy Wardhaugh needed two attempts before he could finally prod the ball over the line – it was a messy affair, but they all count.

Jimmy almost put Hearts into the lead ten minutes later, when his snap shot looked as though it was in all the way until Alan

Wyllie somehow managed to palm the ball clear. Jimmy was not to be denied and in the twenty-seventh minute he lashed a goal-bound Willie Bauld header high into the net past an astonished Wyllie.

In the second half Freddie Glidden, so commanding against Rangers the previous week, had been troubled throughout by Willie McSeveney. Gordon Marshall was also having his 'moments' but he could not be blamed for the visitors' equaliser when the whole defence were caught out as Ian St John got his second of the game. The 'Well man was convinced he had won a penalty when he tumbled in the box with fifty-one minutes gone, but the referee was having none of it. As play went on around him, he picked himself up just in time for the ball to break to him and, unmarked, he swept the ball into the net.

Moments later it could have been worse, with Gordon Marshall having Bobby Kirk to thank for a goal-line clearance after the young keeper let a free kick from Archie Shaw slip through his hands. While the Hearts defence were unsteady, at the other end of the park the forwards were finding it difficult against a back line excellently marshalled by Shaw, who was ably assisted by Charlie Aitken and Bob Gilchrist. When Hearts did break through, they found Alan Wyllie a tough nut to crack. Twice he stopped powerful headers from Willie Bauld.

There was a real let-off for the Gorgie men in sixty-five minutes, when McSeveney brushed off Freddie Glidden's challenge and burst through on goal. The big centre rounded Marshall but, in doing so, took the ball slightly wide and, with the goal gaping, he somehow managed to put the ball over the bar. Hearts might have sneaked it fifteen minutes from time when Wyllie allowed yet another Willie Bauld header out of his grasp. Unfortunately for the Maroons, he managed to twist himself round and grab the ball before it could cross the line. No goalkeeping error to help them out this week.

Hearts: Marshall, Kirk, Thomson, Mackay, Glidden, Cumming, Young, Murray, Bauld, Wardhaugh and Crawford

The 'A' team had fared better through at Fir Park but like the first team, they had got off to the worst possible start. The opening quarter had been even before Rea took advantage of a defensive mix-up in fifteen minutes to put the home side one up. Things got worse when seventeen-year-old Willie Hunter, who had been signed from Edina Hearts, headed in a second goal five minutes before the end of the half. Things looked bleak, but a spirited fightback in the second half saw Hearts take the points.

Danny Paton was first to reduce the leeway and when Johnny Hamilton levelled it there was only ever going to be one winner. Hugh Goldie put the Tynecastle youngsters in front and then hit the back of the net again to put the game beyond doubt by scoring his second and Hearts' fourth.

Hearts 'A': Newman, Parker, Mackenzie, Bowman, Milne, Higgins, Paton, Conn, Goldie, McFadzean and Hamilton

HEARTS v MANCHESTER CITY (FLOODLIGHT FRIENDLY)

Their performance against Bobby Ancell's men was roundly panned in the press the following Monday, but there was no time for the team to reflect on the dropped point, as two days later the Manchester City team coach pulled up at Tynecastle for another 'floodlight friendly'. Given that the defence had been so heavily criticised for their performance, it was perhaps a surprise that the only two changes from Saturday's team were Blackwood and Hamilton replacing Young and Crawford respectively.

The City team, containing such luminaries as Bert Trautmann, ex-Hibee Bobby Johnstone and fellow Scot Dave Ewing, had been narrowly defeated 2–1 at Highbury on Saturday but were performing well in the English First Division. A deputation from Tynecastle, including Tommy Walker, met the team at Turnhouse airport around midday. They were then taken to the Roxburghe Hotel and entertained to lunch. By the time the dispirited crowds trooped out of Tynecastle later that day, perhaps the Hearts board were not feeling as generous to the men from Manchester: soundly beaten 5–3, Hearts had once again shown that they were not at their best playing under the lights.

It had all started so differently when, with twelve minutes played, Jimmy Murray opened Hearts' account. Following a foul on Bobby Blackwood by Bill McAdam, Dave Mackay took the free kick and Jimmy Murray was on the spot to head over Bert Trautmann. Four minutes later, Willie Bauld latched on to a defence-splitting pass from Mackay and blasted an unstoppable left-foot shot from the eighteen-yard line that whistled past the City goalkeeper. It looked as though the Maroons were on 'easy street'. However, for the second game in a row Freddie Glidden looked unsteady and on a couple of occasions Gordon Marshall had to be alert when dealing with his pass backs. Three minutes from the break City pulled one back, when another moment of hesitancy by Freddie allowed Joe Hayes to take advantage. As Bobby Kirk raced across to cover, he could only deflect the shot beyond Marshall.

In the second half City manager Les McDowall made a tactical change that saw his team come even more into the game. Bobby Johnstone started playing deeper, his runs and sweeping passes causing the Hearts back line all sorts of bother. In fifty-five minutes City grabbed a deserved equaliser when a clearance by Freddie Glidden only went as far as Paddy Fagan. He took the ball to the bye-line and crossed perfectly for Hayes to net his second. It took them only a further three minutes to make it 3–2, although Bobby Johnstone looked yards offside when he audaciously lobbed the ball into the net from well out.

Spurred into action, Hearts came back to equalise in the seventy-third minute with Johnny Hamilton squaring a free kick to John Cumming. His drive was going well off target but Jimmy Murray managed to 'get in the way' and diverted the ball into the net.

City continued to trouble the Hearts rearguard and, when Dave Mackay slipped trying to cut out a McAdam through pass seven minutes from the end, Bobby Johnstone blasted the ball into the net for his second of the game. The agony did not end there: right on time Hayes, left to run through on goal, flicked the ball over the advancing Marshall and Billy McAdam, running in from a suspiciously offside position, had the easiest of jobs to trundle the ball into an empty net.

Hearts: Marshall, Kirk, Thomson, Mackay, Glidden, Cumming, Blackwood, Murray, Bauld, Wardhaugh and Hamilton
Manchester City: Trautmann, Lievers, Sear, Barnes, Ewing, Warhurst, Barlow, Hayes, Johnstone, McAdams and Fagan

The game had given Tommy Walker a few headaches. Was the title challenge going off the rails? Not only were there still obvious problems in defence, but both Bobby Kirk and Willie Bauld had picked up injuries. The groin injury to Bauld also put him out of consideration for the Scottish team to play Wales, which was to be announced later that week.

Perhaps now showing signs of strain and fatigue, the squad were probably glad to hear that the game arranged against Newcastle at St James' Park on 13 November had been postponed. It had been announced that Manchester United's European Cup tie against Dukla Prague at Maine Road (City had the benefit of floodlights and United didn't) to be played on the same evening was to be televised. Directors of both Hearts and Newcastle agreed that this innovation might affect the gate and decided to wait until a later date.

After a practice game at Saughton enclosure on Wednesday, 6 November manager Walker announced the team to make the visit to Palmerston on Saturday. With the absence of Kirk, Bobby Parker came in for his first start of the season. In a major surprise, John Cumming was pushed forward into the outside-left position, with George Thomson taking over at no. 6. Ian Crawford swapped from the left to right wing and Alex Young moved to centre in place of the injured Bauld. To complete the shuffle, big Tam Mackenzie made a welcome return at left-back.

A SHOCK DEFEAT (NOVEMBER)

QUEEN OF THE SOUTH v HEARTS

With all the changes to the side, the Hearts faithful that made the journey south might have been more than a little wary. The editor of the match programme had noted the poor performance against City, even going as far as suggesting that because 'Queen's have a habit of doing well against Edina's darlings', they would emerge with both points at 4.10 p.m (it was a 2.30 kick-off). To counter the difference in the league he wrote, 'Placings on the league ladder could suggest only one outcome, but if that were a reliable guide, no one would ever win over £200,000.' The Lottery was still a few years away, but the football pools were on the go, so I presume it was a reference to that. However, if you were not lucky enough to win the pools, Queen's offered for the first time that season a chance to win big money in the form of a 'lucky programme'. The holder of the lucky number drawn at half time would receive a voucher (it did not state what the voucher was for) to the value of £1 (no, I have not missed out any zeros).

The Jam Tarts' first-half display was more than enough to shatter his dream of gaining any points, as they played some neat football, scoring two goals in the process. Particularly pleasing was the form of the defence, with the return of the two veterans Bobby Parker and Tom Mackenzie having a steadying influence.

Hearts went in front after twenty minutes when the ball was played from Young to Wardhaugh to Mackay, whose headed pass found the in-form Jimmy Murray with his back to goal. Quick as a flash, Jimmy produced a spectacular overhead kick that beat advancing Queen's keeper Roy Henderson. Jimmy was on target again minutes later, when Bobby Parker broke up an attack and 'hoofed' the ball down the middle. Alex Young latched onto the kick and sent Murray through with a precision pass that allowed the inside-right to bulge the net comfortably.

Good saves from Henderson prevented further scoring, one in particular from Jimmy Wardhaugh being the pick of the bunch. At one stage the keeper had to be helped out by his centre-half, Alan

Elliot, who bravely put his head in the way of a John Cumming 'rocket' from twelve yards out. It took all of the 'magic' from the trainer's sponge to enable him to continue.

Hearts began the second forty-five with only ten men – not, as you might think, to give Queen of the South a sporting chance, but because Bobby Blackwood had sustained a leg injury and stayed in the dressing-room for some treatment. Although not able to play at anything like 100 per cent, he made it back on to the park just in time to see John Cumming marking his debut in the front line with a goal. In the fifty-third minute Dave Mackay floated in a free kick and Cumming rose above the defence to head home. Hearts really were flowing, although the opposition Queen's were providing was not too stiff. Jimmy Wardhaugh thought he had added to the total but his effort was ruled out after he was caught narrowly offside.

The fourth goal was not long in arriving and, like the first, it was a wonderfully worked affair. Jimmy Murray drifted past former Tynecastle team-mate Dickie Whitehead and then Jimmy Greenock with ease. He then moved the ball onto Bobby Blackwood, who picked out Jimmy Wardhaugh, who in turn knocked it on for Alex Young to steer the ball home.

As Hearts continued to dominate, in a goalmouth 'stramash' of Arthur Montford proportions, John Cumming thought he had scored the fifth. Having initially signalled a goal, the referee consulted a linesman and then chalked it off for an offside decision against Alex Young in the build-up. During the melee Jimmy Murray injured his ankle and required lengthy treatment before coming back on the park to limp on the right wing for the rest of the game.

With four minutes left and against the run of play, Jim Patterson grabbed a consolation for the Doonhamers when he beat Gordon Marshall with a header after Bobby Tasker had crossed from the left.

The Hearts team who got back to winning form was:
Marshall, Parker, Mackenzie, Mackay, Glidden, Thomson, Blackwood, Murray, Young, Wardhaugh and Cumming

Although the 'firsts' won, the 'A' team could only manage a draw against their Queen of the South counterparts at Tynecastle. It had started so well for them when Alfie Conn saw a twenty-five-yarder hit the post with Bill Smith well beaten. Johnny Hamilton was similarly out of luck with a couple of early attempts. But it should have been the visitors who went ahead after a slip by Jimmy Milne let in Stewart: Newman did his chances of a contract no harm at all when he brilliantly turned away the forward's low strike.

It was all Hearts after that and Hamilton, Paton and Conn all had passed up gilt-edged chances to break the deadlock. They were to rue those misses, as the opening goal came from the visitors. With only seconds remaining in the half, Stan King broke through the Hearts rear guard and slotted home.

The second period saw Hearts race into attack and it took only two minutes before they had levelled the game. Danny Paton did well out wide and his cross was inch-perfect for Hugh Goldie to nod home. It looked like Hugh had repeated the feat only a minute later, but this time his effort was ruled out for offside.

It was a tight game and with both sides going all out for the winner. The tackles began to fly in and Johnny Hamilton took exception to a particularly robust challenge from Jimmy McGill. Both players found their way into the referee's book after a short burst of 'handbags'. That turned out to be the last action of the game as the second string had to settle for a disappointing draw.

Hearts 'A': *Newman, J. Thomson, Lindores, Bowman, Milne, Higgins, Paton, Conn, Goldie, McFadzean and Hamilton*

Victory against Queen of the South came at a price: along with the leg injuries to Bobby Blackwood and Jimmy Murray, Alex Young had turned an ankle. With Bobby Kirk and Willie Bauld still not fully fit, there was considerable doubt over the team that would line up against Partick Thistle in the re-arranged fixture two days later.

It turned out that only Bobby Blackwood was unable to take his place, with twenty-one-year-old Danny Paton stepping up from the reserve side that had stuttered to the 1–1 draw with Queen's reserves on Saturday. 'Danny' – or more accurately Robert – was a lifelong Hearts fan who had been signed from Newtongrange Star and was doing well in the 'wee team' with his name regularly on the scoresheet. As with many a lad of his age at the time, he listed his favourite hobby as 'old tyme dancing' – perhaps good practice for some fancy footwork to mesmerise the Partick defence.

PARTICK THISTLE v HEARTS

The criticism of the last few weeks had obviously had an effect on the back line, as they set the foundation for a comfortable win, although two quick goals put the Hearts in the driving seat after only thirteen minutes. Bobby Parker was solid throughout the game but his veteran partner, Tam Mackenzie, found the tricky George Smith hard to handle. On these occasions he was able to count on Freddie Glidden covering up, Freddie being the rock on which the win was built. Behind the defence, Gordon Marshall had a far better game than of late, producing some good saves when called upon. His stop from a free kick by Scotland international Jim Davidson was the pick of the bunch.

The scoring began in the ninth minute when the Partick keeper, Tommy Ledgerwood, could only palm a shot from Young back to the centre's feet; Alex made no mistake with his second chance. Four minutes later and quick thinking by Dave Mackay saw him baffle the Partick defence, when his long throw found John Cumming at the far post. Quick as a flash, John headed towards goal and another blunder by the Thistle goalkeeper allowed him to get his name on the scoresheet for the second week in a row as the ball rolled into the net to put Hearts two up.

The defence had been in commanding form, but there were a couple of lapses that saw Gordon Marshall firstly having to dive at George Smith's feet, then save well from Partick's no. 9, Jimmy Keenan, to allow Hearts to maintain their advantage. But he was beaten five minutes before the break when Bill Crawford pulled Thistle back into the game after being left unmarked at a corner.

Hearts' riposte was swift and it only took the men in maroon three minutes to restore their two-goal advantage when Jimmy Wardhaugh notched the third after being set up by the industrious Dave Mackay. In the second half Hearts seemed to be content to contain Partick and did so with ease. Although there was no further scoring, Dave Mackay was unlucky not to round off a great all-round performance with a goal when, in the dying seconds, his thirty-yard drive came thumping back off an upright.

Hearts: Marshall, Parker, Mackenzie, Mackay, Glidden, Thomson, Paton, Murray, Young, Wardhaugh and Cumming

The two points put Hearts three clear at the top of the league from nearest rivals Raith Rovers and Hibs, with the three teams now having played the same number of games. However, in the ten games played, Hearts had already scored forty-one goals compared to twenty-one by Raith and twenty-three by Hibs. The much-maligned defence had conceded only nine times, a record only matched by Rovers. With the visit of bottom club Queen's Park next up it was difficult to see Hearts slip up on the following Saturday. Despite the fact that the amateurs had managed to grab a draw in their last meeting in the League Cup, the team were more willing to remember the 9–2 hammering they had dished out to the same opponents two weeks earlier.

It was just as well that the team had performed so well at Firhill and that they had picked up no further injuries, as by Saturday they had lost their manager – albeit temporarily. On Friday, 15 November Tommy Walker had complained about feeling unwell when he was working at Tynecastle in the late evening. After he returned home, he became so ill that his wife had to call an ambulance. He was taken to Chalmers Hospital where it was diagnosed that he had appendicitis and he was operated on immediately. On the Saturday morning the hospital announced that Tommy was making good progress. He would remain in hospital for at least a week and then need further time to recover. Chairman Nicol Kilgour broke the news that he would take over management of the team (now where have I heard that before?) as well as Tommy's secretarial duties. As might be expected, the team that ran out at Tynecastle that afternoon was the same team that had taken on Partick.

HEARTS v QUEEN'S PARK

Mr Kilgour's managerial career could not have got off to a better start as the Gorgie men once again demolished the Hampden club, this time by an 8–0 scoreline. They could have matched the nine-goal tally they had hit back in August, had Davie Mackay not missed a penalty. On this occasion the destroyer-in-chief was the majestic Alex Young, who bagged himself a hat-trick. His display was described by 'Raeburn' of the *Evening News* as 'leading his forwards on a gay footballing frolic, tearing the Spiders' defensive web to bits'. For the third league game in a row, John Cumming joined Alex on the score-sheet, grabbing a brace from his new outside-left position.

Any of the 12,000 Gorgie faithful who turned out on a miserable afternoon and bought a programme before the game might have been surprised to read the content of 'Points from the Pavilion' (the name for the editorial). Even though it was only mid November, the editor was writing about forthcoming games. Not the following Saturday's fixture away to unbeaten Clyde, but the clash on 28 December with Celtic! As the league stood, Raith Rovers and Hibs were still the nearest challengers, three points behind. They were followed by Clyde and Kilmarnock on twelve points, but both having played two games less, and then came Celtic in sixth spot. What had caught the eye was the fact that they had only dropped one point from the six games they had played. If they won their games in hand, they would be able to go top.

On a more light-hearted note, it was reported in the 'Dressing Room Diary' feature of the programme that 'Little Johnny Hamilton' had made his debut in the East of Scotland Amateur Snooker Championship. Seven of his club mates and two directors had turned up to witness Hammy see off the challenge of a certain A. Bowie of Craigmillar by three frames to nil. Perhaps the Craigmillar lad was intimidated by such a big 'gang'. Johnny's next opponent was to be Mr J. Gillon of Leith on 20 November at 7 p.m. in the Working Men's Club, Infirmary Street. The programme editor hoped that 'there will be a large turn-out of Hearts Supporters'. These snooker tournaments must have been interesting affairs.

The crowd got a taste of what was to follow after only three minutes, when Danny Paton delivered a superb cross for Jimmy Wardhaugh to head towards goal. With Queen's keeper Frank Crampsey posted missing, it looked a goal all the way until Willie Hastie managed to get back to hook the ball clear. He repeated the act in the seventh minute when he was in the right place to clear a Jimmy Murray header off the line.

It was clear that Hearts were in the mood and it would only be a matter of time before they took the lead. Sure enough, the opener came after ten minutes when Alex Young finished off a textbook move that saw him head past Crampsey after Danny Paton had flicked on a Jimmy Murray cross. From that point it continued to be all Hearts but they somehow contrived not to take full advantage of their superiority. They were unlucky at times: Jimmy Murray saw a shot thump the crossbar and then Frank Crampsey's feet denied Jimmy Wardhaugh.

Gordon Marshall had been a virtual spectator but had to look sharp to deny Junior Omand after a rare attack by the visitors. This seemed to encourage the amateurs and Freddie Glidden did well to block a shot from Andy McEwan before Omand put a header wide of the post with Marshall out of position. The mini revival did not last, as Hearts took a firm grip of the game with a quick one-two. In thirty-nine minutes Bobby Cromar was adjudged to have handled the ball in the area. With regular penalty taker Bobby Kirk not playing, up stepped Dave Mackay to slot home the spot kick. Five minutes later and the game was over as a contest when Alex Young crashed home the third.

Hearts started the second half the way they finished the first and five minutes in they got further reward when Jimmy Wardhaugh was on hand to finish off a cross from John Cumming. A further five minutes went by before Alex Young completed his hat-trick in great style. After controlling a punt through the middle, his quick turn beat two defenders, then as Crampsey came out of his goal, Alex coolly lobbed it over the advancing keeper into the net. Alex was unstoppable – well, he would have been had centre-half Ian Drainer not resorted to pushing him to the ground two minutes later when he was through on goal. Dave Mackay placed the ball on the spot for the second time in the game and promptly became the third man to miss that season.

Just after the hour mark, Bobby Parker was out of luck to see his lob come back off the bar, but Johnny Cumming was on hand to nod home the rebound for goal number six. It was Cumming again who increased the tally when he finished off after a great solo run that saw him leave four defenders trailing in his wake. Minutes from the end, Danny Paton scored his first league goal of the season to round off the game in style.

Hearts: *Marshall, Parker, Mackenzie, Mackay, Glidden, Thomson, Paton, Murray, Young, Wardhaugh and Cumming*

At Lesser Hampden, Hearts 'A' had looked a jaded lot against the Strollers, but against the run of play they managed to snatch the lead when Hugh Goldie grabbed his fifth goal in four games after he latched on to a poor back pass by Ron McKinven.

Johnny Hamilton almost increased the lead, but his ferocious volley was well saved by Willie Pinkerton. The amateurs' cause was not helped when Bill Black went down injured with five minutes left in the half. He was limping badly as the trainer led him to the dressing-room and the Spiders played out the rest of the half with ten men.

Black's injury saw him remain in the dressing-room and Hearts took full advantage when Goldie got his second of the game. Jimmy Milne added another from the penalty spot before a further strike from Alan Finlay wrapped up the scoring for the afternoon.

Hearts 'A': *Brown, J. Thomson, Lindores, Smith, Milne, Higgins, Hamilton, Finlay, Goldie, McFadzean and Crawford*

Monday, 18 November and there was good news for the team as Bobby Kirk had recovered from injury and made a return against Motherwell at Fir Park in a Second XI third-round cup tie. Like the first team, the reserves were unbeaten so far and were confident about their trip to the cup holders Motherwell.

In front of 6,000 spectators it was 'Well who took the lead in the twentieth minute through Willie McSeveney, after Wilson Brown did well to parry a vicious drive from former Edina Hearts player Alan Stenhouse. Hearts deservedly equalised in thirty-four minutes when a free kick from Bobby Kirk was deflected by Hugh Goldie to Crawford and Ian just managed to slip the ball behind Frank Duncan in the Motherwell goal. Both sides had chances in the second half, but the game ended 1–1 with the replay being fixed for Wednesday, 27 November.

Hearts 'A': Brown, Kirk, Lindores, Bowman, Milne, Higgins, Hamilton, Blackwood, Goldie, Finlay and Crawford

Although Bobby Kirk had played well in the game it was a surprise when he was named in the side to take on Newcastle United at Tynecastle on Wednesday, 20 November as Hearts continued with their gruelling midweek programme. It was even more of a surprise when he was chosen to replace Danny Paton at outside-right. Bobby had been a winger in his junior days and had filled the position once before during the previous season in a game against St Mirren. There were several good wingers on Hearts' books at the time and even John Cumming was known to take up an outside role, so perhaps temporary manager Kilgour thought Bobby needed match practice no matter where he played.

HEARTS v NEWCASTLE UNITED
(FLOODLIGHT FRIENDLY)

It turned out that the two teams that lined up did not produce much of a spectacle for the 15,000 crowd braving the rain that night. Only

Jimmy Wardhaugh showed any real flair in the forward line that had been in such fine form in the league. Perhaps it was the rough tactics of a poor Newcastle side, already struggling in the English First Division, which disturbed the flow of the team. In particular, the Toon's Jimmy Scoular incurred the home fans' wrath with his 'robust' play.

The experiment of playing Kirk on the wing did not really work, although he did have a hand in both Hearts goals. Bob Stokoe in the heart of the Newcastle defence won just about every ball in the air, snuffing out the threat of Alex Young in the middle. On the occasions when the forwards did breach the United back line, they found Ronnie Simpson in inspired form. The Glasgow man was at his best when he pulled off a superb save from Jimmy Wardhaugh as early as the eleventh minute. Further heroics to deny John Cumming, Jimmy Murray and Wardhaugh again, did more than most to allow his side to earn the draw.

A generally poor first half exploded into life with three goals shortly before the interval, Len White putting the Magpies in front in the forty-first minute. Hearts hit back immediately through John Cumming, when Alex Young met a cross from makeshift winger Bobby Kirk and knocked the ball down for John to stroke the ball into the net. Only a further ninety seconds elapsed before Kirk was in on the act again, supplying a great ball to Jimmy Wardhaugh, who beat Simpson to give the Maroons the half-time lead.

The second half started as dull as the first, with Hearts seemingly uninterested in the game. Their lethargy was punished in the sixty-second minute when Jackie Bell broke free of his marker and sent the ball past Gordon Marshall for the equaliser. It was the north-east of England side that were now looking more likely and Hearts had a lucky escape when a header from George Eastham hit a post and rolled along the line before Marshall managed to grab the ball. Despite the claims of the Newcastle players, referee Phillips waved away their claims. Newcastle might have then snatched an undeserved winner in the dying minutes, when an attempt from Len White came cannoning back off the crossbar with Gordon Marshall beaten.

A SHOCK DEFEAT (NOVEMBER)

Hearts: Marshall, Parker, Mackenzie, Mackay, Glidden, Thomson, Kirk, Murray, Young, Wardhaugh and Cumming
Newcastle: Simpson, Keith, McMichael, Scoular, Stokoe, Franks, Hughes, Eastman, White, Bell and Mitchell

Although it was now an 'unofficial' competition, after the game the British League stood as follows:

	Played	Won	Lost	Drawn	For	Against	Points
Manchester City	2	2	0	0	6	3	4
Hibs	2	1	1	0	5	3	2
Newcastle Utd	1	0	0	1	2	2	1
Hearts	**2**	**0**	**1**	**1**	**5**	**7**	**1**
Spurs	1	0	1	0	2	5	0
Partick Thistle	0	0	0	0	0	0	0

The next night, Johnny Hamilton continued his quest to become the 1957 East of Scotland Amateur Snooker champion. Even although a large crowd turned out to support Johnny, he was beaten three frames to one by his opponent Jack Gillon.

One of the spectators cheering on Johnny that evening was Willie Bauld, who earlier that day had been pronounced fit from the troublesome groin injury that had seen him miss the last three league games. He was restored to the side that was to face Clyde at Shawfield on Saturday. The team was announced by director Alex Irvine, who had taken over selection duties from Mr Kilgour (who then concentrated on the role of club secretary). With Bauld back in the no. 9 jersey, Alex Young took over from Bobby Kirk at outside-right. Bobby was not even picked for the second string that took on Clyde in a reserve league fixture played on the Friday night. Surprisingly, three games in five days were thought to be too much even for him.

The reserves' game itself was a poor affair and Hearts were considered lucky to retain their unbeaten record, which turned out to be an indication of what was to follow the next day. If the Clyde forwards had taken the any of their chances, the Gorgie men would not have been able to complain about dropping both points. They created few chances throughout the game and only had an Alfie Conn effort that went narrowly wide and a shot from Danny Paton that came back off the post on the half-hour mark to show as opportunities to break the deadlock.

Things did not improve that much in the second half and their only chance came with George Campbell having a headed effort tipped over when he was well placed. They were indebted to 'Newman', whom 'Preston' of the *Evening News* identified only as 'an Edinburgh Waverley player', when with only a few minutes of the ninety remaining, he brought off a great save to deny Jim Rowan from winning the game for Clyde. Nevertheless, the unbeaten run continued and all thoughts turned to the first team getting a better result the next day.

Hearts 'A': *Newman, Mackintosh, Lindores, Bowman, Milne, Higgins, Paton, Campbell, Goldie, Conn and Crawford*

CLYDE v HEARTS

Unfortunately, the next day the first team were hit by the same lassitude of the reserves and for the first time in the league Hearts lost both points. Although Clyde were defending an unbeaten home record, they had lost their last three away games and although they were still 'managerless', it was expected that Hearts would be too good for the Bully Wee.

From the first whistle Bassy Keoch gave Freddie Glidden a hard time. This seemed to disrupt the whole half-back line with both Mackay and Mackenzie finding Robertson and Herd difficult to handle. Up front, the forwards rarely troubled the Clyde defence and Tommy McCulloch in goal was rarely tested. John Cumming, still playing out of position on the wing, had a real 'off day' and consequently even the return of 'King Willie' could not stop the Maroons dropping both points. The only highlight of the day was the fact that Willie Bauld notched Hearts' fiftieth league goal of the season in the 2–1 defeat.

A SHOCK DEFEAT (NOVEMBER)

There was a large contingent from the capital in the 20,000 crowd to witness their side almost go one down in the first minute. Jimmy Wardhaugh put Tam Mackenzie in trouble with a misplaced back pass. Harassed by the attentions of George Herd, Big Tam allowed the Clyde man to rob him of the ball. Luckily for Hearts, Gordon Marshall was alert to the danger and managed to get a hand to push away Herd's effort, and Freddie Glidden was swift to react to clear the danger.

Hearts were struggling to contain the home forwards and Keogh should have done better when a free kick from Archie Robertson broke to him only eight yards out. He snatched at the shot and Gordon Marshall was happy to see the ball go wide. The opener was not far away, though, and after both Dan Currie and Tommy Ring had wasted good opportunities, Archie Robertson got the goal Clyde's play richly deserved. The Tynecastle defence was caught out by a pass from Ring to Robertson and the league's leading scorer blasted the ball into the net from close range.

Hearts had been second best, but were unfortunate not to get an equaliser six minutes after Clyde had gone ahead. With eighteen minutes played, Jimmy Murray ran past Finlay to collect a pass from Jimmy Wardhaugh. The inside-right hammered the ball past Tommy McCulloch, only to turn and see the stand-side linesman with his flag up.

That turned out to be only a brief relief from the relentless Clyde attack. Two minutes later, Dan Currie missed two easy chances before an attempted clearance by Tam Mackenzie struck Jimmy Wardhaugh and Gordon Marshall had to be alert to clear the rebound. The keeper was at his best again with thirty minutes on the clock, when he flung himself full length to stop a fierce drive from Tommy Ring. Eight minutes later and it was Gordon to the rescue again, when he denied Herd for the second time during the game. With the half-time whistle only seconds away, he could do nothing to prevent Keogh increasing the lead after Dan Currie had left a handful of Hearts men trailing.

The Tynecastle defending did not improve in the second half, so the travelling support were thankful when the forwards eventually started to get into the game. First Bauld and then Young let McCulloch know that they still posed a threat. Jimmy Wardhaugh came close when his neat lob was fingertipped over the bar for a corner. The resultant kick ended in a frantic goalmouth scramble that saw Jimmy poke the ball just inches wide.

Hearts knew their 'unbeaten' record was in danger and visibly stepped up their play. Jimmy Murray hit one over from twelve yards, then saw another couple of long-range efforts collected by McCulloch. With six minutes to go, Willie Bauld did manage to pull one back following a free kick from Dave Mackay. It signalled a frantic last few minutes as Hearts went all out to retain their unbeaten record. But it was not to be as Clyde hung on and Hearts sank to their first defeat of the season.

Hearts: Marshall, Parker, Mackenzie, Mackay, Glidden, Thomson, Young, Murray, Bauld, Wardhaugh and Cumming

The result meant that Hearts now only held a one-point advantage over Raith, who had beaten Queen's Park 3–2. Hibs, who had gone down 1–0 at home to Celtic, were a further two points adrift

	Played	Won	Lost	Drawn	For	Against	Points
Hearts	**12**	**9**	**1**	**2**	**50**	**11**	**20**
Raith Rovers	12	8	1	3	28	12	19
Hibs	12	8	3	1	27	15	17

As had happened in previous weeks, Hearts were committed to playing a 'floodlight' friendly during the week. This time it was a return fixture against Newcastle United at St James' Park on Wednesday the 27th. However, on Monday no team selection could be announced as Gordon Marshall had injured a hand at Shawfield and Wilson Brown had not yet recovered from his injury that had seen Newman take his place the previous Friday.

When the team gathered at Waverley Station to catch the train on the day of the game, there had been more changes made to the team other than in who was to play in goals. Bobby Kirk replaced Parker at left-back, Jimmy Milne was to be at centre-half and both Bauld and Cumming were left out. Willie, it seemed, had suffered a recurrence of his groin injury and the unlucky John paid the price of a poor performance, having played out of position. With Tommy Walker still in hospital following his operation, directors Irvine, Tait and Ford oversaw the side.

The team that travelled to Newcastle was: Brown, Kirk, Mackenzie, Mackay, Milne, Thomson, Blackwood, Murray, Young, Wardhaugh and Hamilton

Despite the changes to the side, once again the Hearts failed to hit the heights under floodlights, losing out to a poor Newcastle side by two goals to nil. The result would not help the convalescence of Mr Walker, who had now been allowed to leave hospital. The game turned out to be a personal tragedy for Tommy Mackenzie: he tore a cartilage in his right leg during the game and ended up filling the vacant bed left by his manager.

Only 10,260 bothered to turn out to see the Scottish League leaders take on the home side. Newcastle's form so far in the season was poor at best and the 'Toon faithful' had only seen their heroes win twice at St James' Park. Their impression of Scottish football could not have been enhanced from Hearts' performance in the first half. They were probably encouraged after twenty-eight minutes, when Bobby Mitchell skipped past Bobby Kirk and squared the ball to Len White on the edge of the box. The centre found his striking partner, George Eastham, in space and Wilson Brown could do nothing from preventing his side from going one down.

Worse was to follow in thirty-five minutes when Tommy Mackenzie crumpled to the ground after attempting to tackle Gordon Hunter. The big man was immediately helped off the park and played no further part in the game. Willie Lindores came on in his place at the back, but Newcastle went further ahead just before the interval when White scored the Geordies' second.

In the second half Hearts tried to get the ball out wide to either wing, but time and again Jimmy Scoular and Albert Franks managed to cut out the danger. If the ball did reach Johnny Hamilton or Bobby Blackwood, they found that full-backs Alf McMichael and Dick Keith were hard to beat. The result was that Jimmy Wardhaugh, Alex Young and Jimmy Murray were starved of the ball and as a result the hosts ran out worthy winners.

Newcastle were represented by: Simpson, Keith, McMichael, Scoular, Nesbett, Franks, Hughes, Eastham, White, Bell and Mitchell

So, unlike their Scottish League position, Hearts were near the bottom of the 'Midweek' League that stood as follows:

	Played	Won	Lost	Drawn	For	Against	Points
Hibs	3	2	1	0	10	5	4
Manchester City	3	2	1	0	8	8	4
Newcastle Utd	2	1	0	1	4	2	3
Hearts	**3**	**0**	**2**	**1**	**5**	**9**	**1**
Tottenham	1	0	1	0	2	5	0
Partick Thistle	0	0	0	0	0	0	0

On the same evening, Rangers had been soundly beaten 4–1 by AC Milan at Ibrox. The game had been broadcast live by STV so the whole of Scotland could witness what was surely the end of their European campaign early in the competition. Something that would become very familiar to the Ibrox men in years to come.

HEARTS v FALKIRK

Due to the ever-increasing injury list at Tynecastle, it was inevitable that changes had to be made for the visit of Falkirk on Saturday. Going along with public opinion, John Cumming was returned to the side at his rightful position of left-half. To allow this, George Thomson took over from the injured Tam Mackenzie, with Bobby

Kirk partnering him at the back. In the forward line Bobby Blackwood came in on the right, with Alex Young moving back to the middle and taking over again for Willie Bauld, who was still suffering from the groin injury sustained the previous week. Ian Crawford was restored to the left wing following the failed experiment of playing Cumming there. Like Willie Bauld, Gordon Marshall had not recovered from his injury so Wilson Brown kept his place in goal.

The transformation in the team was instant and for the third time in the season Hearts went one over the eight and rattled in nine goals. Incredibly, that took Hearts' goals scored total to fifty-nine; only one other side in the division, Third Lanark, had scored even half of that total.

Despite the rout, hard-to-please 'Dunedin' in the *Evening News* complained about the poor play of both Hearts wing men and commented they were 'not particularly effective and if they had been surely the Maroons would have satisfied the supporters who were yelling out for double figures'. However, both Young and Wardhaugh caught his eye and were both described to be 'in sparkling form'. Alex's four goals were maybe a bit of a clue that he had a decent game! The Hearts support that turned up that day actually saw two hat-trick heroes, as Dave Mackay managed the feat as well as Alex.

The editor of the match programme did not miss the fact that Hearts seemed not to be getting the recognition they deserved and the issue for the game included an article to that effect. 'Give three hearty cheers please, for the city's two senior football teams. Yes! Both Hearts and Hibs are something to be reckoned with in the Scottish football world. The funny thing is, that no matter how Hearts (in particular) fare in a league game, some smart sports writer in a certain type of Sunday newspaper "tears them to shreds". Ever noticed it?' he asked. To emphasise his point he went on, 'Hearts can score the biggest part of a dozen goals and yet be called a poor lot, or "they had no opposition" and so on and so on. Could this be because of a too powerful influence in the West?' Bias from the media . . . I have never heard of such a thing.

Obviously intent on making amends for the previous week, Hearts took the game to the visitors straight from the first whistle. For long spells they were camped in the Bairns' half and the Falkirk defence could do nothing to stop the free-flowing play of the forwards. The onslaught started as early as the first minute, when straight from the kick-off Hearts marched up the park in a move that ended when an effort from Ian Crawford smacked off the crossbar. It only took another six minutes before a clever back-heeled pass from Alex Young allowed Dave Mackay to put Hearts in front when his shot found its way through a packed penalty area.

Hearts' tails were up, with Alex Young leading the way and Bert Slater did well to stop a crisp effort from the youngster with ten minutes gone. As Hearts looked to increase their lead, the Bairns stopper was well positioned to collect a header from John Cumming after John had made a lung bursting thirty-yard run to meet a corner from Bobby Blackwood.

The second goal was not far way and in the twenty-third minute Jimmy Wardhaugh duly obliged. John Prentice, who in his Tynecastle days had been kept out the side by Wardhaugh, allowed a pass from Jimmy Murray to get through to 'Twinkletoes', who provided the finish.

Seven minutes later and inexplicably centre-half Andy Irvine handled a cross from Jimmy Murray. Undaunted by his last miss from the spot and the fact that Bobby Kirk had been restored to the side, Dave Mackay stepped up to take the kick and casually sent the ball down the middle of the goal as Bert Slater dived to his right. That made it 3–0. And it could have been four just before the break, when Falkirk's right-back Alex Parker just managed to get back in time to clear a net-bound shot after Jimmy Murray had beaten Slater.

Hearts went in at half time well in control, so it was against the run of play when Doug Moran managed to pull one back after only three minutes of the second period. The three-goal lead was soon restored when Alex Young got the goal he deserved after fifty-five minutes. Receiving the ball on the right wing, he waltzed around three men before lashing in a ferocious strike that beat Slater, who had obviously been expecting Alex to pass the ball into the middle.

The crowd were baying for more and they were not disappointed when Dave Mackay received a short free kick from Jimmy Wardhaugh and his fierce drive whistled through the defensive wall, giving Slater no chance and Dave his hat-trick.

Hearts were rampant and it was now just a case of 'how many?' Alex Young added to the total when he almost burst the net in the sixty-ninth minute and Falkirk hardly got a touch of the ball before Jimmy Murray headed Hearts' seventh a minute later. It took nearly three minutes before the next goal arrived courtesy of Alex Young after he gladly accepted a pass from Jimmy Murray. Almost ten minutes elapsed before Alex went one better than his skipper, knocking in his fourth of the afternoon. The Brockville side managed to see out the remaining eight minutes without conceding another, but I am sure they could not get back on the team bus soon enough.

The nine-goal wonders were: Brown, Kirk, Thomson, Mackay, Glidden, Cumming, Blackwood, Murray, Young, Wardhaugh and Crawford

So the Maroons were back to their imperial best, even though it was against a wretched Falkirk XI. The big win, coupled with a surprise defeat for Raith Rovers against Aberdeen, helped Hearts stretch the lead at the top of the league. Hibs were now dropping out of the scene as they were surprisingly beaten 3–0 by Queen of the South at Palmerston.

The league table at the end of November stood as follows:

	Played	Won	Lost	Drawn	For	Against	Points
Hearts	13	10	1	2	59	12	22
Raith Rovers	13	8	2	3	28	13	19
Hibs	13	8	4	1	27	18	17

While the high scoring was taking place back in Edinburgh, the reserves did not enjoy the same success and they lost their long unbeaten run when they went down to a shock 2–1 defeat at Brockville.

What made this even more baffling was that they had played for over fifty minutes against ten men after George Marchant, the Falkirk centre-half, had to leave the field injured. Before then, though, the 'wee' Bairns had taken a two-goal lead within the first twenty minutes. Hearts went behind in the first minute when, after a defensive mix-up, John McCole was left completely unmarked and had no difficulty heading into an empty net. Despite pressing for the equaliser, Hearts went further behind when that man McCole was on hand to head his second of the game. Then came Marchant's departure from the field.

Jim Howieson got the visitors off to the best possible start when he reduced the leeway three minute after the interval. Despite their numerical advantage, Hearts could not break down the well-organised home defence and it was ten-man Falkirk who came closest to adding another goal before the end.

Hearts 'A': *Marshall, Mackintosh, Lindores, Smith, Milne, Higgins, Paton, Howieson, Campbell, Conn and Hamilton*

5

CHRISTMAS CHEER (DECEMBER)

Despite the below-par performance, some of the team were selected to turn out for a combined Hearts/Hibs team that had been lined up for a midweek friendly against a Scottish United Services side at Redford Barracks on Tuesday afternoon. Before that, the first team had yet another midweek friendly to play. In common with the reserves, the military provided the opposition in the form of an Army Select on Monday evening.

HEARTS v BRITISH ARMY (FLOODLIGHT FRIENDLY)

Hearts' favourite, Willie Duff – currently on loan to Charlton during his national service – was included in a strong Army side so a good crowd was expected. Willie almost didn't make the game as two military police had to be dispatched to his mother's house to put him under 'arrest' after he was late in reporting back to Army hotel HQ in the town centre. He wasn't the only one to be late on parade, as only 6,330 turned up to watch Hearts lose yet another game under floodlights.

Perhaps it was the heavy fog that had descended on Tynecastle that kept the hordes away, but they were the ones who missed out on what turned out to be an excellent game of football. Special guest for the evening was a certain Mr Bunce of Comely Bank Crescent, who had played for an Army XI back in 1905, two years prior to joining Hearts.

The game had come at the right time for long-time absentee Alfie Conn and he started in place of Jimmy Murray, this being the only change to the side that had thrashed Falkirk. A well-drilled Army side were fired into the lead on sixteen minutes when, against the run of play, Gerry Hitchins collected a pass in midfield then beat two defenders before slipping the ball through Wilson Brown's legs into the net. After some fine saves by Willie Duff at the other end, he was eventually beaten in the thirty-third minute after Jimmy Wardhaugh was able to prod the ball into the net following a pass from Bobby Blackwood.

The Army front line was led by 'Busby Babe' Bobby Charlton and they really found their shooting boots with two quick-fire goals, both scored by Bill Curry in the forty-ninth and fiftieth minutes respectively, which made for an explosive start to the second half. Four minutes later and Alfie Conn marked his return to the side by pulling Hearts back into the game with a well-taken goal.

Swansea's Barrie Jones restored the Army's two-goal advantage in sixty-one minutes when he was able to escape Dave Mackay's attentions, then rifled the ball into the net. Mackay made up for his slip nine minutes later when he beat three men before lashing the ball past Duff. Hearts took up the challenge and went in search of the equaliser. Try as they might, it just wouldn't come and it was the Army who settled the issue when Curry proved he was hot stuff, breaking away to complete his hat-trick eleven minutes from time.

I apologise for the puns, but it was just too good an opportunity to miss; perhaps a job at *The Sun* beckons.

Hearts: *Brown, Kirk, Thomson, Mackay, Glidden, Cumming, Blackwood, Conn, Young, Wardhaugh and Crawford*
British Army: *Duff (Charlton), Parker (Falkirk), McIntosh (Falkirk), Williams (Plymouth Argyle), Spiers (Reading), Sharpe (Spurs), Harris (Everton), Hitchens (Cardiff), Curry (Newcastle Utd), Charlton (Manchester Utd) and Jones (Swansea)*

The next day the young Hearts/Hibs select managed to get some sort of revenge on the Services when they scored a 4–0 victory over a side that included Ian Crawford, who was to be demobbed the following day. Played in a biting wind with difficult underfoot conditions, the scorers were Dobbie (2), Fox and Aitken, who had come on as a replacement for the injured Alan Finlay.

Hearts/Hibs Select: Proudfoot (Hibs), McCalman (Hibs), Lindores (Hearts), Smith (Hearts), Plenderleith (Hibs), Higgins (Hearts), Dobbie (Hearts), Fox (Hibs), Foley (Hearts), Gibson (Hibs) and Finlay (Hearts) (Aitken [Hibs])

All attention now turned to the important meeting with second-placed Raith Rovers at Stark's Park on Saturday. With Tam Mackenzie already ruled out, Hearts had another injury worry in Freddie Glidden who had taken a knock on his knee against the Army. He decided against reporting for treatment on the Tuesday, due to work commitments, so it was assumed that he would be fit for the game.

There was better news, though, when Gordon Marshall was passed fit and he was named in the reserve side to play against Raith at Tynecastle on Friday, 6 December. As it turned out, his comeback game was rescheduled to the following day as Wilson Brown injured himself during training, so Gordon was promoted back to the first team sooner than expected. Because of the goalkeeping dilemma, the reserves named 'Newman' in goal. His 'brother' turned out at centre-half, but it was the more experienced Bowman who shone throughout the exciting 4–3 win.

You might have thought that the 4,000 who went to Tynecastle that night might have been well entertained with a game that finished 4–3 to the home side. Well 3,999 might have been, but the reporter sent by the *Evening Dispatch* to cover the game was not impressed. 'Football served up is not good enough to encourage Hearts fans to make it a regular Friday date', ran his report.

The 'drab' game started with Hearts going a goal behind in thirteen minutes when ex-Hearts signing Bobby Buchan scored for Raith. Although Newman in goal did well to get a hand to his powerful volley, the trialist keeper couldn't prevent it crossing the line. It took seven minutes to get the equaliser, when George Dobbie ran on to a

Billy Higgins pass and left Eric Bruce and Robert Beath trailing as he shot strongly into the net from fifteen yards. A brilliant goal, but the *Dispatch* reporter claimed that it was 'about George's only praise-worthy move of the game'. Despite constant Hearts pressure, the Rovers were the ones who took the lead for a second time, through Chris Cramb. Andy Bowman was adjudged to have fouled promising young-ster James Curran Baxter moments before the break. The left-half took the kick himself: it was missed by the entire Hearts defence, but not Cramb, who sent his header high into the top corner of the net.

It only took thirty seconds of the second period before Hearts were back on level terms when Johnny Hamilton, who had been brought down in the area, gave George Stewart in the Raith goal no chance from the spot. The Gorgie men then started to press home their advantage and that led to Jim Howieson putting them in front after sixty-two minutes. He was on the spot again two minutes later, when he burst through the visitors' defence and sent a well-placed shot low into the corner of the net. Raith were rattled but kept plugging away and, right on the final whistle, Buchan grabbed his second of the game. However, it was too little too late for Raith.

The *Dispatch* reporter summed it up by saying that 'Hearts had it all their own way' (after only winning by the odd goal in seven?) and then finished his report with a warning: 'Brighten up these Friday Frolics or else . . .' Oh yes, the hard-to-please reporter's name? A certain John Gibson.

Hearts 'A': *Newman, J. Thomson, Lindores, Bowman, Newman, Higgins, Paton, Howieson, Dobbie, Conn and Hamilton*

The 'Newman' who had played at centre-half was identified later as nineteen-year-old Henry Clark of Edina Hearts, whose performance was thought good enough to secure him a contract with the club. However, his career at Tynecastle was short lived. After being farmed out to Dunbar United, he was allowed to join Dunfermline without making a competitive first-team appearance. After a year and five appearances for the Pars, he joined Berwick Rangers where, having started only three league matches, he gave up the game. I have tried without success to identify the 'Newman the goalie'. However, being between the posts in a Hearts side that lost three goals in a game probably signalled the end of your career in those days.

HEARTS v RAITH ROVERS

There was no such dilemma for Gordon Marshall. He could have joined the large Hearts support on the terracing at Stark's Park as Hearts brushed aside the challenge of the Fifers. Even the rhyming couplets of 'The Wraith' in the match programme could not inspire the home side. In order to lift his men, the author wrote:

> *Hearts were made to be broken – that's how the old song goes*
> *And this is a game that's vital as everybody knows*
> *Eager though the Maroons may be to win the flag of fame*
> *Their visit can be pointless if Raith's heart's in the game*

If that was not bad enough, the Fifeshire McGonagall went on:

> *Proud Hearts will take a lot of beating*
> *Pulsating thrills at this great meeting!*
> *They shook poor Falkirk to the marrow*
> *And even Cupid with his arrow*
> *Could never stop the Hearts from attacking*
> *And handing out a real shellacking!*
> *With Christmas nigh Fife's Kings of Soccer*
> *Can give no gifts to Tommy Walker*
> *So Rovers don't relax a minute*
> *And every chance that's going – pin it*
> *A sporting tussle with the leaders*
> *A Merry Yuletide to all readers*

Truly dire stuff, worthy of the other Fife poet laureate Jim Leishman.

Although the conditions were treacherous, Hearts found the way to goal after only five minutes. Bobby Kirk turned defence into attack in an instant by finding John Cumming marauding forward. John played a great ball to Jimmy Murray, who knocked it into the middle to give Jimmy Wardhaugh the easiest of chances to put Hearts in front.

Charlie Drummond in the Raith goal was looking uncomfortable, no more so than five minutes later when he failed to hold onto a pile driver from Dave Mackay; Jimmy Murray was there in a flash to put the Gorgie men two up.

Alex Young did not want to miss out. Some superb play saw him breeze past Willie McNaught then Willie Polland, before sending in a low strike that shaved the post. He had an even better opportunity when he latched onto a through-ball but his effort lacked direction and once again the ball went wide. Gradually the hosts started to get back into the game and in quick succession Kirk, Milne and Thomson thwarted Raith's efforts with well-timed tackles.

Despite now having 'downhill' advantage, Raith, in their change strip of black and yellow, could make no real impact on the Tynecastle defence that had really been 'as strong as the old castle rock'. Johnny Cumming was as wholehearted as ever and twice he needed the trainer's attention before carrying on regardless.

In fifty-seven minutes, Hearts sealed the important victory when Bobby Blackwood rode a tackle from Jackie Williamson and floated the ball into Alex Young. Alex headed on to Jimmy Wardhaugh who lashed the ball into the back of the net. Before the end, Young and Wardhaugh combined again, only to see Jimmy's scoring effort cleared off the line by Andy Leigh. Jimmy Murray and Bobby Blackwood could also have added their names on the scoresheet as Hearts ran out easy winners of what had been billed as the 'game of the season'.

Hearts: *Marshall, Kirk, Thomson, Mackay, Milne, Cumming, Blackwood, Murray, Young, Wardhaugh and Crawford*

The following Monday the draw for the Scottish Cup was made at Park Gardens and Hearts were given the task of taking on East Fife away from home. Having scored nine against them at Tynecastle earlier in the season, it was looking likely that Hearts could progress to the next round in a bid for a league and cup double. Our neighbours had been handed a bye in this round so, despite their woeful cup history, they too were confident of making the next stage.

Monday was also the date for the annual Dinner and Dance at the Charlotte Rooms in Edinburgh's West End. Tommy Walker was now well on the way to recovery and was able to attend the function along with his wife Jean. So well was he doing that he was reported to be rarely off the dance floor. Perhaps this was noted by club chairman Mr Kilgour as he made mention in his after-dinner speech that Alexander Irvine had done a marvellous job carrying out the managerial duties during Tommy's absence but that Mr Walker would be back behind his desk very soon!

With the players and guests all wearing 'colourful carnival hats', they listened as the chairman went on to mention the summer tour of Canada and how it was a 'tribute to the attractive and successful football which the Heart of Midlothian play'. He did not mention the arduous journey the team would have to make to play their brand of attractive and successful football.

Two days later, the manager was back behind his desk and announced that Hearts had eventually agreed a £6,000 fee from Charlton for the services of Willie Duff. It had been no secret that Willie wanted to continue to pursue his career down south after playing for the London club while completing his national service with the Royal Horse Artillery. With Gordon Marshall playing so well and Wilson Brown an able deputy, Hearts were well placed for goalkeepers, so the prospect of Willie regaining his place was slim. A transfer was the best for all concerned and so ended Willie's Tynecastle playing days. The Winchburgh man had joined Hearts from Easthouses Lily in 1952 and had been part of the victorious Scottish Cup team of 1956. When he had first started playing he turned out at left-back, but on one occasion while playing juvenile football the regular keeper failed to turn up and Willie took over the yellow jersey. The rest, as they say, is history.

On the same day as Willie went south, so did Rangers' European Cup hopes. Trailing 4–1 from the first leg in Glasgow, they went down 2–0 in Milan – no doubt a sore one for Ibrox faithful. They would be able to take some comfort as only they can in the thrashing the other half of the 'gruesome twosome' received at the hands of Middlesbrough on the same evening. Playing a 'friendly' in the north-east, Celtic were humiliated 6–1 by a Teesside outfit who weren't exactly on the top rung of the English League.

HEARTS v KILMARNOCK

With no further injuries to consider, but with Freddie Glidden and Willie Bauld still not fully recovered, there was no need to change the team that had accounted for Raith Rovers the previous week. Hearts had not yet beaten Kilmarnock in their two previous encounters in the League Cup, so this could have been a 'banana skin' on their title hopes. A convincing first-half display allayed any fears that the home support might have had and although the Rugby Park men fought back well, Hearts ran out worthy winners to continue their march to the title

There was a sizeable contingent from Kilmarnock amongst the 20,000 who packed into Tynecastle to see Hearts get the game under way. They swept straight up the park in a move that ended with Jimmy Murray testing Jimmy Brown with a snap shot that the keeper dealt with comfortably. In the opening seconds Hearts had given the crowd a glimpse of what was to come. Jimmy Murray was in the middle of things again when he passed to Jimmy Wardhaugh but the inside-left hurried his shot and the ball flew over the bar. Dave Mackay was next to give his former colleague something to think about when he tried his luck from twenty yards, but once again Brown was equal to the test.

Despite being on top, Hearts had a scare after thirteen minutes when a cross from Gerry Mays hit the crossbar. The rebound fell to Tommy Henaughan, who flicked it on to Bertie Black. But the inside-forward sent his headed effort over.

Once again, Alex Young was in sparkling form and it all came to fruition in twenty-two minutes. As soon as he received the ball, three Kilmarnock men went to try to snuff out the danger. Quick as a flash, Alex played the ball to the unmarked Bobby Blackwood. The winger's cross was knocked out by a Killie defender but only as far as the in-rushing Dave Mackay. Dave met the ball sweetly with his right foot and Jimmy Brown could do no more than admire the shot as it sailed into the net.

Hearts were in command and, as had happened in the past, it was only the brilliance of Jimmy Brown that kept Willie Waddell's men in the game. A magnificent one-handed save from a drive by Alex Young brought cheers from both sets of supporters but he could do nothing with thirty-seven minutes gone when, in a well-practised move, Ian Crawford flicked on a corner from Jimmy Murray and there was Jimmy Wardhaugh to head home from a couple of yards.

With the half coming to a close, Dave Mackay nearly got his second of the game in what was almost a repeat move of his first, but this time his try from eighteen yards went inches over. The lights came on for the start of the second half as the afternoon took a gloomy turn. Jimmy Brown tried his best to brighten up the proceedings when he donned a natty bright red bunnet to protect his eyes from the false lighting. Perhaps the home defence could have done with a bunnet as well when, in the fifty-fourth minute, they all appeared to lose the ball after Bobby Kennedy sent in a free kick. Kilmarnock centre Gerry Mays did not have any such trouble and bulleted the ball past a startled Marshall.

The loss of the goal did not unsettle Hearts unduly as they continued to take the game to the visitors. Alex Young still had his good form of the first period and posed a constant threat to the visitors. Unfortunately for Alex, he was getting poor support from the rest of the front line. This was no better illustrated than in sixty-eight minutes when the usually reliable Jimmy Wardhaugh scorned an easy opportunity after having been set up by Alex.

Hearts might have rued that miss as, sixty seconds later, Gerry Mays got on the end of a cross from Davie Curlett but, with Gordon

Marshall stranded, he sent his header high over the bar from only a couple of feet. It was certainly a let-off – but, after that, Hearts heeded the warning, visibly tightening things up. Their cause was made easier because Kilmarnock were now virtually playing with ten men as Bertie Black had obviously pulled a hamstring and could do no more than limp along the left touchline. The handicap was too great for the Rugby Parkers and Hearts were able to see out the rest of the game for yet another two points towards the title.

Hearts: *Marshall, Kirk, Thomson, Mackay, Milne, Cumming, Blackwood, Murray, Young, Wardhaugh and Crawford*

Through at Rugby Park the reserves also continued their winning ways and, like the game at Tynecastle, it was the display of the Kilmarnock goalkeeper which kept them from scoring more than they could have.

On a frostbound pitch it was Hearts who adapted more quickly to the treacherous conditions with the experienced Alfie Conn leading the way. Johnny Hamilton was not far behind and it was Hammy who brought out the first save from Ian Ross when his rasping drive was well stopped by the keeper. He came to Killie's rescue again, ten minutes later, when he pushed over a point-blank header from Alfie Conn. Then, twice in quick succession the bar came to his rescue moments before the interval with Hearts pressing for the opener.

After the break, Killie keeper Ross was at it again with another good save, this time from Hamilton. Then for the third time he had the woodwork to thank when Andy Bowman fired one against the bar. It looked like the first goal would never come but with time running out, Jim McFadzean beat Ian Ross with a clever flick. Kilmarnock were down and a few minutes later they were out when Alfie Conn got the goal his play had richly deserved.

Hearts 'A': *Brown, Mackintosh, Lindores, Smith, Higgins, Bowman, Paton, Conn, Dobbie, McFadzean and Hamilton*

CHRISTMAS CHEER (DECEMBER)

Thursday, 18 December saw Tommy Mackenzie released from hospital after an operation on his cartilage. Bravely, he forecast he would be 'back before the end of the season', a sentiment that was echoed by Hearts supporters everywhere. He was in fact 'back' at Tynecastle as soon as Saturday when he got a rousing reception as he took a seat in the stand to watch the team take on St Mirren.

While Tommy was on the mend, there were no new injury worries for Tommy Walker to concern himself with so it was an easy task to say 'same again'.

HEARTS v ST MIRREN

For the second week in a row, Hearts raced into a commanding first-half lead with the first goal coming as early as the sixth minute. Hearts had been pressing right from the off, which led to Saints' inside-left, Duncan McGill, dropping back to help his pressurised defence. As it happens, forwards don't make particularly good defenders and his poor clearance went straight to Davie Mackay, who wasted no time in whipping in a cross. Jimmy Murray didn't need to be asked twice when he rose to nod the ball into the top corner.

Four minutes later and John Cumming made a twenty-yard dash to get his head to a corner from Jimmy Murray. It was powerful enough but lacked direction and the Saints goal survived on that occasion. Charlie Forsyth had to be alert in thirteen minutes, when he raced from his line to just deny Alex Young reaching a sublime pass from Jimmy Wardhaugh.

Having survived the initial onslaught, the Love Street men began to come more into the game but Gordon Marshall remained untroubled as they could not find a way through the well-drilled Hearts backs. After twenty-six minutes the advantage was doubled when a slip by the visitors' left-half Bill Johnstone allowed Alex Young to launch a screamer into the bottom corner of the net.

On the run of play it was no more than the Maroons deserved, but back came the Saints seven minutes later. Another defensive lapse, this time by George Thomson, led to the goal. His weak clearance only went as far as Peter McKay, who produced a tremendous finish. Back came Hearts and five minutes later they restored the two-goal lead when Ian Crawford was obstructed in the box by former Hibs signing John Higgins. There was an element of doubt as to whether the challenged merited a penalty, but Dave Mackay took full responsibility. Although Campbell Forsyth managed to get his fingers to the ball, the captain's kick had too much power behind it and Hearts were 3–1 ahead at the interval.

Hearts made another whirlwind start in the second period, Forsyth being a busy man dealing with efforts from Murray, Blackwood, Wardhaugh then Blackwood again all in quick succession. On the hour mark he did well to stop a marvellous header from Jimmy Murray but was then relieved to see another header by Ian Crawford come back off a post. Hearts hit the upright again minutes later after a shot from Jimmy Murray had beaten the overworked keeper.

A fourth goal was not far away and in seventy-two minutes a cross by Ian Crawford was deflected to Alex Young, who instinctively laid the ball off perfectly to allow Jimmy Wardhaugh to crash home his eighteenth league goal of the season. The points were safe but there was still time for Jimmy Murray to add to the total when he was first to react after Higgins had fluffed a clearance from a Dave Mackay effort in the seventy-eighth minute. In scoring five, Hearts had now completed a goal tally from nil to nine in less than half a season. No other club in British football could claim such a record.

It was all too easy for Hearts and it had been an outstanding team performance – perhaps now the critics would believe that they were serious title challengers, especially since Celtic had gone down to a surprising 3–2 home defeat against Partick Thistle.

Hearts: *Marshall, Kirk, Thomson, Mackay, Milne, Cumming, Blackwood, Murray, Young, Wardhaugh and Crawford*

The reserves also gained two points through in Paisley but were a little less convincing in doing so. It was a close-fought game, with few real chances for either side, and in the opening spell both goal-keepers were virtual spectators. However the game livened up when Alfie Conn tested the aptly named George Budd in the Buddies' goal after thirty minutes; the keeper, though, managed to pull off a decent save. Shortly afterwards, Alfie played in George Dobbie who didn't waste the opportunity to put Hearts 1–0 up.

Hearts continued to press in the second half and did get the ball in the net on the hour mark but Johnny Hamilton's effort was ruled out for a previous foul. Despite playing the better football, they could not add to the lead and at the end it was only Dobbie's goal that separated the sides.

Hearts 'A': Brown, Mackintosh, Lindores, Smith, Glidden, Higgins, Paton, Conn, Dobbie, McFadzean and Hamilton

Before the first team made the journey through to Parkhead the following day, the 'A' team took on their Celtic counterparts in an evening game at Tynecastle on Friday the 27th. Alfie Conn took the opportunity to remind the manager that he could still play a bit, with his late strike helping to keep their title challenge on track.

The game started with Celtic on top for long spells. However it was the hosts who took the lead in thirty-four minutes when Johnny Hamilton delivered a great ball from the wing; it was met by Danny Paton and his first-time shot beat John Bonnar in the Celtic goal. The lead was short lived as the Celts went up the park and got a deserved equalised through their tricky winger Alex Byrne only two minutes later.

As always, Hearts started the second period in determined fashion and, in the first minute of the half, Hugh Goldie tumbled in the box and the referee awarded a penalty that was definitely of the 'soft' variety. Johnny Hamilton did not stop to argue and rapped the ball home to restore the Maroons' advantage.

Again Celtic came back with a quick reply and, seven minutes later, they got their second goal after a defensive slip by Willie Lindores let in Byrne for his second. Two minutes later and another mistake by the unfortunate Willie allowed Matt McVittie to put Celtic in front for the first time in the game.

This seemed to stun Hearts but they could not find a way through a resolute Celtic back line. George Dobbie did have a couple of opportunities but the forward's luck was out on both occasions and it began to look as though the Glasgow men would head back West with both points. However, with only three minutes left, Alfie Conn gathered the ball twenty-five yards from goal and, after a mazy run, smashed the ball into the net to grab the equaliser.

Hearts stood proudly at the top of their League with a record of played 15, won 10, drawn 4 and lost only 1, but it was still not good enough for the reporter from the *Evening Dispatch* who headlined his report with, 'HIBS TO TOPPLE THE WEE HEARTS'. Yes, no prizes for guessing it was that man Gibson again who was talking up the chances of the wee team from Leith in the 'derby' clash arranged for the following Monday. What a surprise.

Hearts 'A': *Brown, Mackintosh, Lindores, Smith, Glidden, Higgins, Paton, Conn, Dobbie, Finlay and Hamilton*

CELTIC v HEARTS

Just like back in October when Hearts had met the other half of the Old Firm, Celtic had suffered an unexpected defeat the week before. This time Partick Thistle had taken the Parkhead men's unbeaten record from them. According to the programme editor, Celtic should not have lost because 'Neilly Mochan's two magnificent goals were worthy of winning any contest'. However, it was not just Neilly who deserved praise because 'another pleasing feature of the game was the splendid control shown by the players in the face of several rather weird decisions by the referee'. Sound familiar?

Hearts made one change to the side that had defeated St Mirren the week before. Andy Bowman replaced the flu-ridden Cumming, but the change did not affect the team and the Jam Tarts recorded their fourteenth league win of the season. They played by far the better football throughout and, after they took the lead through Jimmy Wardhaugh in nineteen minutes, the end result was never in doubt. This was confirmed when Bobby Collins missed a penalty and the irrepressible Alex Young struck Hearts' second, minutes from the end. The game was played on a typically dreich December afternoon which made conditions difficult for both sides. It is interesting to note, however, that neither trainer was called on to tend to injuries during the game. Not something we would see now in any game, let alone a Hearts v Celtic encounter.

As the teams lined up before kick-off, there was a surprise inclusion in the Celtic XI. Vince Ryan, who had been in the reserve side that drew with Hearts the previous evening lined up in the no. 9 shirt.

Eight minutes in and Dick Beattie in the Celtic goal produced a double save to prevent his side from going behind. He did well to get a hand to an effort from Jimmy Murray who had been only eight yards from goal. Then he had to react quickly to smother the ball at the feet of Alex Young as the Hearts man went in for the rebound.

The rain fell steadily, making it difficult for the players to keep their feet. Perhaps that could have explained Ryan's theatrical tumble in the box after twenty minutes when Dave Mackay was in close attendance. Both sides knew that the outcome of the game would bear a significant outcome of the title, so every ball was keenly contested.

Sammy Wilson came inches away from putting Celtic in front midway through the half but Marshall was happy to watch his effort scrape the outside of the post. Hearts' counter came six minutes later when Alex Young went similarly close with an angled shot from the left. When Mr Harvie, the referee, blew for the end of the half, both teams trooped off happy to get out of the rain for fifteen minutes and probably just as glad to still be on level terms.

Four minutes after the restart, Jimmy Murray almost broke the stalemate when, as so often had happened before, he was put through from a defence-splitting pass from Alex Young. His strike looked goal-bound all the way but Beattie stretched out a hand at the last second and Jim Kennedy was able to get back and boot the ball to safety.

In the fifty-seventh minute Vince Ryan went down in the box again. This time there was no one near him and only the state of the pitch could be blamed. If the youngster had managed to keep his feet, Hearts could have found themselves a goal behind. It was the nature of the game that they could have been in front a minute later as Jimmy Wardhaugh ran on to a loose clearance but his vicious shot was an inch too high and crashed back off the bar. He had better luck after twenty minutes of the half when Bobby Blackwood took a short corner to Alex Young, who passed to Jimmy to allow him to crack the ball home.

Celtic were thrown a lifeline courtesy of a generous penalty award by the referee when Ryan took yet another 'tumble' in the box. Justice was done when Collins blasted his kick against the crossbar and the ball bounced away to safety. The miss was crucial to Celtic's chances and, two minutes from time, Alex Young sealed their fate when Dick Beattie could not prevent his header bulging the net.

Hearts: Marshall, Kirk, Thomson, Mackay, Milne, Bowman, Blackwood, Murray, Young, Wardhaugh and Crawford
Celtic: Beattie, Fallon, Kennedy, Smith, Evans, Peacock, Conway, Collins, Ryan, Wilson and Mochan

With the win, Hearts were now leading the way seven points ahead of nearest rivals Hibs and ten ahead of third-place Raith Rovers and Clyde. Celtic trailed by eleven points but had three games in hand. Rangers, who had drawn 1–1 at Pittodrie, were a further point behind but had played four games less. With the New Year's Day game at Easter Road next up four days later, needless to say the whole of Edinburgh buzzed with anticipation.

After the last game of 1957, the League looked like this:

CHRISTMAS CHEER (DECEMBER)

	Played	Won	Lost	Drawn	For	Against	Points
Hearts	17	14	1	2	71	14	30
Hibs	17	11	5	1	39	24	23
Clyde	17	10	5	0	40	18	20

Before the big event, the 'wee' derby took place at Tynecastle on Monday, 30 December and what a game the 10,000 spectators witnessed. The 'A' team, 2–0 down, produced a fantastic comeback well into the second half to record a 3–2 victory. And that was without anyone called Graham Weir in the team. Also not in the team was Alfie Conn – not because he was being considered for first-team duty days later but because he had pulled a leg muscle against the Celtic second string. There was some good news, as Bobby Parker had recovered sufficiently to play after having been out for a few weeks.

It only took an eager Hibs side three minutes to take the lead when an Andy Aitken drive that looked to be going yards wide was deflected into the net by the unfortunate John Mackintosh. There was no doubt about the Hibees' second, seventeen minutes later, when hesitancy in the home defence allowed Thomson to curl a beauty past Wilson Brown. Throughout the first forty-five minutes the home forward line barely troubled the visitors. However, when Johnny Hamilton switched from the left wing to the right during the second half, the game changed dramatically.

It looked as if the Leithers would add to their lead after only nine minutes of the second half when Tommy Slavin sent in the perfect cross that found Aitken. He couldn't take advantage, though, and he sent a poor header over the bar. It was just after this that Hammy switched wings, but it took until fifteen minutes before the end when Hearts finally got their reward. Moving in from the right, Johnny struck a left-foot shot that was blocked by a Hibs defender. The ball broke back to him but, this time with his right foot, he rifled the ball into the Hibs net from ten yards. With four minutes left, Johnny struck again when he thundered a shot against the bar; Jim McFadzean was quick to react and had the simplest of tasks to chest the ball past Jackie Wren. Never-say-die Hearts sensed they could win the game and, in the very last minute of the game, Hugh Goldie sent in a cross from the wing that was knocked back by George Campbell to Danny Paton who notched the winner. A fine win for the reserves – but the big one was the next again day at Easter Road.

The comeback kings were: Brown, Parker, Mackintosh, Smith, Glidden, Higgins, Paton, Campbell, Goldie, McFadzean and Hamilton

6

A HAPPY NEW YEAR (JANUARY)

HIBS v HEARTS

The omens were good for the First XI. Hearts had won six of the Ne'er Day games since the war against the four victories of Hibs, with one drawn game back in 1956. Perhaps more tellingly, it had been ten years since Hibs last won a New Year's Day game at home.

As there were no injury concerns for Tommy Walker after the Celtic encounter, he announced a 'same again' side, with Andy Bowman continuing in place of Johnny Cumming. With a healthy seven-points difference between the clubs, it was the Hearts fans who crossed town in a buoyant mood. The early arrivals among the 50,000 were entertained by music from the Edinburgh City Police Band. Changed days indeed, as most of Edinburgh's finest would now be on duty at the match but not for the crowd's entertainment. It is also interesting to note that back in 1958 there was no reduced entry for children, something that perhaps those who complain about things at Tynecastle these days should think about.

The winter temperatures had taken their toll on the Easter Road surface and the slippery conditions did not allow for flowing football. Many passes went sadly astray and players of both sides in attack and defence had difficulty turning. In an unremarkable first half, it was Joe Baker of Hibs who had the best opportunity of the half. In the first few minutes he managed to hook the ball wide from a good position when Gordon Marshall was left exposed by his defence.

It was Hearts, or rather Alex Young, who managed to adapt better to the conditions but it took until the second half to make the break-through. Kicking uphill, they started to play short, sharp passes from the back and with Jimmy Murray and Alex Young dropping deeper, they gave Hibs problems which in the end they could not answer. Hearts' back line started to have no difficulty containing Gordon Smith, Laurie Reilly and Co. The fact that Smith was not fully fit and that Reilly was playing in an unaccustomed inside-left role did not help the Hibs cause. In contrast, at the other end, although Paterson tried manfully he could not stop Alex Young.

During that unremarkable first forty-five, it was Alex who single-handedly had done his best to relieve the tedium. His colleagues seemed to be suffering from a Ne'er Day hangover and neither goal-keeper had been tested when referee Bowman blew his whistle to bring an end to the half. The fans had not had much to get excited about and it was probably only the contents of thousands of half-bottles that kept them in 'good spirits'.

There was slightly more to cheer in the second period when Hearts raised their game considerably and deservedly broke the deadlock. Eddie Turnbull had been untroubled throughout the game, but he failed to make proper contact when trying to clear six minutes after the restart. The ball only went as far as Jimmy Wardhaugh, who whipped in a cross that found Alex Young. Despite having been the best man on the park, Alex took that moment to be affected by the jitters of his team-mates. His first strike lacked power but Leslie made a mess of the save and the ball broke back to the Hearts man and Alex managed to scramble the ball into the net at the second attempt.

The goal seemed to settle the Gorgie men and at last they showed the travelling support the standard of football they had become used to. Hibs struggled to cope and it was no surprise when Leslie was beaten for a second time in the seventy-eighth minute. The menace of Alex Young was brought to an end when he was unceremoniously bundled to the ground eighteen yards out. From the resultant free kick Dave Mackay blasted the ball towards goal and, with Leslie throwing himself full length to make the save, the ball ricocheted off Willie Ormond and behind the startled keeper.

A HAPPY NEW YEAR (JANUARY)

Hearts were well worthy of the two-goal lead, but had to survive a scare ten minutes from the end. The Leith supporters screamed for a penalty when a try from Lawrie Reilly hit Bobby Kirk on the arm. Some thought it had crossed the line before Bobby's intervention but all were convinced he 'handled'. However Mr Bowman was not interested and Hearts saw out the rest of the game to continue their derby dominance.

Hearts: Marshall, Kirk, Thomson, Mackay, Milne, Bowman, Blackwood, Murray, Young, Wardhaugh and Crawford
***The vanquished:** Leslie, Grant, Muir, Turnbull, Paterson, Baxter, Smith, Harrower, Baker, Reilly and Ormond*

There was no time for dwelling on the win, as Airdrie were to first-foot Tynecastle the next again day. Using the 'if it isn't broke don't fix it' theory, Tommy Walker once again kept the same side.

HEARTS v AIRDRIE

Overnight, the temperature in Edinburgh had dropped even further and was recorded as the coldest in the UK. No doubt the chill that had descended over Easter Road at 3.45 p.m. the previous day had contributed to that. As Mr Barclay blew his whistle to start the game at 2 p.m. there were many amongst the 19,000 braving the elements who wondered if the game should be played at all. The Tynecastle pitch was white with frost which made the underfoot conditions just as treacherous as the previous day, but Hearts had learnt their lesson and played the same short passing game that had worked so well in the second half at Easter Road. It was Dave Mackay and Andy Bowman who were the architects of this easy victory, their clever link-up play with the forwards being the key.

With Alex Young finding it difficult to break free from the attentions of big Doug Baillie, it was Jimmy Murray, ably assisted by Bobby Blackwood, who took advantage. Jimmy managed it so well, in fact, that he notched a hat-trick in the first twenty-seven minutes.

This was the sixth hat-trick of the season for the team and Jimmy was the fourth player to score one – and it was still only 2 January.

In their previous two games Airdrie had scored eleven times, but against the Hearts they could only count a couple of long-range efforts by their right-back Bill Kilmarnock as genuine scoring attempts.

After seven minutes Bobby Blackwood squared the ball across the goal to Jimmy Wardhaugh, who cheekily back-heeled the ball to Jimmy Murray who then lashed the ball into the net. Fifteen minutes later, Blackwood started yet another move that ended in Hearts' second goal. This time his long cross opened up the Airdrie defence: it found Ian Crawford on the left and when he knocked it back into the middle, there was Jimmy Murray on the spot again to knock it past Bill Goldie. It only took another five minutes before Jimmy had completed his hat-trick. Dave Mackay took a quick throw-in, which was headed into the middle by Ian Crawford, and Jimmy accepted the opportunity to head in his and Hearts' third goal.

In the second half, Hearts continued to put pressure on the visitors. Midway through, their lead was extended to four. The Airdrie back line had been put under pressure the whole game and on seventy minutes John McPhail's rash challenge on Jimmy Wardhaugh in the area gave Dave Mackay the opportunity from the spot. Despite his past failures, the skipper made no mistake on this occasion.

Hearts: *Marshall, Kirk, Thomson, Mackay, Milne, Bowman, Blackwood, Murray, Young, Wardhaugh and Crawford*

After having played three games in five days, you might think the league programme would allow the teams a rest over the festive period and you would be correct. The boys were given the Friday off before travelling to Dens Park to face Dundee.

DUNDEE v HEARTS

Surprisingly, despite the treacherous playing conditions, no player had picked up an injury over the holiday period, so once again the same eleven were chosen to extend the winning run. Once again they did it in style and once again a player hit a hat-trick. Jimmy Wardhaugh was the man this time and, amazingly, this was his hat-trick of hat-tricks for the season: he'd previously hit three against both Airdrie and East Fife.

The kick-off was delayed after a bizarre incident. Dave Mackay had won the toss and decided to take the wind advantage so the teams changed round and lined up, waiting for the referee to get the game under way. Before Albert Henderson could kick off, the ref decided that the light was not sufficient to distinguish the dark blue of Dundee from the maroon of Hearts so he ordered the home side from the park to change into white jerseys.

It didn't matter what colour Dundee wore, as it was the Maroons who went straight onto the attack. Within five minutes they got the first of the afternoon courtesy of Jimmy Wardhaugh. 'Twinkletoes' used the head to beat Bill Brown for the first time after managing to glance a shot from Dave Mackay into the net. It looked like Dave's lob would have ended up in the back of the net anyway, but Jimmy, being the ultimate professional, made sure of the goal. After that great start he turned in a delightful display of football and combined well with Alex Young to allow Jimmy Murray to double the advantage. Dundee had been pressing for the equaliser but Hearts cleared the danger and Alex Young turned defence into attack in a flash when he latched onto the ball. He moved it quickly to Jimmy Wardhaugh, who just as quickly found Jimmy Murray, who had no trouble beating Brown from five yards out.

Although they were behind, Willie Thornton's men were not giving up the ghost and Gordon Marshall was at his best when transfer-listed Albert Henderson beat Jimmy Milne to a long through-ball. He caught it beautifully on the volley but the young goalie was equal to the task to pull off a tremendous stop to deny the Dundee forward. Hearts continued to soak up the pressure and almost scored another 'breakaway goal' when a strike from Alex Hamilton broke off Bobby Kirk to Jimmy Wardhaugh who went on a solo run up the park, only to finish off by putting the ball narrowly past the post. It would have been a sensational finish to the half but perhaps rather harsh on a Dundee side who had battled hard to get back in the game.

Their fightback continued straight from the kick-off in the second half. Davie Sneddon had a chance to grab one back but went down in the box after a crunching tackle from George Thomson. The referee saw no offence and Hearts had survived again. Six minutes in, they gave the Dens Park team a demonstration of just how it should be done. Ralph Mackenzie and Jimmy Black got into a fankle trying to clear the ball on the eighteen-yard line. Jimmy Murray didn't stop to ask questions and lashed the ball into the net to make it 3–0.

For the second game in a row, Hearts had the game won long before the end. Murray, Young and Wardhaugh were leading Dundee a merry dance and, with Dave Mackay orchestrating things from the back, more goals were certain to follow. The captain got the opportunity to get his name on the scoresheet after sixty-five minutes when McKenzie crashed into Alex Young in the box. Referee Morris had no hesitation in awarding a penalty and Davie stroked the ball into the corner of the net.

Ten minutes later, Jimmy Wardhaugh rounded off the scoring when he blasted one home leaving the Dundee keeper floundering. That was 5–0, but it could so easily have been more with Dens full-back Alex Hamilton clearing three goal-bound efforts off the line before the final whistle.

Hearts: *Marshall, Kirk, Thomson, Mackay, Milne, Bowman, Blackwood, Murray, Young, Wardhaugh and Crawford*

After what was described as one of the best all-round team performances of the season, the same eleven men had played four games in seven days, scored thirteen times, conceded none. Nearest challengers Clyde were eleven points behind but had two games in hand, while third placed Rangers were thirteen points adrift having played four games fewer.

To round off a good day for the club, the reserves continued their winning ways when they recorded a 2–1 victory at Tynecastle. With the playing surface still slippery from the recent frost and snow, the players found it hard to keep their feet despite the layer of sand that had been put down by the Tynecastle groundsmen. As a consequence the play was littered with mistakes from both teams but it was the young Hearts side that always looked the more likely. After twenty-five minutes Jim Howieson put them ahead when, despite a valiant effort by Jim Ferguson in the Dundee goal, his powerful effort found the net. He got a second ten minutes later after he had been set up by fellow Dunbar man Alan Finlay.

After the turn-round, Hearts seemed content to hold onto their two-goal lead and only an angular drive from Danny Paton that ended in the side netting looked like adding to their advantage. Dundee slowly managed to get back into the game and got a goal back through George O'Hara. Despite the setback, Hearts remained in control and ran out worthy winners.

Hearts 'A': Brown, Parker, Lindores, Smith, Glidden, Higgins, Paton, Howieson, Dobbie, Finlay and Goldie

Still missing from any Hearts line-up was Willie Bauld, as he continued to have trouble with a groin injury sustained during the only defeat of the season at Clyde in November. X-rays taken in late December had proved inconclusive and it was decided that Willie would enter hospital for further tests. It was hoped that this would clear up the injury once and for all and the 'King' would be back in time for the run-in to the end of the season. Unfortunately this did not turn out to be the case and, as history records, Willie had played his last game for the Maroons that season.

Although 8 January turned out to be a bad day for Willie, another Hearts player had cause for celebration. George Thomson learned that he had been selected along with Dave Mackay and Alex Young for the Scottish Under-23 team that was to take on their English counterparts at Goodison the following Wednesday. It was just reward for George, who had been turning in sterling performances since getting his chance after taking over from flu-struck John Cumming in October.

Signed in 1953 from Edinburgh City, George had been sharing the left-half position in the reserves with Billy Higgins until he moved forward to inside-left for two games in September. In the games against Hibs and Partick he showed his versatility by scoring in both but it was after his move to the left-back position for cover for Tom Mackenzie that he really shone through. Now he was being asked to fill the left-half role for the Under-23s the following week – a versatile man indeed.

The trio were also in the side that Tommy Walker announced the following day for the next game against Partick Thistle at Tynecastle. It was no surprise when the same XI that had done so well the previous week were given the nod. Although recovered from injury, John Cumming was still not thought to be fully match fit so Andy Bowman continued in the no. 6 jersey. A new injury victim was Bobby Parker: it was announced that he was suffering from a 'whittle in a finger' and would be absent from the second-string game.

HEARTS v PARTICK THISTLE

With the side being the same as the last few games, there was no shock when both points stayed in Gorgie. This time a comfortable 4–1 victory saw Hearts continue on their march to the title. They had now scored eighty-six goals in the campaign and attention was beginning to focus on goal-scoring records. First in sight was the ninety-two that Hibs had scored when they won the title in '51–52 and then there was the ninety-nine (the most of any team that season) that they scored when finishing third in '55–56. With thirteen games to go, both those targets looked likely to be met and the all-time record of 119 by Motherwell in '31–32 was under threat. Even though Hearts would play thirty-four games, as opposed to 'Well's thirty-eight, the current scoring average of four a game would see the team better the record considerably.

Beaten by lowly Queen's Park the previous week, Dave Meiklejohn's men were no match for the Tynecastle scoring machine. Hearts played some delightful free flowing football and the four first-half goals were just reward for yet another scintillating team performance. In fact, the Jags were fortunate that the team eased off in the second period – and once again the 'penalty hoodoo' returned with Dave Mackay failing to convert. This, however, did not detract from Dave's all-round performance, later described in the *Evening News* as 'imperious'. His play was the perfect combination of defence and attack and, with Alex Young being in sublime form up front, it ensured that Thistle keeper David Thomson had a very busy afternoon.

As the cold spell continued, there was no change to the treacherous playing conditions, but Hearts soon got the measure of the problem and came close to opening their account after eight minutes. Alex Young was fouled thirty yards from goal and Andy Bowman floated the ball into Jimmy Murray, who stared in disbelief as he watched Thomson magnificently turn away his header from six yards.

Six minutes later and it was Thomson to the rescue again as he dived full length to deny Alex Young. Alex was at his brilliant best and was involved in the move that led to the opener two minutes later. He received the ball from Davie Mackay, then scampered away down the right; after looking up, he whipped in the perfect ball for Jimmy Murray to head in Hearts' hundredth goal in all competitions for the season.

The pressure on Patrick's defence was relentless, with the wing-halves and inside-forwards catching the eye in particular. Dave Mackay scored for the fourth game in a row in the sixteenth minute. He ran on to a low cross from Ian Crawford and, without breaking stride, struck a vicious left-foot drive from eighteen yards that flew into the net via the inside of the upright. More sharp passing moves followed. After twenty-eight minutes it was three, when Jimmy Wardhaugh finished off a move that began when a clearance from Jimmy Milne was headed on by Jimmy Murray. With the Partick defenders static, Wardhaugh was onto the ball in a flash and steered it home from twelve yards.

On the few occasions Partick were allowed to push forward, they did not hold much of a goal threat, although Tommy Ewing battled on gamely up front. Three times Gordon Marshall was called on to deal with decent efforts from the winger and three times he answered the call without too much trouble. With thirty-nine minutes gone, Ewing's strike partner, Alex Wright, had better luck when he rode past half-hearted tackles from George Thomson and Jimmy Milne before he fired the ball into the top of the net.

Losing their first goal of 1958 only served to annoy the Tynecastle team and Bobby Blackwood, who had been tormenting the Jags' back line throughout, restored the three-goal advantage two minutes before the end of the half. He collected a pass from Alex Young and then left three men trailing in his wake before smashing the ball over the despairing Thomson.

The game was over as a contest and, although they continued to pass the ball well, Hearts in the second half never really carried the same threat as they had done in the first forty-five. Alex Young set up Jimmy Wardhaugh fifteen minutes in but, with all the time in the world, Jimmy snatched at the ball and sent it wide of the post with David Thomson stranded. Five minutes later and they wasted an even better chance to increase the lead when they were awarded a penalty after the Jags' left-back Frank Donlevy brought down Alex Young in the box. As had happened in the last two games, up stepped Dave Mackay to take the kick, but he was too casual with his left-foot effort this time and Thomson easily saved his weak attempt.

Hearts continued to press and Ian Crawford was the next to pass up a golden opportunity when he elected to have a go himself from a tight angle when Alex Young was waiting unmarked for his pass. Alex was determined to join the goal-scoring spree and almost did the trick when he blasted in a shot from fifteen yards out: it looked a winner all the way but the Thistle stopper threw himself to his right and managed to keep the ball out.

With ten minutes left, things got worse for Partick when right-half Dave Mathers looked to injure himself making a tackle. After treatment, he was unable to continue and had to be helped from the pitch, leaving Partick to see out the rest of the game with ten men. Hearts failed to press home their numerical advantage, but they had another two points in the bag anyway.

Hearts: *Marshall, Kirk, Thomson, Mackay, Milne, Bowman, Blackwood, Murray, Young, Wardhaugh and Crawford*

If the result was not enough to cheer the Hearts support, I am sure they would have raised a smile with the news that Hibs had gone down to their fourth defeat in a row, this time 3–1 to Rangers. This loss more or less saw the end of Hibs' title challenge, although it did mean that Rangers were still a threat. Clyde remained in the hunt with a 3–1 win over Airdrie, but Celtic's chances were dealt a blow when they could only manage a 1–1 draw with Motherwell.

Through in Glasgow, the reserves matched the 'firsts' and also recorded a comfortable 4–1 victory. It took just fifteen minutes for the Maroons to take the lead when George Campbell took advantage of some slack defending by the home side and easily beat Alfredo Renucci from a couple of yards. It looked as if Hearts would have the opportunity to add to their lead four minutes later when Alfie Conn was felled in the box: it seemed a penalty of the 'stone wall' variety but referee Mr Graham waved play on and, with the visitors still amazed at the decision, Partick centre Bobby Gilmour broke upfield and grabbed the equaliser.

Five minuets later and Gilmour got the benefit of another dubious decision when he was allowed to run in on goal from a conspicuously offside position. This time Wilson Brown excelled himself, thwarting the big forward, and justice was seen to be done. Despite the scare, Hearts were by far the better team and Alfie Conn gave them a deserved lead just after the half-hour mark when he guided home a superb pass from George Campbell. They continued to dominate and were rewarded again when Howieson got the third with six minutes of the half left.

There was no change to the pattern of the game after the restart and Renucci did well to stop a fierce drive from Campbell putting the visitors further ahead. The Thistle defence had no answer to Johnny Hamilton, who had them in knots, but he was badly at fault on the hour when he missed a snip from only five yards. But the Gorgie side and Hammy were not to be denied as he made it four not long before the end.

Hearts 'A': Brown, Mackintosh, Lindores, Smith, Glidden, Higgins, Paton, Howieson, Campbell, Conn and Hamilton

On Monday, 13 January Willie Bauld was allowed to leave hospital after a small operation and was already back in training. So Hearts supporters could look forward to tuning into the first edition of STV's sports programme *Yours In Sport* on Thursday night at 6.30 p.m. to see Willie and the rest of the boys work out in an item that would feature the Hearts.

Prior to that, it was announced that Matt Busby had accepted the job of Scotland manager. Many thought that Tommy Walker should have been given the job, even though the part-time post could have interfered with his Tynecastle duties. Perhaps a third job (remember he was club secretary as well as manager) might just have been too much for the great man. Busby was also in charge of the Under-23 side that, despite good performances by all three Hearts representatives, fell to a 3-1 defeat against their English counterparts on Wednesday evening.

In a game played in thick fog – attended by a mere 19,327, the smallest crowd ever to watch an Under-23 international in England – it was the English who showed more flair and were able to turn defence into attack to good effect. However, when Alex Young latched onto a pass from George Thomson to put the Scots ahead in the seventh minute, it looked as though the youngsters could go on and record a good victory over the Auld Enemy. It was not to be, however, as just before the end of the half, George Thomson hung onto the ball a bit too long and was robbed by Wolves' Jimmy Murray, who fired in the equaliser.

Before they had time to regroup, the young Scots went behind to a goal by a youngster called Jimmy Greaves. In a fairly even second half, Scotland looked to have every chance of getting back on terms. However, ten minutes from the end, Dick Beattie in the Scotland goal flapped at a cross and the ball fell to Hayes, who tapped the ball into the net. Despite the loss, it was a decent display by the Scots, with Dave Mackay in particular showing he was ready to step up to full international honours.

Back at Tynecastle, things had gone well for Willie Bauld and he was named to lead the reserves against East Fife on Saturday. Also back from injury and in the side was John Cumming, who had been out of action since the defeat against Clyde. With Bobby Parker, Freddie Glidden and Alfie Conn also turning out, it was an attractive alternative for fans who were not going to make the trip to the Kingdom.

Not playing for the 'A' team, though, was Johnny Hamilton. He had been promoted to the First XI in place of Ian Crawford, as the former Cameron Highlander was suffering from a groin injury. In the last few games it was fair to be said that Ian had not been showing the form of the previous season. The outside-left berth was becoming something of a problem area, with Cumming and Blackwood also having been tried. Now it was Hammy's turn – but word was that if he did not take his opportunity Willie Bauld would be the next to wear the no. 11 shirt.

Across in Glasgow, Celtic announced that they had cancelled their plans to tour South Africa in the summer. No reason was given but it was thought that there would be a large contingent from Parkhead heading to Sweden for the World Cup. On hearing the news, Hearts chairman Nicol Kilgour commented, 'Our tour of Canada goes ahead as scheduled. We do not anticipate just quite as many World Cup call-offs as Celtic.' Didn't he realise Hearts were quite simply the best team in Scotland by a long way? What could he possibly have been suggesting?

EAST FIFE v HEARTS

In the Scottish Cup rehearsal the Bayview men were dispatched 3–0 and Hammy, back after five months out, appeared in his first league game of the season and did his chances of an extended run no harm by grabbing a double. Building on yet another impressive display by the half-back line and with George Thomson outstanding at left-back, the Maroons turned in yet another sound performance that saw them go thirteen points clear at the top.

When the game kicked off, Hearts had the advantage of the blustery wind behind them, but the conditions were probably responsible for Alex Young missing an easy opportunity in an early attack. Alex atoned for the miss after nineteen minutes, following a clever inter-change between Jimmy Wardhaugh and Andy Bowman. His well-placed left-foot shot beat keeper Ronnie McCluskey low to his left and Hearts were one ahead.

There was an early injury scare for Hearts when Jimmy Wardhaugh went down with what looked to be a twisted knee. However, after lengthy treatment he was able to carry on but was still clearly both-ered by the knock. As was the custom with injured players, he took over the left-wing role, with Johnny Hamilton moving inside.

The wind played a significant part again when Hearts grabbed the second goal on the half-hour mark. Johnny Hamilton sent in a corner from the left, the in-swinger caught out everyone and, much to his own surprise, he had made it 2–0. He almost made it three in a more conventional manner five minutes before the break but McCluskey managed to touch his strike onto the bar and away to safety.

The second half began with East Fife showing greater purpose and ex-Hibs man Alex Duchart was just wide of the mark with a header in the opening minutes. Then Jimmy Bonthrone was equally unfor-tunate when he was inches away with a try from twenty yards. Having weathered the storm, Hearts almost added to their lead after sixty-two minutes when Johnny Hamilton saw Neil Bowie rush back to clear the ball off the line with McCluskey beaten.

He was not to be denied and, six minutes later, Jimmy Murray made a great run down the right before unleashing a fierce shot that McCluskey could only parry. The ball broke out to Hammy, who shot low towards goal. Alex Young was standing on the goal-line but had the presence of mind to let the ball run through his legs on its way into the net. The linesman raised his flag against Alex immediately but, proving he was well ahead of his time, referee Gerrard decided that Alex had not been 'interfering with play' and allowed the goal to stand – much to the disgust of the home support.

The game was in the bag but the Bayview men had the opportu-nity to reduce the deficit twelve minutes before the end when they were awarded a spot kick. As the snow began to fall, Jimmy Bonthrone completed a miserable afternoon when his woeful effort hit the post and was cleared to safety.

It was a comfortable victory and a good omen for the Scottish Cup tie scheduled two weeks later.

Hearts: *Marshall, Kirk, Thomson, Mackay, Milne, Bowman, Blackwood, Murray, Young, Wardhaugh and Hamilton*

The win, coupled with a defeat for Clyde at Dundee, meant that Hearts now had a massive thirteen-point advantage over nearest rivals Rangers, although the Ibrox club did have four games in hand.

	Played	Won	Lost	Drawn	For	Against	Points
Hearts	22	19	1	2	89	15	40
Rangers	18	12	3	3	49	28	27
Clyde	20	13	6	1	53	34	27
Celtic	19	10	4	5	40	22	25

While the first team were keeping their league challenge on track, the impressive reserve side were matching the senior side win for win. They got off to the worst possible start and, incredibly, were two down in the first minute. Straight from the kick-off, Robert Leishman ran down the left and played the ball into the middle for Bobby Gillon to open the scoring. Hearts lost the ball straight from the restart and thirty seconds later Leishman had put the visitors two up.

The experienced side hit back and before Jim Howieson scored in the thirty-fourth minute, McFadzean, Paton and Bauld had all passed up good chances. The game was all square two minutes later when Peter Smith netted his first of the game. He put Hearts ahead with his second as the game saw three goals in a four-minute spell.

It could have been four in five minutes, as the Fifers were handed a chance to equalise almost immediately when they were awarded a penalty. But Jock Adie blasted the ball high over the bar, much to the relief of the home crowd. They paid dearly for the miss, as right on the half-time whistle Jim Howieson got his second goal of the game. So the game that had begun so well for the visitors saw them go in at the interval 4–2 down.

Alfie Conn became the third Hearts man to bag a double with his two goals in the second forty-five, putting the result beyond doubt. But it was the visitors who completed the scoring through the industrious Leishman. With Jimmy Wardhaugh having taken a knock on his right knee at Methill, it was reassuring for Tommy Walker to know that Alfie was ready for a return.

Even John Gibson would have enjoyed this one and the reserves now led their league by three points from Aberdeen, with the added advantage of having two games in hand over the Dons. Could it be that both leagues were heading Gorgie way?

Hearts 'A': Brown, Parker, Lindores, Smith, Glidden, Cumming, Paton, Howieson, Bauld, Conn and McFadzean

The cold snap that had gripped Scotland saw no sign of abating and the Tynecastle pitch was considered unplayable for the Second XI Cup tie scheduled for Monday night. As the week went on, the weather got worse. 'BLIZZARD CHAOS HITS COUNTRY' was the headline in the *Evening Dispatch* on Wednesday the 22nd as everywhere was covered in the white stuff.

It threw the whole country into confusion, but nowhere more so than in Kirkcaldy where Raith Rovers had arranged a 'friendly' against Belgian champions Royal Antwerp. Some 12,000 hardy souls turned out to watch Raith record a 3–1 victory. What they didn't know was that this wasn't the crack outfit as advertised but in fact Waterschie, who had won the Belgian Second Division the season before. They were now at the lower end of the First Division and far from challenging for the title. What made the incident even more remarkable was the attitude of the Raith directors, who found out the true identity of the Belgians prior to kick-off but chose not to reveal it to the paying customers. When questioned about the deception, Raith manager Bert Hardman gave the bizarre explanation that he had been informed that 'Royal Antwerp use the name Waterschie while travelling abroad for convenience sake'. I'm sure it could only happen in the 'Lang Toon'.

The weather didn't affect Jimmy Wardhaugh as he continued to get treatment on his knee injury (picked up against East Fife). All the latest methods were used and the *Evening News* reported that Jimmy was having daily sessions of 'heat treatment under the lamps' and then taking exercise on the 'fixed bicycle'. Willie Bauld had meanwhile come through the reserve game without any ill effect and was now training regularly with the rest of the team at Saughton Park. It may be hard to imagine, but around this time there was many a fan who thought that Willie's best days were behind him and there was a lot of talk of selling him on. Willie was determined to prove the doubters wrong but it would be a hard task for him to get fully fit and then displace Alex Young, who had been a sensation since Bauld's injury back in November.

By the end of the week, manager Mr Walker decided to keep Willie in the reserves for another game. Despite the best efforts of Johnny Harvey and Donald McLeod, Jimmy Wardhaugh's knee injury had not cleared up sufficiently, so Alfie Conn made his first appearance in the league side. There were no other changes for the visit of Third Lanark, as Johnny Hamilton's brace the previous week was enough to see him continue on the left wing instead of Ian Crawford. Back in October, the Hi-Hi's were the first team to not only take a point from Hearts but also to stop the Maroons scoring, so despite their lowly league position, Hearts were not going to underestimate their opposition.

HEARTS v THIRD LANARK

Because of the weather in Edinburgh during the week, the game fell into the 'doubtful' category. Consequently, a pitch inspection was arranged for 10 a.m. and, despite the forecast of further wind and sleet, local referee Arthur Crossman passed the already-solid pitch playable. At 2 p.m. match referee Bobby Davidson made a further pitch inspection, as large puddles had started to gather all over the pitch because of the continuing thaw. Mathie Chalmers and his men got to work mopping up and Mr Davidson was happy to let the match go ahead.

Despite the conditions, a reasonable crowd of just over 15,000 turned up to witness yet another fine display from the Gorgie men. Perhaps it was the opportunity to buy tickets for the forthcoming cup tie at Methil that attracted a few more to the gate. Everyone entering Tynecastle could buy a ticket for the game as they passed through the turnstiles. A simple system that seemed to work – something to reflect on next time you are standing in a queue snaking round McLeod Street waiting to be sold your big match ticket.

Hearts trotted out clad in an unfamiliar blue strip but there was nothing unfamiliar about their start to the game. A minute on the clock and they were one up. The conditions certainly contributed to the opener, for when Bobby Blackwood sent in a corner, the Thirds' defence seemed to be stuck in the mud. The ball found Johnny Hamilton at the far side and, as the defenders slipped and slithered, he returned it into the middle. Alex Young had no trouble keeping his feet and crashed the ball into the back of the net from five yards.

Thirds did not let the setback deter them and they had the chance to level two minutes after going behind. When Bobby Craig whipped in a corner, Dave Mackay went up to head clear but, as he did, the ball hit his arm and Mr Davidson gave the penalty. Once again a Third Lanark player had difficulty keeping his feet and Billy Lewis seemed to slip at the crucial moment with his shot hitting the post before bouncing behind.

If the Thirds' man received brickbats for the miss, he deserved plaudits when he intervened twice to prevent Hearts going further ahead. First, he beat Jimmy Murray to a Bobby Blackwood cross, then he put in a great tackle when Alfie Conn looked like scoring on his return to the team. But it was brickbats again after eighteen minutes, when he tried to dribble the ball out of defence. Bobby Blackwood was onto him in a flash, then cut into the middle. He let fly from fully thirty yards, beating Jocky Robertson to put Hearts two ahead.

A HAPPY NEW YEAR (JANUARY)

Seven minutes later and the diminutive custodian was picking the ball out of the net for the third time. Alfie Conn played a defence-splitting pass for Jimmy Murray and, despite Jocky trying hard to narrow the angle, Jimmy had no trouble in finding the net.

It was a topsy-turvy afternoon for Billy Lewis as again he did well to repel the Hearts attack when goal number four looked on the cards. But then he was posted missing in the thirty-eighth minute when Alfie Conn saw his effort cannon off an up right. Neither the post nor Lewis got in the way of Johnny Hamilton scoring seconds later when he fired in a pile driver from just outside the box.

With a minute remaining in the half, there were chances for both teams. Alfie Conn broke through on goal but unfortunately he left the ball behind, stuck in the mud. It was booted upfield and Johnnie Allan thought he had pulled one back when he beat Gordon Marshall from well out. Unfortunately for the centre-forward, he had been in an offside position when he first collected the ball and his effort was correctly ruled out.

The beginning of the second half saw Hearts toying with Third's, with Dave Mackay pulling the strings. He seemed to start everything and it was he who made the initial pass that led to goal number five. The ball was moved from forward to forward before Johnny Hamilton took a potshot that landed in the back of the net.

Despite being beaten five times already, Robertson was doing well in the Third's goal and was at his best to stop Young, Blackwood and Conn in quick succession from increasing Hearts' lead. He stood no chance when the sixth finally did come after Dave Mackay, on a marauding run forward, was hauled down in the box. Perhaps he was still feeling the effects of the challenge, or mindful of his miss from the spot the previous week, but Davie told Jimmy Milne to take the kick. Despite getting a hand to it, Jimmy's strike had too much power behind it to allow Jocky from keeping the ball out. The like-able Edinburgh lad injured his right shoulder in attempting to stop the ball entering the net, but after treatment and still in obvious discomfort, he elected to carry on between the sticks.

To their credit, Bob Shankly's men never stopped trying and they were rewarded twelve minutes from the end when the Gorgie men dropped their guard to allow Matt Gray to score with a snap shot.

Johnny Hamilton had been looking to become the sixth player to score a hat-trick during the season, but that man Robertson prevented him, earning the distinction with a stupendous save five minutes from time. Hammy had better luck when he turned provider a minute later. Alex Young was fouled out on the left and Hammy played in the perfect cross for Jimmy Murray to volley the ball into the net to make it 7–1.

In the final minute, Third's were awarded their second penalty of the game when George Thomson made a clumsy tackle on Bobby Craig. Johnnie Allan took over the spot kick duties but despite Gordon Marshall guessing correctly, he could only watch in agony as the greasy ball spun out of his hands and into the net.

Hearts: *Marshall, Kirk, Thomson, Mackay, Milne, Bowman, Blackwood, Murray, Young, Conn and Hamilton*

Despite the game at Tynecastle going ahead, the weather had taken its toll elsewhere and both Clyde and Rangers were left without a game. Celtic had squeezed passed Raith Rovers and after the last league game of January, the League stood as follows:

	Played	Won	Lost	Drawn	For	Against	Points
Hearts	**23**	**20**	**1**	**2**	**96**	**17**	**42**
Rangers	18	12	3	3	49	28	27
Celtic	20	11	4	5	42	23	27

The weather was responsible for the reserves being inactive, so they also remained at the top of their division. They did manage to get a game on Monday night when the re-arranged third-round Second XI Cup replay against Motherwell was able to go ahead at the second time of asking. Over 10,000 turned out to see an experienced Hearts side take on 'Well, but sadly the Gorgie faithful witnessed one of the poorest performances by the second string so far that season.

They had started brightly with first-team men Bauld and Crawford combining well to allow Willie to hit a screamer towards the top corner. Former Newtongrange Star player Frank Duncan in the Motherwell goal brought off a brilliant save, managing to push the ball over the bar. It was an early sign of what was to come, with the 'Well goalkeeper giving an inspired performance all evening.

Wilson Brown also had to be alert as Gerry Baker posed a real threat to the Hearts goal, but it was his strike partner Ian St John who eventually opened the scoring in the thirty-first minute when he managed to nudge home from close range. St John was becoming a real nuisance to Hearts, as his two goals at Tynecastle for the first-team clash back in November had been enough to see the club drop their first home point of the season.

At the start of the second half Hearts re-arranged their line-up with John Cumming dropping back to a more familiar half-back role. Smith moved up into the forward line at centre in place of Willie Bauld, who went out to the left wing with Ian Crawford now playing at inside-right. Even with the changes, Hearts did not manage to trouble the Steelmen's back line, ably marshalled by Archie Shaw. However, the shuffle eventually paid dividends fifteen minutes from the end when Ian Crawford managed to lose Shaw and fire a low shot past the despairing Duncan after the keeper could only parry a fierce shot from John Cumming.

It was a real cup tie, now, with both sides going for the winner. Motherwell came the closer but Freddie Glidden was on hand to clear a net-bound shot off the line. There was a controversial moment at the other end when a Motherwell defender used a hand to control the ball just outside the box. Ian Crawford stopped and knocked the ball back to Bobby Parker to take the expected free kick. When the right-back picked the ball up to place it, the referee penalised him for 'handball', much to the disgust of the home crowd.

With only four minutes to go and extra time looming, a cross came in from the Motherwell right; Bobby Parker looked to have it covered all the way but slipped just as he was about to make the clearance. Gerry Baker took full advantage and the 'wee' Hearts were out of the cup. It was their first home defeat and only their second loss of the season. For the second year in succession Motherwell had dashed their hopes of cup success.

Hearts 'A': Brown, Parker, Lindores, Smith, Glidden, Higgins, Dobbie, Howieson, Bauld, Cumming and Crawford

The first team had not even played their first game in the bid for cup success, but the trip to Methil was only a few days away. Jimmy Wardhaugh was winning his fitness battle, so it looked as though the only decision for Mr Walker was whether to pitch him straight back into the fray or continue with Alfie Conn.

On Monday the administrators of the Scottish League had made their decision on the team to meet the SFA selected Scotland XI in the first of three World Cup 'trial' games. The first game had been arranged for the following Monday at Easter Road and the quartet of Mackay, Murray, Young and Wardhaugh had been thought worthy of a place in their side – but not the Scottish side, of course. Bobby Kirk had not made either side but had at least been included as a 'reserve' for the League.

7

ON THE ROAD TO THE DOUBLE (FEBRUARY)

EAST FIFE v HEARTS (SCOTTISH CUP)

For the second meeting in a fortnight, Tommy Walker returned to the same side that lined up in the first game. This meant that Jimmy Wardhaugh, fit again, replaced Alfie Conn in the no. 10 shirt. Despite having the same team, though, they found it a lot harder against a better organised Fife outfit and were fortunate to scrape through to the next round.

From the first blast of 'Tiny' Wharton's whistle, East Fife took the game to Hearts. Neil Bowie and Andy Matthew created good chances early on and Gordon Marshall made a terrific one-handed save from Jimmy Bonthrone after eleven minutes. Hearts were not seen as an attacking force until the fifteenth minute when Bobby Blackwood sent in an inviting cross, but both Alex Young and Jimmy Murray just missed making contact.

The game descended into a dour midfield battle. Johnny Hamilton managed to break free and, although his strike beat Ronnie McCluskey, centre-half Bowie was on hand to save the keeper's blushes. It was Hammy again on the half-hour mark but, once he was through on his own, he chose power over direction and his attempt sailed over the bar when he had the chance to do a lot better.

The opener was not far away and seven minutes later Jimmy Wardhaugh pounced on a poor clearance by George Stewart. His pass found Jimmy Murray and, with a neat turn, Jimmy eluded Neil Bowie before thundering the ball into the net with his right foot.

The lead didn't last long, as the Fifers battled back to get back on level terms four minutes later. George Thomson gave away a need-less corner and when Alex Duchart sent the ball over, Bonthrone was there to head goal-wards. It looked like Gordon Marshall would make a comfortable save until ex-Heart Tommy Neilson, with his back to goal, cheekily back-heeled the ball, wrong-footing the keeper completely. It was probably no more than East Fife deserved and when the teams trooped off at the break, Hearts knew they had a game on their hands.

A stiff breeze had picked up for the start, with the hosts having the advantage, and they used it to good effect. Christie, Duchart and Bonthrone all had decent efforts but some desperate defending kept them out. Dave Mackay had the wind knocked out of him as he got in the way of Bonthrone's strike but after a splash from the magic sponge he carried on regardless.

It was one-way traffic and Gordon Marshall was required to be at his best to stop ex-Hibs signing Duchart putting his side ahead. It looked as though Leishman might break the deadlock but Bobby Kirk came to Hearts' rescue by throwing himself in the path of the winger's shot. It was hard to believe that this was the same side Hearts had taken twelve off in their two previous meetings.

The game had now developed in to a classic cup tie and, despite Hearts being under the cosh, they came the closer to going ahead. Dave Mackay proved that he had fully recovered from his earlier knock when he charged forward. His shot on goal beat the advancing McCluskey but with the ball inches from the line Stewart managed to get back to knock the ball into the stranded keeper's arms.

With twenty minutes left and totally against the run of play, Hearts took the lead. In a rare attack Dave Mackay and then Jimmy Murray both went close but the ball ended up going out for a corner. Johnny Hamilton sent in a trademark in-swinger and there was Bobby Blackwood in the perfect position to slam the ball home from a few feet.

It was a shock for the hosts but still they battled away. Some excellent defending, with Bobby Kirk outstanding, saw Hearts' name go into the hat for the next round.

ON THE ROAD TO THE DOUBLE (FEBRUARY)

Hearts: *Marshall, Kirk, Thomson, Mackay, Milne, Bowman, Blackwood, Murray, Young, Wardhaugh and Hamilton*

The draw for the next round of the Scottish Cup was made in Glasgow on Monday and Hearts received a favourable draw, being paired against Second Division Albion Rovers at Tynecastle. Hibs, who had received a bye in the previous round, were matched against Dundee United away from home; and Celtic and Rangers got their usual tough assignments, against Stirling Albion and Forfar respectively.

Monday, 3 February was a memorable day for Alex Young. It was his twenty-first birthday but his celebrations had to be curtailed as he had to play for the League XI against a Scotland XI in the World Cup 'trial' match played at Easter Road that evening. A remarkable crowd of 45,436 turned out at night to watch Scotland struggle to a 3–2 victory against the League. Best for Scotland turned out to be Stuart Imlach, who had a hand in all three goals, setting up two and scoring what turned out to be the winner. For the League side, all four Hearts men played their part with Alex Young and Jimmy Murray getting the goals. Dave Mackay had a quiet game but could have given the League side a draw they probably deserved – if he'd not, once again, missed from the penalty spot.

By Wednesday the bad weather that had swept Scotland a couple of weeks earlier had returned with a vengeance, bringing with it more chaos on the roads. It had swept in from Europe, where Manchester United had headed to take on Red Star Belgrade in the second leg of their European Cup tie. United had established a 2–1 lead from the first game in Manchester and were confident of finishing off the job in Yugoslavia. On the morning of the game there was a deep covering of snow on the pitch but an afternoon thaw meant the game could go ahead. United swept into a 3–0 lead by half time through two goals by Bobby Charlton and one by Dennis Viollet and, although Red Star fought back to earn a 3–3 draw, United had safely qualified for the penultimate stage of the competition. As history has recorded, tragedy struck on the journey home and seven players were amongst the twenty-one who lost their lives on the runway in

Munich. More were to follow in the days after the crash, as the whole of Britain mourned; the sense of loss was felt keenly in Edinburgh as, like Manchester, the city had an exciting young team that looked set for a tilt at Europe next season.

Meanwhile, Hearts' preparations for the arduous trip to Aberdeen continued although, with the north-east being worst hit by the blizzard conditions, it looked highly unlikely that the game would go ahead.

On Friday afternoon, Mr Walker made the shock announcement that leading scorer Jimmy Wardhaugh was officially 'rested' for the game. As there had been no recurrence of his recent injury and he was clearly 'available for selection', it looked in no uncertain terms as if Jimmy had been dropped. It was true that he had not been at his best in his last three outings and had failed to score but it was only four weeks since he'd hit a hat-trick against Dundee. The decision became of no consequence at 4 p.m. when the manager received a call from the Aberdeen secretary to say that, because of the layer of snow on the pitch, the game had no chance of going ahead and the referee had officially called off the match.

Another piece of news to come out of Tynecastle was that Willie Duff had finally made his transfer to Charlton Athletic official. Although Hearts had accepted the £6,500 fee for the former Scottish Cup winner some weeks earlier, with Tommy Walker being incapacitated (and all official business went through him) the administration had been delayed. Now, though, Willie's Tynecastle career was at an end.

With all games being postponed, the only football talking-point on Saturday was Scotland's fate for the forthcoming World Cup. The draw, made in Stockholm, pitted them against France, Paraguay and Yugoslavia. With typical Scottish swagger, the consensus of opinion was that the side would easily progress to the next stage by coming either first or second. Señor Lidio Puevedo, chairman of the Paraguayan selection committee, had a different view and he was quoted as saying, 'The draw has been lucky for us: Scotland are a weak side and the main challenge will come from the other two teams.' Time would tell who was right.

Hearts squad 1957–58. Back row: Conn, Blackwood, Lough, Milne, Brown, Robertson, Marshall, Bauld, Higgins, Wardhaugh, Mackenzie. Middle row: McLeod (Asst Trainer), Bowman, McFadzean, Cumming, Smith, G. Thomson, McIntosh, Kirk, Lindores, Harvey (Trainer). Front row: Goldie, Hamilton, Fraser, Mackay, Crawford, Murray, Paton

Tommy Walker organising a training session

Willie Bauld scores the first-ever goal under floodlights at Tynecastle

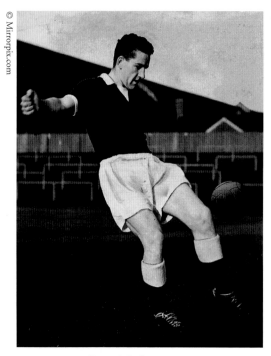

Dave Mackay, 1958

Alex Young's 'offside' goal against Kilmarnock at Rugby Park

Dave Mackay

Willie Bauld

Freddie Glidden

Alex Young

John Cumming

Bobby Parker

Johnny Hamilton

Bobby Kirk

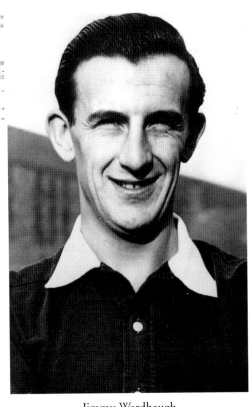

Jimmy Wardhaugh

Tom Mackenzie

Ian Crawford

Alfie Conn

Gordon Marshall saves from Andy Aitken of Hibs at Tynecastle

Jocky Robertson of Clyde, aided by Billy Lewis, stops Jimmy
Wardhaugh from scoring in Hearts' only defeat of the season

The scenes at Love Street after the title had been won

Hearts team group. Back row: Bowman, Paton, Parker, Mackenzie, Marshall, Walker (Manager), Brown, Glidden, Milne, Higgins, Thomson.
Middle row: McLeod (Asst Trainer), Hamilton, Blackwood, Murray, Crawford, Conn, Lindores, Young, Bauld, Harvey (Trainer). Front row: Tait (Director), Kirk, Strachan (Vice-Chairman), Mackay, Kilgour (Chairman), Wardhaugh, Irvine (Director), Cumming, Ford (Director)

League Champions caricatures, a commissioned artwork of all twenty-two players

The team group aboard the *Carinthia* bound for Canada

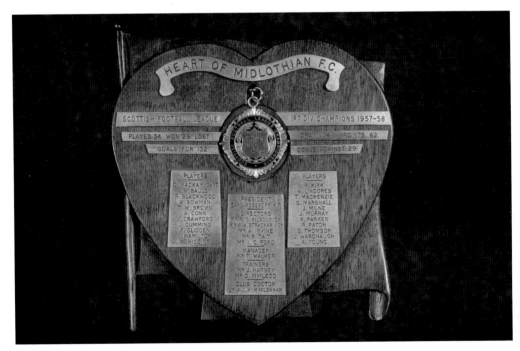

The Championship Medal

On Wednesday, 12 February the international selection committee met in Glasgow to pick the team for the second 'trial' game against Rangers the following week. 'Promoted' to the Scotland select were Jimmy Murray and Davie Mackay but the goal-scoring prowess of Alex Young and Jimmy Wardhaugh was overlooked again. They now appeared certain to be joining the club on the end-of-season tour of Canada and New York. The details of the tour, which would see them play an astonishing nine games in nineteen days, were announced that day.

The next day, with many of the survivors of the Munich air disaster still lying in hospital, Players' Union chairman Jimmy Hill announced that the dependants of the seven United players killed in the crash would receive a payment of £600: £500 would come from the union's own insurance scheme, which only that season had been extended to cover air travel, while the remaining £100 would come direct from the union's funds. Small comfort for the relatives of the famous team.

HEARTS v ALBION ROVERS (SCOTTISH CUP)

Having been out of action for two weeks, perhaps this was the best game for Hearts to pick up where they left off. Albion Rovers were a Second Division outfit and playing away from home – surely they would be no match for the team at the top of the First Division? If Jimmy Wardhaugh had been out of favour prior to the cancelled trip to Aberdeen, he had managed to redeem himself and was included in the side at the expense of Alfie Conn.

Rovers did fight something of a rearguard action with Frank Pattison, who had been listed as their left-winger, actually playing as an extra defender. The Wee Rovers had obviously pinpointed Alex Young as the danger-man and this move allowed their centre-half Bobby Herbert to follow Alex wherever he went. Left-half Pat Glancy then became the stopper in the middle of the defence. This is perhaps the first time the idea of twin centre-halves had been used at Tynecastle. Any time the Tynecastle forwards did manage to break through, they found Alec McFarlane in the Albion goal in fine form.

The visitors' tactics did leave them short of firepower up front, but both Jim Bingham and Matt Carson were big bustling forwards and the Hearts back division had to be on their toes throughout. Jimmy Milne in particular was in sparkling form and probably only he and Alex Young escaped criticism from the home support. During the game the team could do nothing right, with wingers Blackwood and Hamilton coming in for the worst abuse from the terracing. Calls for Willie Bauld and Ian Crawford to be restored to the side were heard throughout as the team toiled. This was Hearts' thirteenth successive win, but you might have mistaken it for their thirteenth successive defeat from the reaction of some of the home support. Disgruntled Hearts fans? Hard to believe, isn't it!

Before the game kicked off, as at every other ground in Scotland, there was a perfectly observed minute of silence in memory of the Manchester United players and staff. This was followed by the City of Edinburgh Band playing 'Abide With Me' as the 23,451 packed inside Tynecastle reflected on recent tragic events.

Not for the first time, Hearts raced into an early lead with Alex Young showing the way after two minutes. Bobby Blackwood made the initial move down the right and his pass was helped on by Jimmy Murray to Alex, who scored from six yards. He was inches away from getting his second three minutes later when Rovers keeper Alec McFarlane initially did well to push out a header from Jimmy Wardhaugh. The ball fell kindly to Alex, who cheekily chipped the ball over the goalie but, agonisingly, the bar as well. Jimmy Wardhaugh and Alex Young continued to ensure the keeper was kept busy for the next twenty minutes; but then, inexplicably, Hearts fell out of the game.

Rovers could have sneaked an equaliser seven minutes before the interval when Alec Harper unleashed a rocket that had Gordon Marshall beaten, but a desperate lunge by Jimmy Milne prevented the ball bulging the rigging. It was at this stage that the home support started to get restless and the players trooped off the field to shouts that were less than encouraging.

Obviously smarting from the criticism from the terracing, Hearts sprang out of the blocks at the start of the second period. Jimmy

Wardhaugh went close with a fierce drive before Bobby Blackwood scored in the fifty-sixth minute to placate the restless fans. This time Alex Young played in a good ball from the left wing and Bobby had time and space to control the ball before smashing it high into the roof of the net.

The Albion refused to capitulate and reduced Hearts' lead seven minutes later when Andy Bowman fouled Matt Carson thirty yards out. Centre-half Bobby Herbert went up the park to take the kick and the big lad had only one thought in mind. He hammered his kick goal-ward and Gordon Marshall might have had a chance to get to the ball had it not taken a wicked deflection on its way into the net. The goal was the signal for the return of the terracing barracking, which began to increase as Albion started to push for a second.

In the seventy-seventh minute, however, Alex Young silenced the critics when he got his second of the game with a well-taken header following a corner by Jimmy Murray. The goal seemed to settle Hearts, as they started to play some of the passing football that they had become synonymous with. But the jitters and jeers resurfaced when Jimmy Murray had two bites of the cherry trying to make it four. First, he hit the upright with a header after he had been left totally unmarked and, when the ball came back to him, Jimmy proved he could miss with his feet as well as his head as he skied the rebound over the bar.

Eventually Jimmy Wardhaugh ensured Hearts' passage into the next round when he scored eight minutes from time. On paper, 4–1 looked like an easy win but it was far from that and the natives were definitely restless as they poured out onto Gorgie Road after the final whistle.

Hearts: *Marshall, Kirk, Thomson, Mackay, Milne, Bowman, Blackwood, Murray, Young, Wardhaugh and Hamilton*

Elsewhere in the cup there were goals galore with Celtic, Kilmarnock, Queen of the South and Queen's Park all hitting seven past their opponents. Rangers managed nine against Forfar but poor old Hibs could only manage a scoreless draw against Second Division Dundee United at Tannadice.

Unlike the first team, the reserve XI were not on cup duty, having been put out of the competition earlier by Motherwell. Instead, they were continuing their quest for their league title with a testing trip to Ibrox. Unfortunately, though, like the game at Tynecastle the home team ran out convincing 4–1 winners. Showing several changes from their last outing, the Hearts reserves went on the attack from the first whistle but Rangers' defence stood firm and soon took a grip of the game. With nine minutes on the clock, Jimmy Millar played the ball in to the unmarked George Duncan and Wilson Brown could do nothing to prevent him opening the scoring from inside the six-yard box.

From the kick-off, Hearts lost possession and Peter Smith upended John Queen to prevent the Rangers man running in on goal. Bobby Orr took the free kick and Don Kichenbrand, left unmarked, headed strongly into the net for the second. Hearts battled back but the combination of stout defending and playing against a strong wind limited them to only a fine try by Alan Finlay that went anywhere near to reducing the deficit before the end of the half.

Playing with the wind advantage after the interval, Hearts set about the home side in determined mood. However, John Valentine at the heart of the home defence was having a commanding game and the Hearts attack struggled to find a way past. When they did, George Niven dealt with anything that came his way and both Ian Crawford and Hugh Goldie saw their efforts comfortably dealt with by the keeper. Despite playing the better football, the Tynecastle men fell further behind in the fifty-seventh minute when Kichenbrand blasted one past Brown for the second time. Five minutes later, 'The Rhino' completed his hat-trick when he rounded Freddie Glidden and slipped the ball into the net.

With Hearts four down, the game was over as a contest, but late in the game Hugh Goldie managed to grab a consolation goal. However, there was no doubt that the loss to one of their nearest rivals was a severe blow to their title challenge.

ON THE ROAD TO THE DOUBLE (FEBRUARY)

Hearts 'A': Brown, Mackintosh, Lindores, Smith, Glidden,
Cumming, Paton, Finlay, Bauld, Crawford and Goldie

The draw for the fourth round was made in the SFA offices on Monday afternoon and there was excitement around Edinburgh when it threw up the prospect of a local derby. Hearts had home advantage against the winners of the Hibs v Dundee United tie.

The following day the second World Cup 'trial' took place, with Rangers providing the opposition at Ibrox. Both Dave Mackay and Jimmy Murray were involved for Scotland, Davie taking over from Doug Cowie of Dundee and Jimmy replacing Alex Scott who was included in the Rangers side. The game itself was a dull affair, with the Ibrox side looking the better of the two. They had taken the lead after six minutes through Murray before Jackie Mudie equalised ten minutes later.

Mudie was Scotland's top man, which sums up the quality of the Scottish team since he was at that time plying his trade with Blackpool *Reserves*. The Hearts duo did their World Cup chances no harm and would get another chance to impress the seven selectors when Scotland took on Hearts in the final 'trial' match at Tynecastle on 3 March.

Wednesday night saw Hibs manage to scrape into the next round of the cup with a 2–0 win in the replay against Dundee United. All Edinburgh now eagerly anticipated the derby encounter on 1 March. And on Friday the 21st there was some good news for Hearts when the SFA announced that the season would be extended to accommodate the backlog of games that had accrued due to the inclement weather of the past few weeks. The final day would now be 3 May and a raft of new fixtures was announced. For once, it did not work in Rangers' favour as they were scheduled to play nine league games in April – plus, like Hearts, they were still challenging in the Scottish Cup.

As far as team selection went, the manager decided to bow to popular opinion and replace Jimmy Wardhaugh with Alfie Conn. Although Jimmy was the team's leading scorer, his form of the past few weeks had not been of the same high standard he had set early in the season. Alfie, on the other hand, had been showing some good form in the second team, as might have been expected, so after missing the last two games he was back in the side for the visit to Fir Park. The Steelmen had lived up to their nickname when they stole a point from Tynecastle back in November, so for the Hearts team there was a real sense of revenge about the game.

MOTHERWELL v HEARTS

The supporters who travelled through to Motherwell expected nothing but a comfortable victory. They might, then, have been tempted to celebrate by taking up the offer of the Motherwell Supporters' Association (Central Branch) who were holding a whist drive after the game. The advert in the programme proclaimed that visiting supporters would receive a warm welcome and for 2/6d (which included tea after whist) they would 'enjoy a good night in good company'.

Perhaps some had enjoyed the 'good company' before the game, as there were still thousands outside as Willie Brittle blew his whistle to get the match under way. Those queuing to get in missed the usual whirlwind start by Hearts: both Dave Mackay and Alfie Conn went close. However, the home side weathered the storm well and then started to pose a few problems themselves.

Jimmy Milne was in the right place in nine minutes when he headed a goal-bound effort from Pat Quinn off the line. Two minutes later and Davie Mackay repeated the trick, this time from an Ian St John strike. Then it was the bar that came to the rescue when 'Well's wing-half Bert McCann rattled the woodwork then put his shot from the rebound narrowly wide.

The Gorgie men were under pressure, but slowly started to work themselves back into the game and Alfie Conn created a good chance for Alex Young with a defence-splitting pass. Unfortunately, Alex snatched at the ball and Hastie Weir was able to make a comfortable save.

It was end-to-end stuff and, after half an hour, Gordon Marshall produced a save right out of the top drawer from Jim Gardiner to prevent Hearts going behind. He denied the centre again a few minutes later when he made another good stop after Gardiner was allowed to run in on goal from an obvious offside position. It was the last action of the half and Hearts counted themselves extremely lucky to be on level terms.

The second half started the same way as the first with Hearts roaring into action. Johnny Hamilton forced Weir to make a first-class save before the visitors went ahead in the forty-ninth minute. The style was reminiscent of so many goals before, with Alfie Conn heading home after a precise cross from Andy Bowman. The difference was that this was Alfie's first league goal of the season

The goal lifted Hearts and they went further ahead ten minutes later in slightly controversial circumstances. Johnny Hamilton had worked his way into the box before he went down from a tackle by Pat Holton. The home crowd seemed to think that Hammy had been somewhat theatrical in his fall but Mr Brittle had no hesitation in awarding the kick. Jimmy Milne stepped up and left Hastie Weir rooted to the spot as the ball flashed past him into the net.

Both sides continued to create chances but it was Hearts who made the game safe fifteen minutes from the end. Again it was a simple affair, with Alex Young mesmerising the home defence before setting up Jimmy Murray, who made no mistake from a few yards out. As the snow started to fall, Hearts were in full flight and Alfie Conn wasted a great opportunity to pile on the misery when he fluffed his shot in front of goal. He more than made up for the miss with four minutes remaining, though, when he ran thirty yards with the ball before crashing in the fourth of the game and Hearts' hundredth in the league so far. Two goals in two outings for Alfie – not a bad strike record and one that should see anyone keep their place in the side. Or was it?

'Ton-up' Hearts: Marshall, Kirk, Thomson, Mackay, Milne, Bowman, Blackwood, Murray, Young, Conn and Hamilton

On the same day, Kilmarnock had held Celtic to a 1–1 draw but Rangers had thrashed Queen's Park 5–1, so at the end of

February the league was turning into a two-horse race and stood as follows:

	Played	Won	Lost	Drawn	For	Against	Points
Hearts	**24**	**21**	**1**	**2**	**100**	**17**	**44**
Rangers	19	13	3	3	54	29	29
Clyde	21	14	6	1	59	36	29

Back at Gorgie, with the reserves it was 'business as usual' as they gained another two points and also scored four against their Motherwell counterparts. They were not impressive in the first half and could easily have been more than a goal down at the break. Twice, John MacIntosh had come to the rescue with goal-line clearances and Wilson Brown distinguished himself with a marvellous save from Gerry Baker. Motherwell finally got the goal their play deserved after forty minutes when Wilson could do nothing to stop a fierce drive from John McPhee.

Hearts started the second half having re-shuffled the forward line to Paton, Crawford, Campbell, McFadzean and Goldie, but it didn't have the desired effect. Motherwell continued to press and they thought they had gone further ahead when Willie Hunter had the ball in the net – only for his effort to be ruled out for a foul by Baker earlier in the move. With just over an hour gone, Hearts were given an opportunity to get themselves back in the game when they were awarded a penalty after Danny Paton was brought down in the box. Ian Crawford took the kick and made no mistake. Motherwell were still recovering from the loss when, two minutes later, Ian Crawford got his second to put Hearts ahead. Ian was in inspired form and, after some good lead-up work by Hugh Goldie, he completed his hat-trick. Motherwell were now a dispirited outfit and Jim McFadzean got goal number four as Hearts gained a certain amount of revenge for their defeat in the Second XI cup back in November.

Hearts 'A': Brown, Mackintosh, Lindores, Howieson, Glidden, Higgins, Paton, Campbell, Goldie, McFadzean and Crawford

8

THE DOUBLE DREAM SHATTERED (MARCH)

Despite Hearts being league leaders by a distance, some things never change in the West of Scotland. At the Gordon Bridge Club in Glasgow, under the auspices of the Scottish Bookmakers' Protection Association (yes, they needed protection back then), Hearts were installed as third favourites to lift the cup. There are no prizes for guessing the two teams who were joint favourites at 3–1. You could get 100–30 on Hearts; Hibs and Aberdeen were quoted at 100–6; and outsiders Clyde were quoted at 8–1. Clyde's odds reflected the fact that they had been paired against Celtic at Parkhead, having given up home advantage and transferred the tie as a 'public safety measure'.

If the SBPA had not made them favourites to win the cup, they did make Hearts firm favourites to progress to the next round. This wasn't just because of the form they had shown in the league, plus the home advantage: across the city, Hibs had to deal with a lengthy injury list; and the previous Saturday, although they scored five times against a St Mirren side that were struggling at the lower end of the league, the hapless Easter Road defence also conceded five. So perhaps it was the poor form of the Hibees that had made the clubs decide the game would not be an all-ticket affair. Only the stand and enclosure were ticket only but by Friday night only the stand was displaying the 'sold out' sign.

For the match, Tommy Walker decided it was time to restore Jimmy Wardhaugh to the side and Alfie Conn – despite the fact that he had scored twice the previous week – dropped out. This decision seemed in tune with 'Edina', who stated in the *Evening News* that

'Conn alas is playing at Second Division speed and is not fast enough for his front-rank colleagues'.

Also replaced was Bobby Blackwood and he made way for Johnny Hamilton who had been moved from the outside-left berth to accommodate the return to senior football of Ian Crawford. Ian's hat-trick in the reserves the previous week had obviously come to the manager's attention and, given his Scottish Cup pedigree, it was hard to argue with him taking his place in the side.

HEARTS v HIBS (SCOTTISH CUP)

The decision not to make the game all ticket looked the wrong one as the queues to get into Tynecastle snaked round the ground before kick-off. Perhaps the good weather, the first for many weeks, had attracted the crowds but a bigger-than-expected 41,666 turned up to witness the latest instalment of the Edinburgh derby.

It was underdogs Hibs who were first to show when seventeen-year-old Joe Baker was given a great chance to open the scoring after only ten seconds – but the young forward made a mess of his attempt, much to the relief of the Hearts back line. They were caught out again a few minutes later when John Grant was left totally unmarked. The full-back had been pushed forward to play in the inside-right position, so perhaps that is how he was allowed to get a 'free' header. Gordon Marshall did well to make the initial stop but excelled himself to get to the rebound before the Hibs man. It was about this time that the crowd at the south-east corner spilled onto the track but the police stepped in to restore order as the game raged on.

Hearts started to get the better of their rivals and, after eight minutes, Dave Mackay was the first to test Lawrie Leslie who was well positioned to stop the skipper's effort. Two minutes later and he didn't do so well when Hearts got the opener. Alex Young headed the ball onto Johnny Hamilton and the wee man then wriggled past two defenders before smashing the ball goal-ward. Leslie got his hands to the ball but could only push it onto the underside of the bar and then it bounced down and out. Neither the referee, Jack

Mowat, nor his linesman seemed to signal the goal even though it had clearly crossed the line. With some Hibs players wanting to play on, Eddie Turnbull picked up the ball and booted it towards the half-way line. Whether or not it was a sporting gesture by Eddie, justice was done and Hearts were one up.

The lead lasted only two minutes before another controversial moment allowed Hibs to equalise. Willie Ormond was given time to fire in a shot that crashed back off the bar. In the ensuing scramble, Gordon Marshall got kicked in the head as the ball broke to Joe Baker and, despite a valiant clearance attempt by Bobby Kirk, it was 1–1.

This was a rough tough game of football and Andy Bowman received a long lecture from Jack Mowat for an over-enthusiastic tackle on John Grant. Other fierce tackles started flying in all over the pitch as both sides fought to gain the upper hand. The game settled into a midfield battle before Joe Baker broke free to give Hibs the lead. He got the ball on the half-way line and beat Jimmy Milne for speed as he ran in on goal. With the Hearts defence trailing, he unleashed a shot from twenty yards that flashed past Gordon Marshall. The smile was wiped from the Hibs man's face seconds later, however, when his name entered the referee's book after he clattered into Jimmy Milne straight from the restart.

Hearts stormed back, looking for the equaliser, but could not find the net – due in the main to some inspired goalkeeping by Lawrie Leslie as Hibs held firm and went in at the break a goal to the good.

At the start of the second half, John Grant came out with his right arm strapped against his chest. It was a recurrence of a shoulder injury he had sustained in a previous game so he had to play out the half with the handicap. This seemed to inhibit the Hearts players from tackling Grant as every time he received the ball the defence backed off, a sporting gesture but one that was to come back to haunt them.

Hearts flew into the attack straight from the kick-off and Jimmy Wardhaugh had a couple of chances to get them back on terms before he did the trick in forty-nine minutes after a blunder by Leslie. Johnny Hamilton tried his luck with a snap shot but the keeper let his harmless effort fall to Jimmy who was able to roll the ball into the empty net.

Hearts were well on top and Hibs were reduced to breakaway raids that came to nothing. Alex Young and then Jimmy Wardhaugh both missed glorious chances to put Hearts back in front but poor finishing was their downfall. They got a lesson in the art in the sixty-sixth minute when Joe Baker was able to complete his hat-trick following another quick break from the back.

It could have been a whole lot worse as, a minute later, John Fraser was inches away with a shot that hit a post then bounced away to safety. If Fraser didn't make the game safe then, he did in the eighty-first minute when he played in a great pass to Joe Baker. With Hearts claiming – and the linesman signalling – offside, Joe didn't stop before hammering the ball into the net for his fourth of the game.

The game seemed to be over and the Gorgie faithful started deserting the terracing but Jimmy Murray gave them faint hope when he pulled one back a minute from time. It was nearly a magnificent comeback when Dave Mackay took a tumble in the box with seconds remaining but Mr Mowat disappointed the home fans again and ignored the claims. It turned out to be the last action of the game and Hearts were out of the cup.

Hearts: *Marshall, Kirk, Thomson, Mackay, Milne, Bowman, Hamilton, Murray, Young, Wardhaugh and Crawford*
Hibs: *Leslie, Paterson, McClelland, Turnbull, Plenderleith, Baxter, Fraser, Grant, Baker, Preston and Ormond*

At the same time as the First XI were tumbling out of the cup, Hearts' reserves gained another two points towards their title with a comfortable win at Palmerston Park. With Freddie Glidden marshalling the defence, they were the better side throughout, although they only had a George Campbell goal to show for their first-half superiority.

Soon after the resumption, Jim McFadzean put Hearts further ahead when he finished off a flowing move involving Billy Higgins and Hugh Goldie. Peter Smith then scored a quick brace which looked to have put the issue beyond doubt. However, Queen of the South had other ideas and hit back twice before the final whistle. Despite the loss of the goals, Hearts were never in danger and returned to Edinburgh with the points safely in the bag.

Hearts 'A': Brown, Parker, Lindores, Howieson, Glidden, Higgins, Paton, Smith, Campbell, McFadzean and Goldie

HEARTS v SCOTLAND (FLOODLIGHT FRIENDLY)

On Monday 3 March, as 2,000 teenage girls flocked to the Usher Hall to scream at American singing sensation sixteen-year-old Paul Anka, 30,000 slightly older men flocked to Tynecastle to scream at Scotland's footballing sensations taking on the best the rest could offer. This was the third and last 'trial' game before Scotland gathered for the World Cup in Sweden. It was fair to assume that these would be the men who would carry the hopes of a nation in the summer. This was reinforced when a tailor visited the Scotland dressing-room before the game to measure the players for clothing for the trip.

It was the Hearts attire though that caught the eye as the music of the pipes and drums of the 1st Battalion the Black Watch played the teams onto the park. This was the first time the crowd had been treated to the sight of the now legendary 'candy stripe' jersey. A natty white satin shirt with narrow maroon stripes had 30,000 tongues wagging before the game began.

Alfie Conn for the injured Jimmy Wardhaugh was the only change to the side that had been knocked out the cup. If they had been poor against Hibs on Saturday, they certainly set about Scotland with renewed vigour. Throughout the first forty-five minutes it was Hearts who played the better football. Alex Young in particular gave Charlton's John Hewie what Bill Heaps of the *Evening Dispatch* accurately described as 'the run around'. Even the hard-to-please 'Tron Kirk' reported that Hearts gave 'an exhilarating display of snappy, clever football'.

Alex's dominance of Hewie was evident when he scored Hearts' first goal. Ian Crawford played the ball in to Alex who was standing twelve yards out. In one swift movement he sold the Charlton defender an outrageous dummy and then hit a low shot on the half-turn. Tommy Younger dived to his right but could do nothing about it and Hearts were deservedly ahead. The Maroons (or should that be Candy Stripes?) continued playing some excellent football but couldn't manage to increase their advantage due in the main to some resolute defending by the Scottish back line.

However, they could not hold out forever and ten minutes into the second half they capitulated once again. It was no more than the Gorgie side deserved when Johnny Hamilton collected the ball on the half-way line and beat Eric Caldow with ease. He took a few strides forwards before hitting a rasping left-foot drive from thirty yards that saw Younger picking the ball out of the net for the second time.

Two minutes later, Scotland hit back through Hibs' Willie Ormond, who incidentally had been a third choice for the team after injuries had ruled out firstly Jim Imlach of Nottingham Forest and then his replacement, Partick's Tom Ewing. Willie Fernie made good progress down the wing and his cross found Ormond who headed home. Despite the setback Hearts continued to dominate, so it was a real shock when Bobby Collins drew the sides level in the sixty-sixth minute with a snap shot that deceived Gordon Marshall.

It was now end-to-end stuff but it was Hearts who settled the issue with only minutes left. Fittingly, Dave Mackay, having played a true captain's part throughout the game, got the winner. He won the ball just outside the box and, after leaving three defenders in his wake, fired towards goal. Tommy Younger managed to block the shot but failed to hold the ball and he could only manage to push it out to Davie following up. Once again, the shot went towards goal and, once again, the Liverpool man somehow managed to keep out his effort. But the big keeper was not as lucky this time as Davie steered the rebound home at the third time of asking.

At last, Hearts had won a game 'under the lights' – and in memorable fashion.

THE DOUBLE DREAM SHATTERED (MARCH)

Hearts: Marshall, Kirk, Thomson, Mackay, Milne, Bowman, Hamilton, Murray, Young, Conn and Crawford.
Scotland XI: Younger (Liverpool), Haddock (Clyde), Caldow (Rangers), Docherty (Preston), Hewie (Charlton), Baird (Rangers), Fernie (Celtic), Collins (Celtic), Brown (Luton), Mudie (Blackpool) and Ormond (Hibs)

As a reward for their historic victory, Hearts were not rewarded with a 'day off' but were told to report for duty at Tynecastle as usual. What they didn't appreciate was that Tommy Walker had arranged for them to take part in the new anti-tuberculosis campaign that was being carried out in Edinburgh during the month of March. TB was a real threat and the health authorities wanted everyone to have an X-ray to help prevent the spread of the killer disease. Everyone who had an X-ray received a smart badge to wear with pride and they were also entered into a prize draw, the top prize being a new house at 139 Caroline Terrace.

Mr Walker was chairman of the Gorgie and Dalry X-ray campaign committee and had agreed to take the team en masse to have the X-rays done. So on Tuesday, 4 March, the team turned up in full training gear at Springwell House to become the latest recruits to the campaign. Sadly no player won the new house. That distinction eventually went to Mr Burnie, a thirty-six-year-old bank clerk at the time – and who knows, he may still be there to this day.

In the next few days Hearts saw fit to arrange a very busy schedule for themselves. They agreed to meet Queen of the South on the Monday of the following week in the fixture originally cancelled due to the cup tie against Hibs. It had been re-scheduled to be played on the Wednesday after the Scotland game but was then further postponed due to the Dumfries side having to replay their cup tie against Kilmarnock.

Incredibly, they also decided to bring forward by twenty-four hours what would be a vital league encounter with Celtic. The game would now be played on the Friday night to avoid a clash with the Hibs v Third Lanark Scottish Cup tie at Easter Road the following afternoon.

Even more remarkable was the fact this game had been scheduled to be the last game of the season for Hearts on 26 April. With the season already extended due to postponements throughout the season, both Hearts and Celtic had agreed to play on what was a 'blank' Saturday but in courtesy to Hibs it was changed again.

It was a happy bunch of shareholders when the Association gathered in the Royal British Hotel for their annual dinner on Thursday the 6th. The main speaker for the evening was Mr W. D. Barnetson, at the time Managing Editor of the *Evening News,* and the speech he gave tackled the problems within the game. Football was now 'big business', he observed, and 'dwindling gates, waning interest, the growth of stay-at-home fans due to TV coverage and the ever-widening gap between revenue and expenditure' all had to be tackled if football was to flourish, according to Mr Barnetson. He added that every club had to be run on sound economical lines or they would run the risk of grave crisis and 'extinction in the case of many clubs'. Sentiment and local patriotism were not enough in some of the over-clubbed areas where too many clubs were trying to draw from too small a population, he observed.

Finally, he broached the subject of the run-down state of some clubs' stadiums. 'One thing the bigger clubs must face up to is the provision of covered accommodation and far better amenities,' he said. The expense would be a long-term investment, 'but it would be well worth it'. He then suggested that a better standard of football was required to bring the fans flocking back through the turnstiles – although considering the achievements of Heart of Midlothian already that season, perhaps this was maybe not the best place to be making the point. However, who could really argue when he declared that 'better coaching is required' and added, 'Why not a real national coaching scheme?' In his reply for the guests, the Editor of the *Scotsman,* Mr A. E. Dunnett, carried on the point and told the assembly that 'football is far too cheap' and that 'it would be well worth double the price if that meant giving the spectators the comfort and amenities they deserve'. Good to see things have moved on so much since 1958.

Having got back on track with a dramatic victory over the Scotland 'probables' on Monday night, Tommy Walker thought the same XI would be good enough to see off the challenge of already-relegated Queen's Park at Hampden. That meant that Alfie Conn retained his place at inside-left, also meaning that Jimmy Wardhaugh was once again consigned to the reserves. Jimmy was not the only one of what could have been thought of as regular first-team men named in the side to take on the 'Strollers' at Tynecastle: Bobby Parker, Freddie Glidden, John Cumming and Willie Bauld all joined him in the 'A' side selected by the manager. With three games in six days coming up, though, these regulars might expect to be called into first-team action sooner rather than later.

QUEEN'S PARK v HEARTS

It was top against bottom as the amateurs got the game under way and, with the knowledge that Hearts had already rattled in seventeen goals in the three previous meetings between the clubs, the Hearts support in the meagre 8,200 crowd stood back and expected a goal rush. What they had maybe forgotten was that Hearts had not scored in their last outing to the national stadium back in August; they were soon reminded when their favourites went behind after six minutes.

Malcolm Darroch and Eddie Perry combined well out on the wing and the inside-left sent in a teasing cross. Gordon Marshall seemed unsure what to do and only succeeded in pushing the ball out as far as Hugh Stevenson who gladly accepted the gift to put the home side ahead.

There was no doubt about it, Hearts were stunned, but playing against the wind, they could not find a way through. The nearest they came to the equaliser was when Davie Holt almost put a free kick from Andy Bowman through his own goal. Luckily for the amateurs, his header was 'accurate' and just cleared the bar. Although Davie was to go on to be a Tynecastle stalwart during the '60s, he never scored during his time in Gorgie. Who knew back then that this was the closest he would come to scoring for Hearts? It took twenty-five minutes before Willie Pinkerton had a save to make: the Hearts man with the honour was Jimmy Murray but he couldn't direct his header beyond the keeper.

Still the Spiders pressed. In one attack, with half an hour gone, Dave Mackay thumped into Malcolm Darroch. Despite receiving attention from the trainer, the amateur had to leave the field for further attention. The home crowd were incensed that Davie was not cautioned for his challenge and from then on he was barracked every time he was on the ball. With five minutes left in the half, Hearts' numerical advantage paid off. Alex Young beat a couple of men before sending the ball into the middle but, as the keeper came to collect, Alfie Conn nipped in front of him and put the ball into the unguarded net.

The home side's inside-left, Darroch, was unable to continue after the break so Queen's had to play the second half with ten men, and for six minutes they equipped themselves well. It took a highly controversial goal to put Hearts in front and for once it looked like they got a break from a referee. Jimmy Murray was adjudged to have been at least two yards offside when he got the ball and the linesman certainly agreed. 'Tiny' Wharton did not and signalled Jimmy to play on. The linesman signalled again when Jimmy seemed to have run the ball over the bye-line before crossing for Alfie Conn to get his second of the game. Despite the protests of the Queen's players, Mr Wharton refused to consult his assistant and the goal stood. Now if only Hugh Dallas had treated Andy Davis in similar fashion!

Hearts were on Easy Street but had a scare when Dave Mackay pulled up suddenly. When he went to the side of the pitch for treatment, the standside crowd were not slow to wish him a quick recovery, or something to that effect. With their good wishes ringing in his ears, but still not fully recovered, he rejoined the game in the forward line with Jimmy Murray dropping back to right-half. It didn't weaken the effectiveness of the forwards so, when right-back Ian Harnett missed a through-ball in the sixty-second minute, Alex Young was on hand to pounce and make it 3–1.

Although Hearts were the better team, there was no spark their play; even the reliable George Thomson was caught out by Hugh Stevenson and resorted to a rather harsh tackle to stop the forward pulling one back. Needless to say, that didn't please the Hampden faithful – nor did the fact that the referee took no action against the Hearts man. 'Tiny' did eventually put a Hearts name in the book when Alex Young took his frustration out on Ian Harnett with five minutes to go. Four minutes later, Dave Mackay sealed the points when he swung his 'good leg' at the ball and it deflected off Ron McKinven on its way past Pinkerton.

Hearts: *Marshall, Kirk, Thomson, Mackay, Milne, Bowman, Hamilton, Murray, Young, Conn and Crawford*

Back in the east, the reserves had gone one better and scored five without reply. With a slight sprinkling of snow on the pitch, Hearts kicked off minus Bobby Parker, whose place had been taken by John Mackintosh – a plasterer to trade, who had been doing his national service with the Cameronians in Germany. He had signed from Larkhall Thistle in August 1951 and was considered to be a great sporting 'all-rounder' (something that might have helped when Hearts had challenged the Meadows XI at cricket before the start of the season).

Hearts took the lead in twelve minutes when Peter Smith received a sublime pass from Jimmy Wardhaugh and tapped in from six yards. Jimmy was running the show and was unfortunate not to add to the lead when he headed against the bar with twenty-four minutes gone. It was his old partner, Willie Bauld, who started the move that led to the second after thirty-five minutes. He played an inch-perfect thirty-yard pass that set Danny Paton free and from his cross Smith ensured that Hearts went into the break two up.

Jimmy Wardhaugh was out to prove a point and he had the ball in the net minutes after the restart. Unfortunately, the linesman had ruled that he had done so from an offside position. But there was nothing wrong when he netted number three with a wonderful header from a John Cumming free kick after fifty-seven minutes.

Willie Bauld was not to be left out and a typical header four minutes later from a spot-on cross by Hugh Goldie brought about the next goal. Jimmy was not to be outdone when, after a further four minutes had gone by, he stroked home number five.

Hearts 'A': Brown, Mackintosh, Lindores, Howieson, Glidden, Cumming, Paton, Smith, Bauld, Wardhaugh and Goldie

HEARTS v QUEEN OF THE SOUTH

On Monday night Queen of the South were the scheduled visitors to Tynecastle, but around midday snow started falling heavily in Edinburgh. By 5 p.m. the snow had eased but it had left the pitch completely white and what we would consider to be 'unplayable'. Nothing, though, was going to stop Hearts' march to the title and sterling work by Mattie Chalmers and his assistant, Willie Montgomerie, saw the lines and goal areas cleared and the rest of the pitch 'rolled' to compact the snow. I am certain that, had both the referee and Queen's not made such long journeys, the game would have been called off; but, having made the trip from Aberdeen, Mr Devine obviously did not fancy just turning round and heading home so the game went ahead.

The weather took its toll on the gate and Hearts' lowest crowd of the season so far – 11,000 hardy souls – took their places to see if the Maroons could continue their chase for the championship. Despite the fact that both Dave Mackay and Jimmy Milne had taken knocks on Saturday, both were pronounced fit enough to take their places in an unchanged side.

Hearts found it difficult to play their normal passing game in the atrocious conditions and for long spells of the game, despite all their efforts, it looked as though this might be the first stutter since the defeat at Clyde back in November. Queen's employed the 'long-ball' tactic to good effect, with the Hearts rearguard finding it difficult to turn on the snow-covered surface. The conditions were the same for both sides, though, and Hearts almost benefited when the visitors' right-back, Alex Smith, slipped when trying to make a clearance and missed the ball completely. His namesake, Willie in goal, had to rush from his area to make the clearance with Alex Young running in.

Twenty-four minutes had gone when Robert Crosbie met a cross from Jim Patterson and headed over a bewildered Gordon Marshall into the net. Stunned, Hearts went on the offensive but the visitors' defence put up stout resistance. They managed to hold off the home forwards until eight minutes before half time when, with the Queen's players claiming for handball against Alex Young, Jimmy Murray was on the spot to grab the equaliser.

After the resumption, Hearts started in determined mood and they had a great chance to take the lead in the forty-ninth minute. Cutting into the box, Alex Young was impeded by Alex Smith and Mr Devine had no hesitation in awarding the penalty. Unfortunately, Jimmy Milne then became the newest member of the 'missed penalty club' when his strike sailed high over the bar.

There then followed a procession of missed opportunities with Jimmy Murray missing in front of an open goal and then Alfie Conn shooting straight at the keeper when he was handily placed. There was another penalty claim when Bobby Blackwood took a tumble in the box but this time the ref was not in such a benevolent mood. When Ian Crawford put the ball over the bar when it looked easier to score, the anxiety levels amongst the crowd began to grow palpably.

The Gorgie men had a third penalty claim turned down when the unfortunate Alex Smith clearly handled the ball in the area midway through the half. Referee Devine was not convinced and the game raged on. With only two minutes remaining, Alfie Conn harassed Smith while he was trying to clear. The full-back hit a pass back to his keeper but again the conditions played their part and the ball eluded the custodian, trickling into the net via the inside of the post. The cheers that echoed round the ground were certainly more of relief than for the quality of the goal but as the old saying goes, they all count.

Against all that had gone before, Hearts managed to put a gloss on the scoreline when, in the last minute, left-back Jimmy Binning sent Bobby Blackwood 'spinning' in the box. Mr Devine could not deny this one and up stepped Jimmy Milne for a second time. There was no mistake this time, as Jimmy slammed the ball past Willie Smith and Hearts had won 3–1.

Hearts: Marshall, Kirk, Thomson, Mackay, Milne, Bowman, Blackwood, Murray, Young, Conn and Crawford

As the crowds wandered home to defrost, news filtered through that Rangers had dropped a point against Kilmarnock. There followed a lot of talk about the next game at Tynecastle against Celtic, which had now taken on the title of championship decider.

On Thursday, 13 March the Scottish League announced the side that would oppose the English League in Newcastle two weeks later. It meant a further honour for Davie Mackay and a first 'cap' at the level for Alex Young. Despite the goalscoring feats of the Jimmies Murray and Wardhaugh, neither were included in the team. Jimmy Murray did at least get a mention in the 'reserves' but he was not one of the two 'to travel'.

Throughout the week, the big thaw continued and by Friday the Tynecastle pitch, although heavy, was free from the snow covering that had made conditions so difficult on Monday night.

There had been talk all week that John Cumming might be drafted back into the side in a straight replacement for Andy Bowman. Andy had been doing well since taking over from Cumming, coincidentally against Celtic back on 28 December. But it was thought that John was more composed on the ball and this could be an all-important factor against the Celts this time round. As it was, the only change to the team turned out to be that Jimmy Wardhaugh replaced Alfie Conn, who had not recovered from a leg injury sustained on Monday night.

Victory would almost guarantee the title and, to add even more spice to the occasion, both sides went into the game with unbeaten records: Hearts unbeaten at home and Celtic unbeaten away from home. Something had to give.

HEARTS v CELTIC

After playing in front of the lowest home gate of the season on Monday, Hearts ran out to the biggest gate on Friday night. Not one of the 35,000 spectators could have imagined what a thrill-packed game they were about to witness.

It was apparent straight from the first blast of referee Massie's whistle that Hearts were, to use modern-day parlance, 'up for it'. They were not unduly put out by the use of the unusual new 'white' ball, and took only three minutes before going ahead through Ian Crawford. Alex Young wrestled possession of the ball from Willie Fernie just inside Celtic's half and slipped a great pass out to Bobby Blackwood. Bobby found Jimmy Wardhaugh twenty yards from goal and then Jimmy, with his left foot, hit one right out of the top drawer. Dick Beattie in the Celtic goal did well to get to the ball but he let it slip from his grasp and Ian Crawford beat John Donnelly in a race to it and swept the ball home.

There was no let-up in Hearts' play and four minutes later they were two up. Once again Alex Young found Bobby Blackwood who hit an angular drive from ten yards that beat the Celtic keeper all ends up. The men from Parkhead were shell-shocked but they got a break when, for once, Dave Mackay did not come out on top after a tackle. The skipper had to be carried off the field by Johnny Harvey and Donald McLeod for attention after taking a kick on the thigh. But what a cheer he received when he returned to the fray after a few minutes' treatment of the 'magic sponge'. It was obvious, though, that he was still suffering and he took up a position on the left wing, with Jimmy Wardhaugh dropping back to right-half.

Still Celtic could not get into the game and, despite playing with only ten fit men, it was Hearts who looked the more likely to score. In fact, it was the injured Dave Mackay who could have been the next name on the scoresheet. Left unmarked by the Celtic defence twice, he was picked out by Jimmy Wardhaugh and twice Dick Beattie had to look lively to stop his shots.

Despite being in the ascendancy it was Hearts who lost the next goal, in the thirty-first minute. Alex Byrne received the ball out on the left and his dipping volley dropped over Marshall and into the net: 2–1 and it was definitely 'game on'. It was to and fro for the rest of the half but neither side could get the next goal that could be so vital to the outcome of the game.

When the sides came back out, there were few in attendance who believed that the sides could serve up as exciting a half as the one they had already witnessed. How wrong they were. In a repeat of the first half, Hearts scored two goals in the first seven minutes of the half to take the wind out of the Celtic sails.

Immediately after the resumption, the hirpling Mackay headed the ball on to Alex Young who squared to Ian Crawford. The outside-left wasted no time in restoring Hearts' two-goal advantage with Dick Beattie unable to stop his low drive. Six minutes later and the lead was increased to three. Again it was the Alex Young–Bobby Blackwood combination that did the damage. Alex passed to Bobby wide on the right and his precision cross was met by Jimmy Murray, giving the Celtic keeper little chance with a superb header.

At 4–1 Hearts were coasting but, as happens so often, the Glasgow side were handed an opportunity to get a foothold back in the game. In the fifty-seventh minute, Sammy Wilson was adjudged to have been impeded in the penalty area and Bobby Collins made no mistake from the spot. Celtic tails were up and Hearts now looked as though they were hanging on. Corner after corner was conceded as the Hoops went in search of another goal to bring them right back into the game. Outstanding in the heart of the defence was Jimmy Milne who shackled the dangerous Billy McPhail throughout, time after time diving into tackles to break up promising attacks. Despite his heroics, even he could do nothing when an attempt from Alex Byrne was not cleared properly, the ball falling to Eric Smith who netted easily.

It was 4–3 and beginning to look as if the game was slipping away from the Gorgie men but the title was up for grabs and they summoned up one last effort to put the game beyond the visitors. With fourteen minutes to go, Hearts were awarded a free kick just outside the box, Jimmy Wardhaugh played the ball into the area and once again

Jimmy Murray rose above the Celtic defence to head past Beattie. Some things never change and at that point a wine glass landed in the penalty area from behind the goal. It is unlikely that the perpetrator, John Turner (18) of Glasgow, was suggesting that Jimmy celebrate the goal with a sip of fine wine, but what a sophisticated young man he must have been to be drinking his 'Buckie' from a glass!

Time was running out, Hearts were handed the perfect opportunity to put it beyond the Glasgow side when Bertie Peacock was adjudged to have handled a shot from Alex Young in the box. Up stepped Jimmy Milne but, for the second time in the week, he failed to convert as his effort flew over the bar. It didn't matter, though, as Mr Massie blew the final whistle moments later and Hearts had won a thriller 5–3.

The cheers that reverberated around Tynecastle as the players left the park could be heard for miles around. Now Hearts only needed nine points from their remaining seven games to ensure the league flag flew over Gorgie for the first time in sixty-one years. Happy days indeed.

Hearts: Marshall, Kirk, Thomson, Mackay, Milne, Bowman, Blackwood, Murray, Young, Wardhaugh and Crawford.
Celtic: Beattie, Donnelly, Fallon, Fernie, Evans, Peacock, Collins, Smith, McPhail, Wilson and Byrne

Although Rangers had six games in hand, Hearts had already won ten games more and were a telling eighteen points clear. It was no wonder that the Hearts support were preparing to celebrate in the next few weeks.

	Played	Won	Lost	Drawn	For	Against	Points
Hearts	27	24	1	2	112	22	50
Rangers	21	14	3	4	60	60	32
Celtic	24	12	5	7	51	51	31

On Monday the 17th, Motherwell manager Bobby Ancell put an end to speculation that he intended to make Hearts an offer for the services of Willie Bauld. Despite being back to full fitness after the troublesome groin injury that had kept him out the side since November, Willie had not been able to force his way back into the first team.

There was also news of another long-term injury victim, big Tam Mackenzie. Tam was Hearts' longest-serving player, having joined the club from Haddington Athletic on New Year's Day 1942. He had been out of action for five months with a career-threatening cartilage injury but Tam announced he was now focusing on making his return to first-team action on the club's summer tour of Canada and the USA. After sustaining the injury against Newcastle United, he spent two weeks in hospital after 'going under the knife', as the press so delicately put it. After that, he had a further fortnight of rest and the famous Tynecastle 'heat treatment under the lamps'. Then, under the watchful eye of Johnny Harvey, 'Mac' continued with light training and strengthening exercises until he was fit enough to take part in the regular Tuesday and Thursday practice sessions at Saughton enclosure. The trainers had now decided he was ready for a game in the reserves and he was named in the team to take on Airdrie at Broomfield that night.

The return of Big Tam to the team did nothing to help their performance, though, as they could consider themselves lucky to escape with a draw after being second best for most of the game. Airdrie had given Hearts notice of their intentions early on when Willie McLean was out of luck when his shot came back of the post. Hearts' only reply was when Danny Paton had set up Hugh Goldie but the inside-left made a hash of his attempt and put the ball over with only the goalie to beat. They paid the price after twenty-nine minutes when Airdrie took the lead. Ian Reid broke down the left, his cross eluding the Hearts defence to allow Jimmy Sharkey to head past Wilson Brown. Ten minutes later and Hugh Goldie was presented with an opportunity to atone for his earlier miss. However, this time he was unlucky not to score when his shot beat the keeper but was cleared off the line by 'Newman'.

In the second half, Hearts shuffled the forward line in an effort to get back in the game but despite the changes it was Airdrie who continued to look the better outfit. Sharkey was just too ambitious when he left three or four men trailing but then lashed the ball over when a couple of his team-mates were better placed to score. Then Airdrie went even closer when a head flick from Dunbar hit the base of the post with Wilson Brown beaten. Hearts were riding their luck but it paid off four minutes from time when Danny Paton got on the end of a cross from Johnny Hamilton to smash in the equaliser.

Hearts 'A': *Brown, Mackintosh, Mackenzie, Howieson, Glidden, Higgins, Paton, Campbell, Bauld, Goldie and Hamilton*

A name missing from the reserves and the first team announced for the game against Clyde on Wednesday night was that of Bobby Parker. Bobby's last First XI appearance had ironically been in the 2–1 defeat against Clyde on 23 November and he chose 19 March to announce his retirement from the game. He had never been able to properly straighten his left leg after the operation on his cartilage that had kept him out of the '56 Scottish Cup final. Now at thirty-three and struggling with a knee injury, he decided to call time on his Tynecastle career and concentrate on his business interests: he owned two newsagent shops, in Gorgie Road and at St Andrew Square bus station.

Dave McLean had signed Bobby from Partick Thistle in 1947 in an exchange deal that saw left-winger Jimmy Walker heading in the opposite direction. At that time Bobby had been turning out at centre-half for Thistle and he played in the same role for Hearts in his first few starts. He made his debut in a 3–2 League Cup tie defeat away to Airdrie on 16 August that year. After he'd had a season in the heart of the defence, manager McLean decided he would make a better right-back and Bobby assumed that role against East Fife on 9 October 1948. Bobby Dougan made his debut in the centre-half position vacated by Parker and a certain Conn, Bauld and Wardhaugh played together for the first time up front!

Although he had missed out on the Scottish Cup final, he had had the honour of leading the side in the historic 4–2 defeat of Motherwell in the League Cup final two years previously. This was not his first medal in senior football and it is worth noting that he was part of the Partick Thistle side that defeated Hibs 2–0 in the 1945 Summer Cup final.

Despite being rock solid in defence, Bobby was never recognised at full international level although he did gain a 'B' international appearance against France in Toulouse. He was thought good enough to captain the side that day but no further honours came his way. Not a new story as far as Hearts are concerned, I suppose. Ever since Thomas 'Tammy' Jenkinson became the first man from Gorgie to represent Scotland – and scoring on his debut in 1887 – he was never chosen again. From that day Hearts players don't seem to have gained the recognition they deserved. If you consider that Jenkinson's feat of one game, one goal was repeated in later years by Thomas Breckinridge (1888), Thomas Chambers (1894), Thomas Robertson (1898), Barnie Battles (1930) and finally Alfie Conn (1956), you start to get the picture. Add to these guys the achievement of Albert Buick (1902), who scored in both his appearances, and then the classic example of the great Andy Black, who scored the three times he was selected, and there might be enough there for a conspiracy theory to develop.

HEARTS v CLYDE

Hearts had to start the game against Clyde minus the club captain as Davie Mackay had not recovered from the thigh knock he had picked up against Celtic. To cover for his absence, Andy Bowman moved over to right-half with John Cumming returning to the team on the left.

Clyde had featured prominently in Hearts' last league title success sixty-one years earlier when a thumping 5–0 win confirmed them as champions. Having been the only team to have beaten Hearts in the league so far, their visit on the Wednesday night was eagerly anticipated. Surely after such a stirring win against Celtic on Friday night, the Gorgie men would exact their revenge? It did not turn out that way, though, and Johnny Haddow's men managed to make the trip back to the west with yet another point wrestled from the league leaders. It took a goal two minutes from time to save Hearts from being beaten for a second time and they were somewhat fortunate to get away with a 2–2 draw. They showed none of the silky play of the past and for long spells of the second half it did not look likely that they could even gain a point.

The forwards were clearly missing the drive of Dave Mackay and their cause was further hindered when deputy skipper Jimmy Wardhaugh received a knock early in the game. After twenty minutes, the Tynecastle outfit created their first good opening when Bobby Blackwood cleverly beat two men but Jimmy Murray couldn't capitalise.

Clyde were not to be outdone and in the thirty-fifth minute had their own chance to break the deadlock. Jimmy Milne did well to break up an attack but then decided to pass back to Gordon Marshall. His pass was woefully short and the big keeper had to look smart to beat the in-rushing Johnny Coyle to the ball. Coyle was not to be denied and four minutes later got the goal Clyde's play richly deserved. Tommy Ring made a good run from midfield before passing to Archie Robertson, who in turn found Coyle. His strike took a deflection off the unfortunate Milne and the ball spun agonisingly over Marshall into the net.

George Herd gave Hearts a few scares early in the second half before Jimmy Wardhaugh, still struggling with his leg knock, almost grabbed the equaliser. He managed to produce a terrific shot on the half-turn but Tommy McCulloch was up to the task just managing to tip the ball round for a corner. But McCulloch was not as agile in the seventy-first minute when he allowed an Alex Young effort to slip through his legs after he looked to have the ball covered.

Hearts hardly deserved to be on level terms, so when Johnny Coyle restored Clyde's lead three minutes later the outlook was as bleak for Hearts as the weather. By this time the game was being played in what only can be described as blizzard conditions. It looked like referee George Mitchell might have to abandon the game if Hearts were to get anything out of the match. When everything seemed lost, Bobby Blackwood worked his way down the right and cut in along the bye-line. He pulled the ball back for Ian Crawford to prod it into the net for an unexpected equaliser.

Prophetically, the football correspondent for the *Scotsman* ended his report with the words: 'On this showing Clyde appear to have a good chance of winning the Scottish Cup'. How right he was! In a similar vein, in the programme for the game the editor commented that Hibs would be making their first Scottish Cup semi-final appearance since 1951. He added, 'They have not won the cup since the war' – without, however, mentioning what war.

Hearts: *Marshall, Kirk, Thomson, Bowman, Milne, Cumming, Blackwood, Murray, Young, Wardhaugh and Crawford*

There was another late goal scored that night but unfortunately for Hearts it was Rangers' Jimmy Millar who grabbed the winning strike seconds from the end at Ibrox. Prior to Millar's spectacular winner, it was looking like Rangers would also drop an unexpected point at home. Falkirk had taken a first-half lead but Rangers fought back and went 2–1 ahead. The battling Brockville outfit hit back through former Hibs man Doug Moran and it seemed like they would hold out until Millar's intervention. So the Ibrox men moved a point closer to Hearts. But surely Hearts had already established too big a gap – or had they?

There was no real good news anywhere for the club that day, as even the reserves crashed to their worst defeat of the season when they suffered a 6–1 reverse against the wee Bully Wee. It all looked so different in the first half when some clever play seemed certain to pay dividends. The defence however were soon cut open with monotonous regularity and the eager Clyde forwards took full advantage.

The veterans of the side, Tam Mackenzie and Freddie Glidden, looked the most unsure and it was Freddie who was badly at fault for the first four Clyde counters. The opener came when he managed to deflect a harmless-looking attempt beyond his own keeper. He was then caught out of position when firstly Charlie Brown and then David Thomson got goals two and three respectively. It got worse for poor Freddie when he tried to dribble the ball out of defence and was dispossessed by centre-forward Archie McHard, who wasted no time in blasting the ball past Wilson Brown. McHard got his second and Clyde's fifth following another defensive lapse, which at least this time did not involve Freddie. After John McLaughlan had raised the tally to six, Hugh Goldie managed to get a consolation for the visitors.

Hearts 'A': *Brown, Mackintosh, Mackenzie, Howieson, Glidden, Higgins, Paton, Smith, Dobbie, Finlay and Goldie*

A bad night all round for the title challenge of both first and second strings but, like the first team, the reserves were still on top of their league, albeit with not such a comfortable advantage. The Reserve League standings were as follows:

	Played	Won	Lost	Drawn	For	Against	Points
Hearts	23	17	2	4	73	29	38
Aberdeen	24	16	5	3	57	34	35
Rangers	25	14	6	5	62	37	33

FALKIRK v HEARTS

Dave Mackay was free from injury in time for the trip to Brockville, so Andy Bowman moved back to his rightful position and John Cumming returned to reserve team duty. With the team taking a familiar look, they made a very familiar start to the game. After only two minutes Alex Young got on the end of a corner from Bobby Blackwood but Andy Irvine had taken up a position at the far post and was able to head clear.

It served as an early warning to the Bairns and, if further evidence of Hearts' intent was needed, Alex Young threatened again in the fifteenth minute: Jimmy Murray cushioned a header into his path but Alex blasted the ball over. With Hearts 'in the mood', the opening goal was not far away and four minutes later it duly arrived. This time Alex kept his shot down but Bert Slater could only push the ball out into the path of Jimmy Murray, who stroked the ball home.

Falkirk struggled to contain the Maroons and, five minutes after opening the scoring, the visitors went two up. Out on the right wing, Jimmy Wardhaugh picked out Ian Crawford and the left-winger didn't need to break stride as he thundered the ball into the back of the net.

Hearts were rampant and Gordon Marshall could only stand and admire they play of the forwards, as he had been given nothing to do. After thirty-three minutes Dave Mackay pulled up injured. It looked as if it was a recurrence of the foot injury that first bothered him in the game against Queen's Park a few weeks earlier. After a couple of minutes of treatment he decided to carry on, although it was obvious he was still experiencing considerable discomfort. The side didn't allow Dave's handicap to upset their rhythm and they went three up a minute later. It wasn't the most aesthetically pleasing effort but it counted when Jimmy Murray squeezed the ball in at the near post, following a melee in the box.

When the break came Falkirk, who had not lost at home since November, must have wondered how they were only three down, so great was Hearts' superiority at that stage. The Bairns could hardly be worse in the second period and they did start the half by testing if Marshall was still awake. Falkirk's centre, John McCole, hit a high one but Gordon dealt with this easily and pushed the ball over.

That was it where Falkirk were concerned, as Hearts took over. After fifty-two minutes Alex Young thought he had done enough with a strong header but he stood in amazement as he watched the ball skim the top of the bar. He had better luck with an hour gone when his header from a Bobby Blackwood corner sailed into the net past his boyhood pal, Tranent man Bert Slater. The two had played in the same Midlothian Schools side and had become firm friends when they both joined Broughton Star.

The points were safe but Hearts looked as though they wanted to match the nine they had scored against their opponents the last time they met back in November. Jimmy Wardhaugh was denied by a marvellous save by Slater and yet another goal-bound header by Alex Young was cleared by Alex Parker.

Ten minutes from the end, Falkirk managed to stage a late rally with Jimmy Milne needing to clear off the line from Derek Grierson and George Thomson having to repeat the trick from John McCole two minutes later. With a minute left, Gordon Marshall did well to keep a clean sheet when he brought off a magnificent save from Grierson. It just wasn't Falkirk's day, but it was Hearts'.

Hearts: Marshall, Kirk, Thomson, Mackay, Milne, Bowman, Blackwood, Murray, Young, Wardhaugh and Crawford

When the Hearts team arrived back in Edinburgh, Davie Mackay was sent straight away for an X-ray on the foot injury that gave him so much bother during the game. After the examination, the doctor revealed that he had 'broken a bone in his small toe and that there was a crack on another on his right foot'. The word 'metatarsal' was probably not invented in those days.

It meant that Davie would miss out on representing the Scottish League against the English counterparts on Wednesday night and a possible call-up to the full side for the Home International against England at Hampden in April. More importantly, as the injury would take four to five weeks to heal, he would miss the run in to the end of the season.

If one Hearts hero was out of action, another was showing that he was fully fit and ready for the fray. In the reserve game Willie Bauld ran the show from beginning to end and scored two headed goals into the bargain. Hearts fell behind when McCormack opened the scoring for the visitors but that was just the signal for Willie to make his mark. Danny Paton provided the opportunity from a right-wing cross for 'The King' to majestically rise above the Falkirk defence and bullet in the equaliser.

The 1–1 scoreline was just about right for the first forty-five minutes but it was all change after the break. Willie was in superb form and his control and distribution were a joy to watch as he gave the youngsters around him a masterclass in the footballing arts. He covered every inch of the pitch and he and Johnny Hamilton mesmerised the young Falkirk side by swapping positions time and again. It was from one of Willie's forays on the left that Hearts took the lead when his cross was met by Alan Finlay to make the score 2–1.

Danny Paton was revelling in the opportunities Willie was providing and he got his name on the scoresheet after seventy minutes to make it 3–1. In the closing stages Willie drifted back into the middle again, accepted a neat pass from Johnny Hamilton, then created just enough room for himself to beat Bobby Brown in the Falkirk goal with a crisp shot.

Hearts 'A': Brown, Mackintosh, Mackenzie, J. Thomson, Glidden, Higgins, Paton, Smith, Bauld, Finlay and Hamilton

On Wednesday, 26 March Alex Young was the lone Gorgie representative who turned out for the League team at St James' Park after Davie Mackay's withdrawal. Sammy Baird of Rangers took Dave's place and, despite providing the pass for St Mirren's Tommy Gemmell to equalise, it was fair to say he had the most uncomfortable of evenings in a 4–1 defeat.

Despite wearing the no. 9 jersey and being expected to lead the attack, Alex was forced to play most of the game in midfield; and although he provided many good passes for his colleagues he never looked like getting his name on the scoresheet. It was a disappointing performance but he still looked good enough to be included in the initial squad of forty for the World Cup that was to be announced in a couple of weeks' time.

THE DOUBLE DREAM SHATTERED (MARCH)

HEARTS v RAITH ROVERS

With Dave Mackay being ruled out through injury, John Cumming was recalled to the side at right-half after his long spell in the reserves. The enforced change was the only one necessary from the side that ran Falkirk ragged the previous week.

Despite the league title being within sight, a meagre 9,000 – the lowest crowd of the season – turned out for the game against Raith Rovers. True, it was a miserable afternoon with the rain that had been falling steadily since Friday afternoon now turning to sleet. Perhaps the Edinburgh public took it for granted that the flag would fly over Tynecastle. The hardy souls attending the game could really have gone home at half time as Hearts tied up both points in the first period.

At kick-off the enclosure and stands were packed to capacity, for Hearts had taken pity on those standing on the terracing and allowed them cover from the weather. Despite this unusually generous offer, there were still a few who preferred to stay where they were for whatever reason – which led to a rather unreal atmosphere in the ground. The playing surface was 'heavy' to say the least but the mud did not stop the Hearts playing some scintillating football from the first whistle and it took all of three minutes before they scored the first of the afternoon. Jimmy Wardhaugh once again deputised for Dave Mackay as skipper and he played a captain's part in the first goal. After tantalising the Raith defence, he squared the ball from the bye-line back to Jimmy Murray, who rattled home the goal that equalled Motherwell's 1932 goal scoring record of 119 in a season.

Four minutes later and they had established the new record and, fittingly, it was Jimmy Wardhaugh who got the goal. Bobby Blackwood sent a high one in from the right and it reached Ian Crawford on the far side; he hit it back into the middle where Jimmy was waiting to nod it into the net despite the best efforts of Andy Leigh and Raith keeper Charlie Drummond. Although this was his twenty-fourth league goal, it was surprisingly his first strike in the league since 11 January when Hearts had beaten Partick 4–1.

179

Despite the absence of Dave Mackay, the half-backs, with John Cumming in particular, were outstanding. Time after time they dealt with everything Raith could muster. Consequently it was Hearts who got the next goal, which came in the twenty-sixth minute, and once again Ian Crawford was the architect. He controlled a beautiful cross-field ball from John Cumming then played his own inch-perfect pass inside to allow Jimmy Murray to guide the ball home.

The Fifers had no answer and the game was put beyond their reach after only thirty-four minutes when Alex Young headed in number four after getting the best of a challenge for a high ball with Drummond.

It could have been five four minutes later when Jimmy Wardhaugh had the ball in the net again following some good lead-up play. His 'goal' was ruled out, however, as although not offside himself, he was denied by the linesman who deemed that Alex Young was.

At the start of the second half, both sides had made a change of strip; Hearts were now wearing the 'candy stripe' and Raith had changed into yellow and blue stripes. The half also saw a change of fortune for both sides. Raith came more into the game as Hearts sat back knowing that the game was won.

But after only two minutes, Bobby Blackwood almost had the ball in the net in an unusual incident. He fell heavily in going for a ball that was collected by Drummond. As the keeper hesitated to see if the Gorgie man had injured himself, Bobby got up and gave the Raith goalie a hefty shoulder charge. The startled keeper dropped the ball but managed to scramble it away to safety. Although within the rules, Bobby's barge had, according to Bill Heeps in the *Evening Dispatch*, 'infringed the unwritten rules of sportsmanship'.

That was the closest Hearts came to adding to their tally, with both Jackie Williamson and Jim Kerray coming close to pulling one back for the visitors. Their pressure finally paid off with fifteen minutes to go when former Hearts man Johnny Urquhart beat Gordon Marshall at the second attempt after the keeper couldn't hold his initial effort.

THE DOUBLE DREAM SHATTERED (MARCH)

The record breakers: Marshall, Kirk, Thomson, Cumming, Milne, Bowman, Blackwood, Murray, Young, Wardhaugh and Crawford

In scoring four times, Hearts had now set a new record with an average of just over four per game. Head of the pile was Jimmy Murray, a man who although having been at Tynecastle for seven seasons and starting the season in the reserves, had now scored twenty-eight times in the league. He was behind Jimmy Wardhaugh in all competitions but he had not played in the League Cup campaign and only got his chance after Alfie Conn had been injured. His scoring record had now put him on the verge of being selected for the World Cup – a remarkable turnaround in fortune for the former Merchiston Thistle man.

Nearest challengers Rangers had been held at home by Motherwell and even although they still had six games in hand over Hearts, the Maroons needed just two points from four games to see them crowned champions.

	Played	Won	Lost	Drawn	For	Against	Points
Hearts	30	26	1	3	122	25	55
Rangers	24	16	3	5	66	37	37
Celtic	27	14	6	7	62	37	35

Like the senior side, the reserves kept up their winning ways, this time by 4–2 in Kirkcaldy with Willie Bauld and Alfie Conn teaming up to great effect. Although they started brightly enough, they went behind in the eighteenth minute when Wilson Brown couldn't hold a fierce drive by Ernie Copeland and the ball fell nicely for Ronnie Tainsh to put the home side ahead.

Willie Bauld was leading the line in his usual fashion but should have put Hearts level when, with only the keeper to beat, he shot straight at the trialist playing in goal for the Rovers. But 'Newman' was well beaten when Johnny Hamilton scored a superb solo goal after he went on a dazzling run, beating three or four defenders before slipping the ball behind the advancing keeper. Three minutes later and Willie Bauld made his mark on the game when he put Hearts in front with a ferocious shot from twenty-five yards that flew into the top corner of the net.

In the second half, Hammy was the tormentor-in-chief and, with the prompting of the little winger, both Willie Bauld and Alfie Conn got their names on the scoresheet. Raith managed to reduce the deficit but it was Hearts who looked more like adding to their tally. Jim Foley being the biggest sinner when, from a pass from Johnny Hamilton, he was left in front of an empty goal but missed the ball completely.

Hearts 'A': *Brown, Mackintosh, Lindores, Thomson, Glidden, Howieson, Foley, Paton, Bauld, Conn and Hamilton*

9

CHAMPIONS AT LAST (APRIL)

With everything looking bright at Tynecastle, it is reasonable to expect that everyone would have been very happy, but Hearts being Hearts, step forward one Alex Jackson. Alex, a twenty-one-year-old provisional signing from Shettleson Juniors, had been doing his national service while attached to Hearts for the previous two years. When he was demobbed, he claimed he had been given an assurance that on conclusion of his service he would be called up to Tynecastle. Hearts, on the other hand, wanted him to see out the last two months of the season at Shettleston, not an unreasonable suggestion. After discussions Tommy Walker said, 'My directors and I consider that Jackson has been handsomely treated as a Hearts player and Jackson knows it. We had a gentleman's agreement with Jackson owing to him being previously stationed in Germany. That agreement still holds good as far as Hearts are concerned.'

Private Jackson thought otherwise and walked out on the club, going south to listen to offers made by Everton (who had been tracking him after their former player Tommy Jones had played against him in a junior international), Fulham and Birmingham City, eventually opting for the Midlands club. A classic case of a player thinking he was too good for the club then being 'tapped' by another outfit: at least that sort of thing could never happen today . . . could it?

Wednesday, 2 April and Hearts' reserves headed through to Ibrox for the first leg of the League Cup semi-final. It turned out to be a game of contesting styles, Rangers utilising the 'long punt' while Hearts played the usual short passing game that had well served both First and Second XIs alike. It was Rangers who looked the more likely to break the deadlock, though, with both Jimmy Walker and Billy Simpson wasting good chances in the opening phase. It was a 'full-bloodied' cup tie with players from both sides flying into tackles. At the heart of the defence, Freddie Glidden was outstanding and he was ably assisted by Willie Lindores, keeping the shackles on Ibrox danger-man Bobby Morrison.

Despite the good showing of the back line, Wilson Brown was the busier of the two keepers. After twenty-five minutes he threw himself full length to push a rasping twenty-yarder from John Queen over the bar. Five minutes later it looked like he would be beaten by Rangers inside-left Jimmy Walker but John Mackintosh got back to clear the shot from the line and the keeper was able to recover, gathering the follow-up attempt from Morrison.

With the referee's whistle for the end of the half seconds away, Hearts went behind when they failed to deal with a cross from Bill Simpson and former Dalkieth Thistle and Hearts player Harry Melrose blasted the hosts in front.

Three minutes after the restart, Hearts were back on level terms. Johnny Hamilton and Billy Higgins combined well and from fully twenty-five yards Billy's swerving shot caught out Charlie Wright in the Rangers goal. This was the signal for the game to explode into life and, after sixty-two minutes, Hearts went ahead. When they were awarded a free kick thirty yards out, Danny Paton hit a screamer that Wright only caught sight of as it came bouncing out from the back of the net.

The lead did not last long, as straight from the kick-off Rangers went up the park and equalised: Queen accepted a pass from Simpson, with his shot from just inside the box catching out Wilson Brown. Again the sides did not remain level for long as Hearts repeated the trick of regaining the lead straight from kick-off. This time Johnny Hamilton showed that he could also hit long-range efforts and, once again, Charlie Wright could do nothing as the ball whizzed past him into the net.

There was no doubt the game had developed into an exciting cup tie and it didn't take long before Rangers hit back when they snatched an equaliser in the sixty-eighth minute. Bill Simpson robbed Freddie Glidden of the ball on the half-way line, he fed it to Harry Melrose and, with Freddie out of position, Rangers' inside-left Jimmy Walker had the easy task of heading home his cross.

Hearts really should have taken an advantage back to Edinburgh but the form they had shown made them firm favourites to progress to the final to play either Hibs or Aberdeen, who had to battle out the other semi-final.

Hearts 'A': *Brown, Mackintosh, Lindores, J. Thomson, Glidden, Higgins, Dobbie, Paton, Goldie, Smith and Hamilton*

The following day, Jimmy Cowe wrote an article in the *Evening Dispatch* reflecting that Saturday could be a historic day for Edinburgh football. Hibs were due to travel to Hampden to take on Rangers in the Scottish Cup semi-final and Hearts were to visit Kilmarnock looking for the two points that would bring the league title back. He pointed out that an Edinburgh Double had in fact happened before, back in 1894–95 season, when Hearts won the title and St Bernard's had beaten Renton 2–1 in the Scottish Cup final. Sadly, given Hibs' cup record and Hearts' league record since then, the closest the two senior teams had come to the Double was in 1902–03: that season, Hibs won the league and Hearts made the cup final but were beaten 2–0 by Rangers.

Interesting stuff, but the main thrust of the *Evening Dispatch* article lay in its final paragraph: 'Rest assured, however, if the "double" does come to Edinburgh it will be well watered down by the peeved pundits in the West.' To emphasise the point, the author highlighted that when Hearts had gained the draw at home against Clyde, they had been branded 'lucky'. Although Rangers toiled against Falkirk that week, they were not castigated in the same manner. 'Was it lucky Rangers?' he asked. 'Oh, no. Don't you know? Rangers produced a great glorious, wonderful, gorgeous, tremendous, skilful, superlative fightback win. BAH!' Bah indeed – but with no west-coast bias in the media these days, you can only wonder how frustrating it must have been for Hearts and Hibs supporters back then . . .

As Mr Cowe rightly pointed out, Hearts' trip to Rugby Park was the most important they had played for some time. If they could secure a win, the title was theirs for the first time in sixty-one years. Significantly, on their last visit to Kilmarnock on the opening match of the League Cup, Hearts had gone down 2–1. This time the Rugby Park outfit would be facing a vastly different side. Only Marshall, Kirk, Wardhaugh and Crawford remained, as Tommy Walker once again said 'same again' when announcing the team on Thursday afternoon.

KILMARNOCK v HEARTS

A large contingent of the Gorgie faithful left rain-soaked Edinburgh en route to Kilmarnock, convinced this was to be their day. Unfortunately, it was not to be and the celebrations had to be put on hold as Killie frustrated the Maroons in a 1–1 draw. But perhaps the biggest source of frustration to the away side was referee Mr Crossley. With the game delicately poised, Alex Young thought he had scored when he rose majestically to head home. At first the goal was awarded but after consulting the linesman Mr Crossley changed his mind and ruled it out for offside.

Jimmy Wardhaugh had won the toss and chosen to kick with the strong wind advantage. Jimmy Murray was the first to get the benefit when he latched onto a through-ball from 'captain for the day' Wardhaugh and sent a shot zipping along the deck from ten yards. It looked in all the way until Jimmy Brown dived full length to turn the ball away; how Hearts must have regretted letting Jimmy go. However, they had the younger Gordon Marshall in goals now and he distinguished himself with good saves from both Bertie Black and Gerry Mays as the game raged from end to end. Despite the handicap of playing against the wind, it was the home side who looked the more threatening.

Just before the half-hour mark, the Hearts keeper went for a cross from Dave Burns but only managed to push it out to Tommy Henaughan. With Gordon still on the ground, Bobby Kirk was there to clear his snap shot. After that scare and much against the run of play, it was Hearts who took the lead through Andy Bowman. This was Andy's first goal for the team but what a goal it was. He got the ball on the half-way line after Johnny Cumming and Jimmy Wardhaugh had broken up yet another Kilmarnock attack. He took a couple of strides forward, looked up, then lashed the ball past Jimmy Brown into the net from fully forty yards.

The goal had an immediate effect on the visitors and, seven minutes later, they had the ball in the net – through that Alex Young 'offside' header mentioned earlier. It was certainly a contentious decision, as the referee had been better placed than the linesman in the first instance and it was clear to everyone in the ground (apart from the linesman, that is) that there were two Kilmarnock defenders on the line when Alex 'scored'.

Despite concerted pressure, the Hearts had to settle for the one-goal lead at half time but started the second period desperate for the second goal that would surely be enough to lift the title. Jimmy Brown just beat Alex Young to a free kick from Johnny Cumming in the opening minutes but he was beaten by Jimmy Murray in the fifty-second minute. Unluckily for Jimmy, the ball thundered back off the bar and just when it looked likely he would put the rebound in the net, he was foiled by the linesman flagging him offside.

Kilmarnock still plugged away and grabbed a deserved equaliser with an hour gone, although it took a huge slice of luck to beat the impressive Gordon Marshall. The Hearts defence were unable to clear the ball in the area properly when Killie right-half Bobby Kennedy collected the ball around the penalty spot. With his back to goal, he hit the ball on the turn; Gordon had it covered all the way until George Thomson, trying to clear, only succeeded in deflecting it beyond the keeper.

The goal took the wind out of the Maroons' sails and for the next thirty minutes there was no doubt they were fortunate to hold out. However, Jimmy Milne was in inspired form, denying the hosts further clear-cut chances. In the end the Gorgie men finished the game grateful to be a point closer to clinching the flag.

The point they gained, though, was significant in as much it meant that Hearts had broken yet another record. They had now amassed fifty-six points, one better than Rangers' post-war record achieved the previous season. So in a week they had created new goal-scoring and points records. With three games still to go, who could tell what the team would achieve?

Hearts: Marshall, Kirk, Thomson, Cumming, Milne, Bowman, Blackwood, Murray, Young, Wardhaugh and Crawford

That Saturday was also a disappointing day for our friends from Easter Road. Having made it through to the semi-final of the cup, they were held to a 3–3 draw at Hampden by Rangers. Like Hearts, though, they had another chance at glory the next week when their replay was scheduled for the following Wednesday *afternoon*. Because Hampden did not have floodlights, it was to be a 4.45 p.m. kick-off – handy for anyone from Leith wanting to attend. The teams were playing for the right to meet Clyde, who in the other semi had seen off a rather lacklustre Motherwell side.

For another Scottish side with a Hearts connection, it was a better day: once again, Newtonmore Camanachd triumphed in the Shinty Cup final, beating Oban Camanachd 3–1 in Inverness to win the trophy for the fifteenth time. Right, so where's the Hearts connection? It transpired that Tommy Walker had sent a telegram with the message, 'Greetings, captain Newtonmore Camanachd Club. Every good wish from all at Tynecastle Park.' The reason Tommy had sent well wishes up north and not to Hampden? Mr and Mrs Walker spent their annual summer holidays in Newtonmore, of course. Well, you could hardly imagine them spending their vacation in 'sunny' Leith now, could you?

The reserves' outing against Kilmarnock had been postponed due to the weather conditions as the constant rain had made the Tynecastle pitch unplayable for once. Edinburgh had been lashed by rain of storm proportions since Friday. At least it was a change from the snow blizzards of a few weeks earlier. With the season running out, it was important to get the fixture played as soon as possible and both teams agreed to meet on Monday, 7 April.

A crowd of 5,000 turned out to watch what became the 'Johnny

Hamilton show'. Kilmarnock lined up with former Hearts favourite Bobby Dougan and the exotically named import from South Africa, Vernon Wentzell. The Hearts side included 'Newman' on the right wing, the trialist turning out to be Cruickshanks from Dundonald Bluebell, who turned in a reasonable performance; but right from the off it was 'Hammy' who tormented the visitors. Kilmarnock right-back John Malloy suffered most from his mazy runs and the defender's frustration began to show with his tackles growing cruder as the game progressed. Despite not getting any protection from the referee, Johnny showed commendable restraint and time after time set up good chances for his colleagues. In the twenty-seventh minute, Malloy brought an end to another promising Hamilton run but this time was punished by referee Carroll. Willie Lindores took the resultant free kick and found Danny Paton some twenty yards from goal. Danny didn't hesitate and he lashed the ball first time past Ian Ross in the Killie goal.

From that moment on, Ross did well at keeping the 'wee' Hearts at bay. Despite both Danny Paton and 'Newman' showing up well, there was no way past the Kilmarnock keeper 'Newman'. The win took Hearts another step closer to winning the title. They now had forty-four points from twenty-seven games, five points ahead of closest challengers Rangers and Aberdeen.

Hearts 'A': Brown, Mackintosh, Lindores, Thomson, Glidden, Higgins, Newman, Paton, Campbell, Smith and Hamilton

On the same day as the reserve game, in Europe AC Milan announced they would withdraw from the European Cup if they could not play their semi-final on the dates they stated. They were due to play Manchester United but, because of the air disaster, United's fixture list was somewhat congested. United had requested that the games be played on 14 May and 21 May but Milan insisted on 16 April and 14 May. The club's secretary, Signor Carlo Montanari, stated: 'If the organisers insist, we shall be forced to retire from the competition.' A fine example of Italian sporting spirit which continues to this day.

The following day turned out to be an important day for football in Edinburgh when the SFA selectors announced the team to face England at Hampden on Saturday week. In the side for the first time was Hearts' Jimmy Murray. Despite the Maroons proving to be the best team in Scotland by a long way, Jimmy was the only Gorgie man to make the side. Hearts fared slightly better in the initial World Cup squad for Sweden that was also announced. In the forty were Murray, along with Alex Young, Jimmy Wardhaugh and Dave Mackay; however, this list had to be trimmed to twenty-two, so it was not guaranteed that any would make it to Vasteras (where Scotland would play their first game, against Yugoslavia).

Also that day Hibs managed to beat Rangers in the cup semi replay. They had even managed to survive a last-minute scare when Murray had the ball in the net but his strike was disallowed after the linesman signalled that Ralph Brand had handled prior to the ball being poked home. In the final they would meet Clyde who on the same evening had been hammered 6–2 by Celtic, so there was now every possibility of an Edinburgh Double. Surely not!

On the other side of Edinburgh, all the focus was now on the game at Paisley when Hearts could seal the League title once and for all. With no further injury worries, Tommy Walker entrusted the task to the same men that had come up short the previous week. Supporters were in buoyant mood throughout Edinburgh but no more so than at 60 Gorgie Road, where Merchiston Hearts formally opened their new social club. Despite the importance of the next day's game, Tommy Walker took time out to perform the official opening ceremony. Along with Dave Mackay, Bobby Parker and Johnny Harvey, Tommy met club president David Delworth and club secretary Arthur Delworth to do the honours. Another VIP guest that evening was Hibs' Lawrie Reilly, whom the club presented with a clock as a token of the high esteem in which the members held him.

The Merchiston club had been running for a number of years previously and the prime movers in the early days were Tommy Alston and Charlie 'Pop' Delworth. The club had grown to a hundred strong before a breakaway group went off to form the Ardmillan branch of the Supporters' Association. Once again, they built up the numbers before a second group formed the Harrison Supporters' Club. Undaunted, Charlie – ably assisted by his three sons, Arthur, David and Robert – ensured that the Merchiston club carried on. The club had flourished to the extent that they were able to buy their own premises at the end of 1957 for the princely sum of £5,000. It could now be that the first function that they would hold would be a party to celebrate clinching the flag.

ST MIRREN v HEARTS

It was a perfect afternoon for football, with the sun shining brightly, but the nerves that ran through the team were evident from kick-off. The estimated 8,000 who'd made the trip from Edinburgh did not witness the same scintillating football that had been the trademark of the team throughout the season. Twice the Hearts went into the lead but twice they allowed St Mirren to peg them back. It looked like the winner would never come until, perhaps fittingly, Alex Young scored fifteen minutes from time.

It was Alex who had opened the scoring after only six minutes with one of the easiest goals he scored all season. Slipshod defending by former Hibs stalwart Archie Buchanan allowed a lob from Jimmy Murray to run through to Alex, who was quick to sweep it into the net from close in.

A great start, but Hearts failed to capitalise. They had a let-off in ten minutes when John Cumming fouled Tommy Gemmell just outside the box. Veteran David Lapsley made his way up from his right-back position to take the kick but was out of luck when his effort thumped back off the crossbar.

It turned out that this was all the Buddies had to offer, as Hearts took control and went in search of the second. The vital goal almost came in the twenty-fifth minute when Alex Young spotted Jimmy Wardhaugh in space and gave him the perfect opportunity with his pass. However, Buchanan made a last-gasp lunge to block Jimmy's shot and the ball fell nicely for Jim Lornie, the Love Street keeper, to make an easy save.

Bobby Blackwood had the home defence mesmerised and time and again he set up his colleagues. One sixty-yard run in particular gave Jimmy Wardhaugh a glorious chance but once again he failed to tuck it away. Jimmy was playing well, though, and his clever back-heel pass to Jimmy Murray ten minutes before the interval almost led to the inside-right making it 2–0. Unfortunately Jimmy screwed his shot a few inches wide and the Saints goal survived intact till the half-time whistle.

After the restart, the home side began to take the game to Hearts and Bobby Kirk needed to be sharp to clear the danger when Jim Miller threatened. Hearts weathered the initial storm and hit back through a Jimmy Wardhaugh effort in the fifty-third minute but once again the ball shaved the woodwork. Moments later, Alex Young was denied by a superb save from Lornie, who couldn't hold Alex's initial left-foot drive but managed to gather the ball at the second attempt.

It was against the run of play, then, when Willie Reid's men got their equaliser through Vince Ryan, a recent signing from Celtic, who scored after fifty-nine minutes. A quick break from defence by Saints ended with Hearts conceding a corner. Miller swung the ball over and, with the defence hesitant, Ryan was there to knock it over the line.

Hearts' reply was instant. Jimmy Murray made headway down the right-hand side until he was barged off the ball by Jacky Neilson. Johnny Cumming sent the free kick into the middle and, much to the delight of the away support, Jimmy Wardhaugh restored the lead with a well-placed header.

Then Jimmy Murray went within a whisker of making the game safe in the sixty-seventh minute when his long-range lob had the keeper beaten – but it dropped onto the top of the net. From the goal kick, Tommy Bryceland got the ball and played it to John Wilson, who smashed the ball high into the roof of the net from an acute angle.

Hearts had been pulled back again but the point would still be good enough to win the title. However, they almost slipped behind when Bryceland forced Gordon Marshall into producing a brilliant save. Then, with the away support nervously looking at their watches,

Alex Young got the goal that sealed the league title. Ian Crawford floated the ball in from the left, with the home defence appealing for offside, then Alex just beat Jim Lornie to the ball and flicked it over the keeper's head and into the net. There was only seventeen minutes left and the League flag was as good as won.

There was one downside towards the end of the day when Andy Bowman's name found its way into the referee's book. When Hearts won a throw-in, some of the home support gave Andy abuse for taking what they thought to be too long at getting the ball back into play. Slightly miffed, Andy gestured that he would throw the ball in their direction instead. His action left Mr Gallacher with no real option but to book Andy for 'ungentlemanly conduct'.

There was one final scare when, with time running out, Jim Miller looked to have pulled Saints level for a third time. However, his effort was rightly ruled out for offside and Hearts played out the remaining few seconds comfortably. At the final whistle the relief from the travelling Hearts support was palpable as they staged a mini invasion of the Love Street pitch. Hearts were champions despite not playing the brand of scintillating football that they had been renowned for throughout the season. Despite the fact there were jeers amongst the cheers, the celebrations could begin in earnest.

The League Champions: Marshall, Kirk, Thomson, Cumming, Milne, Bowman, Blackwood, Murray, Young, Wardhaugh and Crawford

When the team returned to Edinburgh, they stopped at the Harp Hotel in Corstorphine Road for a meal. It was a routine that was followed most weeks after away games but this week was a little bit special (although it was to be the only time that the players marked the achievement with anything close to being called a celebration). The team and officials who had been at Paisley were joined by the likes of Freddie Glidden, Tommy Mackenzie, Willie Bauld and Alfie Conn, who had all been with the reserves at Tynecastle that afternoon. Who could have imagined at the beginning of the season that

Hearts would have won the league without these stalwarts in the side?

Earlier in the day they had taken part in a 5–2 demolition of the St Mirren colts at Tynecastle. The game had got off to a rip-roaring start with Hearts taking the lead straight from the kick-off. Saints' left-half Bobby Holmes got in the way of a Willie Bauld rocket but the ball broke kindly to Alfie Conn who knocked it past George Budd from six yards. Time on the clock: ten seconds!

The Buddies hit back two minutes later when former Hearts favourite Bobby Flavell did all the lead-up work for Rodgers, who gave Wilson Brown no chance from close range. It certainly was end-to-end stuff, the rest of the half being played at a hectic pace. Just before the interval, Hearts managed to grab the lead when Willie Bauld controlled a cross from Hugh Goldie then cleverly back-heeled the ball to the in-rushing Peter Smith, who blasted the ball into the net.

Five minutes after the restart and Hearts doubled their advantage when Smith got his second of the game, applying the finishing touch to a knock-down from Alfie Conn. It was around this time that news of the game through in Paisley started to filter through the crowd. Another couple of goals from Willie Bauld and a counter by St Mirren were almost incidental as the realisation set in that the league flag would be flying at Tynecastle for the first time in over sixty years.

The 5–2 win meant that the reserves now held a five-point lead with six games left to play. It looked like they could well emulate the first team with their own title.

Hearts 'A': Brown, Mackintosh, Lindores, J. Thomson, Glidden, Higgins, Paton, Conn, Bauld, Smith and Goldie

With the title now wrapped up, some of the team were looking forward to what they could achieve next season. Jimmy Wardhaugh was looking forward to the challenge of European football, as Hearts had become the first side from Edinburgh to actually qualify for the European Cup. Jimmy showed he was aware of the challenge that lay ahead when he said, 'Our style of play is not very different from that of the Continentals. Over there the strategy is pretty much the same.' He went on to exlain: 'A case of push and run, many of the attacks starting from the back, always on the lookout for the opportunity to build up a "push". This is almost similar to our own game during the season that has ended with out league success'.

Even the *Evening News* was predicting great things in Europe for the team, as Bill Heeps wrote: 'They are ready as they ever will be to take on the Real Madrids, the Milans and the Rheims [ah, whatever happened to the mighty Rheims?] of the Continent'. He added, 'I am pinning my faith in Hearts doing well in the European Cup because they have pinned their hopes in team-work all season' Unfortunately, as we all now know, it did not quite work out that way when Hearts were well beaten by Standard Liege in the first round.

As would be expected, the Lord Provost, Ian A. Johnson-Gilbert, offered his congratulations to the club. However, his choice of words perhaps revealed his true feelings when he wrote: 'The glory of sport must never be clouded by success alone. Nevertheless there is a sense of achievement when success has overcome defeat and victory is assured. Our most cordial congratulations must go to Heart of Midlothian Football Club in their hour of triumph. Edinburgh is proud of the victory.'

When he added 'I am assured by good sportsmanship and skilful play', it was obvious that Ian was not a regular at Tynecastle. Then, probably revealing the reason why, his message of congratulations continued: 'I am sure every jubilant Hearts supporter will now join with me in extending our good wishes to Hibernian Football Club and hope that they succeed in bringing double honours to the City'. Aye right, Lord Provost!

Hearts' success could not go unnoticed and one of the main men behind the triumph was Johnny Harvey and his revolutionary training and tactics. On Monday 14 April, East Fife approached Johnny to take the reins at Methil. It was an attractive offer to take over from current East Fife boss Jerry Dawson and Johnny asked for twenty-four hours to think it over.

Johnny had taken over from former head coach Johnny Torbet in 1951 and in that time had overseen the most successful era there had ever been at Gorgie. Prior to that, in his playing days, he had played for the Fifers although he never set foot on Bayview. In fact he only ever played once for the club and in that game he won a Scottish Cup winners medal. The remarkable turn of events happened in 1938 when Johnny was playing for Hearts. He had learned his trade along-side such luminaries as Alec Massie and Andy Herd. Then Herd was transferred to East Fife and he was part of the side that reached that year's Cup final. Unfortunately for Andy, he received an injury in the 1–1 draw with Kilmarnock and would not make the final. East Fife's manager, Dave McLean (who would soon become Hearts manager), needed a replacement urgently and contacted Hearts about Johnny's availability. A transfer was agreed and Johnny played in the side that triumphed 4–2 after extra time. A few days later he re-signed for Hearts, having only played 120 minutes for East Fife.

Back with the reserves, and that night Willie Bauld was named to lead the front line at home to Rangers in the second leg of the League Cup semi-final. George Dobbie was the man to drop out. Maybe it was Willie's name on the list, or the fact that the first leg had been such an exciting affair, but 14,000 were attracted to Tynecastle for the game. However, if they had been hoping for the excitement of the first game they were sadly disappointed. The first half was a dull affair with neither side creating a scoring opportunity. Luckily for the big crowd, there was a marked improvement in the second period. The game opened up when Hearts deservedly went into the lead nine minutes after the restart. Throughout the game 'The King' had been creating good chances for his fellow forwards but none seemed able to take advantage. In the fifty-third minute he decided to have a go himself but Rangers' full-back Johnny Little managed to get in the way of his shot and the ball broke to Peter Smith, who provided the finish.

It was not long before Hearts had the ball in the net again: Danny Paton chased a long ball through the middle and Charlie Wright in the Rangers goal could do nothing about stopping his fierce strike.

His celebrations were short lived when the referee altered his decision to award the goal when his linesman signalled that Danny had used a hand to control the ball before putting it in the net.

With time running out, they had an even better chance to secure the game five minutes from time when they were awarded a penalty after Danny Paton had been pulled down in the box. Up stepped Johnny Hamilton but once again the Hearts penalty hoodoo struck when he put the ball wide. Luckily the miss didn't matter and they saw out the last few minutes to reach the final for the second year in a row. There they would meet either Hibs or Aberdeen. Indeed it had been Aberdeen who had beaten them the previous year: after going down 2–0 at Pittodrie they lost out 3–2 to the Dons' youngsters in the home leg. So there was a possible chance of revenge.

Hearts 'A': *Brown, Mackintosh, Lindores, J. Thomson, Glidden, Higgins, Hamilton, Paton, Bauld, Smith and Goldie*

The next day the fine form of the reserves was recognised at Under-23 level when the Second XI Association selectors included Billy Higgins and Johnny Hamilton in the reserve team for the return game against Holland in Amsterdam. It was to be the last Under-23 team to be chosen by the Association, as future teams would come under the auspices of the full International and Selection committee of the SFA. The whole idea of the Under-23 team had been the brainchild of a group of club administrators who wanted to further youthful talent for future international sides. They had started without funding from the SFA but the games proved popular with the public and now the ruling body wanted to get involved.

Neither Hearts player would actually get a game unless there was an injury to the first-choice team but Hammy did have the distinction of being one of three who'd make the trip no matter what. Neither Dave Mackay nor Alex Young, who both played in the first game at Tynecastle, were considered this time round as Hearts' rearranged encounter with Rangers had been scheduled for the same evening.

The trainer to the Under-23s was to be Johnny Harvey who, after having had a discussion with the Hearts board and then giving it careful consideration, announced that he was going to decline East Fife's offer to become their next manager. Johnny listed his 'long and happy association' with the Gorgie club as his reason for turning down the job, but it was more than likely that the fact that the Bayview club's fortunes were definitely on the wane and Hearts' were definitely not.

With Jimmy Murray in Girvan with the Scottish team preparing for Saturday's international against England, there was an enforced change to the Hearts side that travelled to Aberdeen on Wednesday afternoon. Jimmy, along with Alex Young, had been the only 'ever-present' in the thirty-two league matches played so far; but that evening his place would be taken by Alfie Conn, who he had replaced way back at the end of August.

ABERDEEN v HEARTS

The new league champions took the park to warm applause from a small Pittodrie crowd of 10,000. The low attendance could have been explained by the 6 p.m. kick-off but they were not in such appreciative mood when Ian Crawford opened the scoring in controversial circumstances in the fourteenth minute.

Alex Young took a quick free kick to Ian Crawford, the winger ran in on goal and as he did a whistle was clearly heard. Thinking it was referee 'Tiny' Wharton wanting the kick to be retaken, the Aberdeen defence stopped but Ian didn't and promptly put the ball in the net. Despite the protests of the Aberdeen players, the goal stood and Hearts were on their way. However, it was to be no easy ride for the Maroons and their defence had to stand firm against the spirited Dons. At times they rode their luck and Jimmy Milne and Bobby Kirk both had to make goal-line clearances from Graham Leggat after Gordon Marshall had been beaten.

Time after time, Marshall himself thwarted the home attack and, midway through the second half, he received a nasty injury for his troubles. Bravely diving at the feet of Norrie Davidson, Gordon took a kick to the head. He lay motionless on the turf and there was great concern amongst his team-mates, but after treatment from Johnny Harvey, Gordon bravely signalled he was able to carry on.

With fifteen minutes left, Hearts sealed the points when, against the run of play, Jimmy Wardhaugh met a cross from the right perfectly and headed the ball home to make it 2–0. The goal deflated the home side and Hearts took full advantage and added to their tally with two further strikes in the last five minutes from Alex Young and then Andy Bowman.

Hearts: *Marshall, Kirk, Thomson, Cumming, Milne, Bowman, Blackwood, Conn, Young, Wardhaugh and Crawford*

In the dressing-room after the game, Gordon Marshall admitted that he could remember nothing of the ninety minutes. The Aberdeen club doctor diagnosed severe concussion but when the team returned to their hotel Gordon was still suffering. A second opinion was needed and this time it was decided that he should be taken to Aberdeen Infirmary for an X-ray as a precautionary measure. Johnny Harvey accompanied him to hospital where, after examination, it was revealed that there was no damage to his skull. However, it was confirmed he was suffering from concussion and so he was kept in overnight for observation.

He was still not fit to travel when the team made their way back to Edinburgh the next morning, so Gordon had to suffer the delights of hospital food for a further twenty-four hours. On Friday he received the 'all clear' and was driven back to Edinburgh by Johnny Harvey, who had remained up north while Gordon was hospitalised. He at least had nearly two weeks to recover as the final game of the season, ironically against Rangers, was not to be played until the end of the month.

On the same day that the first team had taken care of Aberdeen at Pittodrie, the reserves could only manage a draw against the Dons' 'A' side. It was a top-of-the-table clash and could have gone a long way to deciding the Reserve League title, but by the end of the after-noon nothing was decided with Hearts still holding a slight advantage over their northern rivals.

It was the same line-up that had faced Rangers earlier in the week and the tiredness in the limbs was beginning to show. Only Johnny Hamilton and, to some extent, Willie Bauld, rose above the medioc-rity throughout.

All the scoring came in the first half with the visitors going ahead in fifteen minutes. Bobby Bryans waltzed past Higgins, Lindores and Glidden in turn before unleashing a ferocious shot that – despite a valiant effort by Wilson Brown – hit the back of the net. The lead didn't last as 'King' Willie got the colts back on level terms when he effortlessly controlled a Willie Lindores free kick in the box. His shot cannoned off Willie Clydesdale and the deflection left Aberdeen keeper John Ogston stranded.

Aberdeen regained the advantage with thirty minutes gone after outside-right John Boyd cut along the bye-line and squared the ball to Graham McInnes, who made no mistake from eight yards out. Hearts battled back and with five minutes left in the half, Hugh Goldie put them back on level terms when he got his head to a high ball from Smith.

Despite the promptings of 'Hammy' there was no further scoring in the second forty-five, although Willie Bauld missed an easy chance after being set clear by Johnny. Both sides had to settle for the draw which left Hearts four points ahead of the Dons with four games left to play.

Hearts 'A': *Brown, Mackintosh, Lindores, Thomson, Glidden, Higgins, Hamilton, Paton, Bauld, Smith and Goldie*

The games were coming thick and fast for the reserves and they were back in action two days later when they made the journey to Dens Park in a rearranged fixture from the start of the season. Well, most of the team made the journey but a trialist due to play in place of Freddie Glidden failed to turn up. Jimmy Milne was given the call and took his place in the side that also saw the forward line reshuffled with Alfie Conn and George Dobbie taking over from Willie Bauld and Hugh Goldie.

Hearts were on top from the first whistle and had the chance to take the lead as early as the sixth minute when future Everton stalwart Jimmy Gabriel upended Johnny Hamilton in the box. Danny Paton took the resultant kick but fired wide. It was a miss that they were to rue fifteen minutes later when David Dunsmuir gave the home side the lead. Thinking it was going over the bar, Wilson Brown made no effort to stop the ball as the inside forward's looping header found the net.

Hearts stepped up the pressure in the second half but could not find a way past Pat Liney in the home goal. However, with five minutes left, Danny Paton atoned for his earlier miss from the spot when he headed powerfully into the net after a great run and cross from George Dobbie.

Hearts 'A': Brown, Mackintosh, Lindores, Thomson, Milne, Higgins, Paton, Conn, Dobbie, Smith and Hamilton

The following day, Scotland took on the 'Auld Enemy' at Hampden, and it was a proud day for Jimmy Murray who was chosen to make his international debut. Unfortunately for Jimmy, it was a miserable performance by the team and the Scots went down 4–0. It was Scotland's worst ever defeat at Hampden (and only once previously had the English inflicted a bigger victory – but that was back in 1888, when they had gone one better at 'First Hampden Park'). Despite the embarrassing reverse, Jimmy could hold his head high and it was he who probably came the closest to getting Scotland on the scoresheet. First, in the twenty-fifth minute, he fired just wide and then, fourteen minutes later, he brought a wonderful save from Eddie Hopkinson when the big keeper managed to tip his net-bound shot over the bar. Then just before the break, the Bolton goalie again denied Jimmy when he courageously dived at the Gorgie man's feet with Jimmy ready to strike.

The result was a great disappointment to Jimmy, but his misery was compounded when he reached the dressing-room after the final whistle. On the park he had swapped his jersey with Bill Slater but Scotland trainer Dawson Walker told the new boy that it was just not the done thing and ordered him to get his Scotland strip back from the Wolves defender. We can only imagine how acutely embarrassing it must have been for Jimmy to interrupt the jubilant England side and ask for the jersey. When he returned with the blue strip, he might have expected that he would be allowed to keep the memento of his memorable day but again he was sadly disappointed: the trainer took the jersey from him and that was the last that Jimmy ever saw of the strip.

On Sunday night, the Heart of Midlothian Supporters' Association held their first rally and concert in the Usher Hall and were a little more generous than the SFA. It was a happy coincidence that Hearts had a league title to celebrate but the main point of the evening was to honour club stalwart Bobby Parker, who was hanging up his boots at the end of the season. Two thousand turned out to see star of stage and screen Moira Lister present on behalf of the Association a tape recorder to the former skipper. In reply, he made an emotional speech expressing his thanks and his regret at giving up the game. There to see him collect his award were John Harvey, Mattie Chalmers, Ian Crawford, George Thomson, Bobby Blackwood and Dave Mackay. Dave had another important date the next again day when he would go into hospital to have his foot X-rayed to assess the progress on his toe injury. Davie was desperate to lead his side out against Rangers a week on Wednesday and, if the bones had knitted sufficiently, he could commence training in an effort to be fit on time.

Over at Easter Road, another club stalwart was taking his final bow. Lawrie Reilly made his final appearance for Hibs, against Rangers, on Monday the 21st. Much to the delight of the crowd, he managed to grab a goal in a comfortable 3–1 victory and was applauded from the park by both sets of players at the end.

HEARTS v BRITISH ARMY (FLOODLIGHT FRIENDLY)

To keep the side ticking over, Hearts took on the British Army at Tynecastle on Wednesday, 23 April. The team showed one change from the side that had beaten Aberdeen. With Jimmy Murray returning from international duty, Alfie Conn made way for him to take up the inside-right berth. Gordon Marshall had fully recovered from his head knock and was able to take his place between the sticks.

An Army XI had beaten the Gorgie side 5–3 back in December, so here was the opportunity to make amends. And make amends they did. Although the Army side contained many 'stars', they did not have the cohesion of the Tynecastle men and even when Bobby Blackwood had to go off in the thirty-eighth minute after taking a knock, it did not upset the home team's rhythm. His replacement was Johnny Hamilton who had been watching the game from the stand, and when he appeared he got a tremendous ovation from the crowd.

He slotted easily into the attack and, after only a minute on the park, initiated the move that led to the first goal. His pass found John Cumming and his old team-mate Willie Duff could do nothing to prevent the ball heading into the net. Just as John was about to celebrate his strike, up popped Falkirk's Alex Parker, who showed the Army keeper how it should be done – by stopping the ball with his hands. Duff did not learn the lesson and Ian Crawford made no mistake from the spot.

After the break, Hearts continued the onslaught and Willie Duff did well on a number of occasions to keep the scoreline down. But he was helpless in the fifty-seventh minute when Jimmy Wardhaugh hit the bye-line and, after beating Parker (yes, he was still on the park: there was no sending-off for deliberate handball in those days), squared the ball for Jimmy Murray to slot home number two. Murray nearly added to the tally moments later but Duff was equal to the task and it was the Army who snatched the next goal. Sixty-one minutes gone and Pat Quinn latched onto a long through-ball from Bill Curry; with the Hearts defence slow to react, he lobbed the ball neatly over Gordon Marshall and the Army were back in the game.

Eleven minutes later, Hearts' two-goal advantage was restored when Johnny Hamilton chipped the ball to Jimmy Wardhaugh, who in turn laid the ball off to Alex Young who accepted the chance gladly. This inflicted the Army's first defeat in Scotland: they had previously seen off the challenge of both Hearts and Hibs and drawn with Dundee the previous week. There could be no argument that Hearts were the better side and the only complaint the 15,000 crowd had at the end was that Hearts had played in the 'candy stripe' jerseys again. The strip was a hit with a section of the crowd but, unbelievably in my opinion, was disliked by the majority.

Hearts: Marshall, Kirk, Thomson, Cumming, Milne, Bowman, Blackwood (Hamilton), Murray, Young, Wardhaugh and Crawford *Army XI: Duff (Charlton), Parker (Falkirk), Ferguson (Newcastle United), Williams (Plymouth), Plenderleith (Hibs), Petts (Arsenal), Wilson (Rangers), Hitchens (Aston Villa), Curry (Newcastle United), Quinn (Motherwell) and Ewing (Partick Thistle)*

It was a quiet week at Tynecastle after that, as they prepared for the final game of the season. Dave Mackay had been given the thumbs-up to start light training and joined in the sessions at Saughton Park. The big question was, would he be fit enough for the Rangers game? According to Dave himself it looked unlikely for, although the bones had healed, he was still feeling a 'reaction' and reckoned he would not be fully fit in time. This also put in doubt his inclusion in the twenty-two that would head to the World Cup, as the seven selectors were due to make their final decision the following Monday.

At the end of the week the reserves travelled through to Parkhead to take on Celtic, a game played in the afternoon owing to the Glasgow club's lack of floodlighting. Straight from the whistle the second string put on a dazzling display to light up the dull afternoon, with Peter Smith heading home a cross from Danny Paton after only four minutes.

The half continued with both Alfie Conn and Willie Bauld showing the sort of skills that set them apart from the others. Despite their dominance, though, they could not add to their tally and the home side were fortunate to go in at the break only a goal down.

In the second half the Hoops stepped up their game and it was Hearts who were under pressure. When Mike Jackson beat Wilson Brown with a vicious free kick from twenty yards to equalise, it looked as though the points might be staying in the west. However, some excellent saves by Brown and stout defending by Willie Lindores and John Cumming, in particular, ensured that the colts gained another point in their quest for the title.

Hearts 'A': Brown, Mackintosh, Lindores, Thomson, Cumming, Higgins, Paton, Conn, Bauld, Smith and Hamilton

As Hearts prepared for their first title celebrations in over sixty years, our friends from Leith were hoping for their first cup celebrations in over fifty years. Tragically, it was not to be and on Saturday, 26 April they went down 1–0 to Clyde in front of 95,000 (which incidentally included the entire Tynecastle playing staff) at Hampden Park. To be fair, their cause was not helped by an early injury to their inside-right, Andy Aitken, which left him limping badly for most of the game. But when Clyde took the lead after thirty minutes there was no way back for sad Hibs and their Scottish Cup misery continued for another year. Well, another fifty years and counting, actually.

Before the first team completed their fixtures for the season, the reserves still had a few games left in their title challenge. On Monday the 28th, when Tommy Steele disappointed a few thousand young girls by cancelling his sell-out concert at the Usher Hall due to being knocked unconscious the previous evening when he had been mobbed by fans in Dundee, the Hearts reserves disappointed a few thousand of their fans as well when they travelled through to Cathkin Park confident of yet another two points. Oh how wrong they were, with Freddie Glidden in particular having the unhappiest of evenings.

Firstly, he allowed George McCallum to run in on goal and, despite a valiant attempt by Wilson Brown, the Thirds' centre made no mistake for the opener. Before the interval McCallum was through again, but went down from Freddie's challenge. Alex Harley put away the resultant spot kick and Hearts were two down.

Despite the best efforts of Johnny Hamilton, it didn't improve in the second half; in fact, it got worse. A header from Jimmy Welsh gave the Hi-Hi's a third and then outside-right George Carmichael went clear twice to hit goals four and five. To complete a miserable night for Freddie, he found his way into the referee's book after being too animated when questioning a decision.

Hearts 'A': *Brown, Mackintosh, Mackenzie, Thomson, Glidden, Higgins, Hamilton, Campbell, Bauld, Smith and Goldie*

The defeat was an unexpected blow to the title challenge. However, with only one game left, they still held the edge over the Dons who the same evening had been in action against Hibs at Easter Road, battling it out for the right to meet Hearts in the final of the Reserve League cup. Once again, there was no cup joy for Hibs. They had done well to lead 2–1 at the end of ninety minutes, with this making the aggregate score 3–3 after they had gone down by the same score-line at Pittodrie in the first leg. In extra time, two goals by the Dons' Hugh Hay were good enough to see Aberdeen through to what would be a repeat of the previous year's final.

If the other side of town was smarting from two cup defeats in three days, the west of Edinburgh was gearing up to celebrate.

HEARTS v RANGERS

The first sign of success the 36,000 fans got to see as they flooded along the roads in Gorgie was that Hearts had produced a 'Souvenir Programme'. It was the same size as the normal edition but what made it special was, on the front cover, a picture of the coveted league trophy – rather than of a player, as was the custom. The other difference was that the price had doubled and supporters were being charged sixpence for this little piece of history. The first case of Hearts supporters being exploited, perhaps?

Inside the programme there was a picture of the current playing squad (black and white, of course) and a message from the club president, Lord Rosebery – a man of few words, it seems, as his message read: 'I send my heartiest congratulations to you all on a wonderful performance.' Even Hibs' manager, Hugh Shaw, was more eloquent when he wrote, 'Heartiest congratulations from the management and staff of Hibernian FC on your splendid achievement. May we wish you good luck on your Canadian tour and assure you that everyone at Easter Road consider that no more worthy ambassadors of Scottish football have crossed the Atlantic Ocean.'

Further on in the programme the usual match reviews were reduced to teams and scorers to accommodate a 'Congratulations Corner', where good wish messages from individuals around the world were printed. It was truly global and South Africa, Hong Kong, Canada, Belgium, USA, Ireland and Tasmania were all represented. Supporters' clubs had not wasted time offering their felicitations: as well as the Supporters' Association, messages from the Stockbridge and Battersea London branches appeared. Perhaps the most exotic of all was from the colourfully named Rarity Roberts of the Leith Harbour, South Georgia Hearts Supporters' Club. In a letter addressed to Tommy Walker but sent to the *Evening Dispatch* (I would have thought 'Tynecastle Park, Edinburgh' might have sufficed) Rarity wrote, 'Heartiest congratulations self and team. Well done. Poles apart but confidence never flagging.' Who could have put it better?

For the final game of the season, Hearts made one change to the team that had beaten Aberdeen. Bobby Blackwood had not recovered from the injury he received against the Army and, with Johnny Hamilton in Amsterdam on Scotland Under-23 duty, Danny Paton came in for his third start of the season.

If this was a game that had nothing but pride at stake, it was Rangers who set about proving a point. Straight from the kick-off the 'Gers roared into attack but resolute defending and no small degree of good luck kept the visitors at bay. However, the Rangers forwards had to share the blame for not putting the Ibrox side ahead earlier than they did. When Bobby Kirk failed to cut out a high ball from Davie Wilson, the ball fell to Johnny Hubbard in acres of space and it looked like he could not miss. But miss he did, as he hit the ball into the side netting when it looked easier to score.

After quarter of an hour, though, Ralph Brand showed the way. A neat move between Hubbard and Wilson ended with the Rangers winger chipping the ball into the middle where Brand was able to shoot low past Gordon Marshall.

Hearts were clearly second best at this stage, but managed to hold the score at 1–0 until half time. Even a dressing-room pep talk did not help improve matters, as the 'Gers continued where they left off. Only some desperate goal-line defending by Kirk, Milne and Thomson kept them from increasing their advantage. Then Gordon Marshall excelled himself after he was caught slightly out of position when Ian McColl lobbed the ball goal-ward. Somehow Gordon managed to twist himself backwards to push the ball over the bar to safety.

Despite the Rangers pressure, Hearts kept plugging away and fifteen minutes after the break they grabbed the equaliser. Danny Paton had been having a quiet game, even contriving to miss a glorious opportunity in the first half when Jimmy Wardhaugh had set him up. On this occasion, it was Danny who sent Jimmy away through the middle but Wardhaugh's run was interrupted when he was brought down by Willie Telfer. From John Cumming's free kick, Jimmy made a perfect run across the static Rangers defence and was able to hook the ball home.

This could have been the signal for Hearts to take control of the game but it was Rangers who continued to look the more likely side. It continued that way until the final minute but, with the referee Mr Mitchell glancing at his watch, Jimmy Wardhaugh collected the ball in midfield. In one swift move he turned Ian McColl, then sidestepped past Harold Davis. From fully twenty yards he sent a cracking left-foot drive just inside Billy Ritchie's right-hand post. The noise that greeted the goal was deafening and how fitting it was that Jimmy was receiving the plaudits. The goal had not only beaten Rangers but had also taken Jimmy to the top of Hearts' league goal-scoring charts with twenty-eight, one ahead of Jimmy Murray. In total, Jimmy had scored thirty-seven times but even that remarkable strike rate was not good enough to top the list, as Clyde's better run in both cup competitions allowed John Coyle and Archie Robertson to beat Jimmy's tally.

No matter who finished top of the goal-scoring charts, it was Hearts who had finished top of the league and a win over Rangers was probably the perfect denouement to an almost perfect season.

Hearts: Marshall, Kirk, Thomson, Cumming, Milne, Bowman, Paton, Murray, Young, Wardhaugh and Crawford
Rangers: Ritchie, Shearer, Little, McColl, Telfer, Davis, Duncan, Wilson, Murray, Brand and Hubbard

It was a great night at Tynecastle, but there was disappointment elsewhere. There was no joy for Johnny Hamilton over in Amsterdam as he sat in the stand watching the Johnny Harvey-coached Scotland Under-23 side slip to a 2–1 defeat.

The reserves did not fare any better either. Playing their second game of the week, they went down for the second time. Following Monday night's thrashing from Third Lanark, the colts made the short trip to Methil.

Freddie Glidden paid the price for his poor display and Peter Smith took his place in the side. He could not prevent 'Newman' scoring the goal that gave East Fife the victory over a lacklustre Hearts outfit. At the end of the game, however, they did learn that they had in fact won their league, since nearest rivals Aberdeen had also faltered. So Hearts had completed a unique championship double.

They had the chance to make it an even better season by winning the Reserve League cup, the first leg of which was scheduled for a week on Wednesday.

Hearts 'A': Brown, Mackintosh, Lindores, Thomson, Smith, Higgins, Dobbie, Campbell, Bauld, Foley and Goldie

After the game, some of the players due to go on the club tour of Canada and North America received the 'reward' of having their vaccination injections from the club doctor. There was only just over a week before Hearts set out on their tour of Canada and Tommy Walker had announced a squad of seventeen who were to make the trip. With Jimmy Murray and Dave Mackay heading to Sweden, Billy Higgins and Danny Paton were promoted and would set sail from Greenock to Montreal aboard the good ship *Corinthia*. Well, they hoped she would be a 'good ship', as the journey would take six days. On arrival in Montreal they would head off to Toronto to play the Ontario All Stars on 23 May. After that, further games in New York, Edmonton, Toronto (again), Sudbury and finally Montreal were planned. It was then back on the boat for another six days before returning to Greenock on Thursday, 19 June.

While the news of being included on the trip was welcome for some, there was less good news for others. On the same day, Mr Walker announced the 'retained' list for the following season. Missing from the list were the names of Bobby Parker, George Dobbie, John Thomson, George Campbell, Jim Howieson and Jim Foley. Bobby Parker had previously announced his retirement but the others had all at some stage during the season played some part in the successful reserve team. A team that could still round off the most successful season ever by winning the Reserve League cup.

While the first team kept up their fitness with light training and golf outings, the reserves were kept 'hard at it' in a bid to bring back yet another trophy to Tynecastle. The first leg of the League Cup final was played at Pittodrie on Wednesday, 7 May. Back into the side came Alfie Conn and – fresh after sampling the delights of Amsterdam – Johnny Hamilton. The side was further strengthened by the inclusion of Jimmy Milne and Danny Paton from the senior side that had beaten Rangers and both men played a significant part in the outcome of the game.

Three minutes before the end of what had been a dull opening period, Willie Bauld opened the scoring in his own inimitable fashion. He latched onto a Billy Higgins pass from defence and took on the Aberdeen defence single-handed. Despite a last-gasp lunge by centre-half Bill Stephen, Willie could not be shaken off the ball before he stroked home, leaving 'Tubby' Ogston helpless. It was perhaps harsh on the home side, who had peppered Wilson Brown throughout the half, but it was a lesson on finishing by the 'master'.

The home side did manage to get back into the game when Jimmy Milne conceded a penalty in the fifty-second minute, bringing down Hugh Hay in the box. The Aberdeen inside-forward had to be helped from the field before left-back Willie Clydesdale beat Brown with a well-placed shot.

Although Aberdeen were playing with ten men, it was the Dons who came closer to going in front. Wilson Brown brought off a superb save to deny Billy Little, whose shot looked like sneaking in at the post until the keeper got down to turn it round for a corner. It took nearly fifteen minutes before Hay came back on to fill the left-wing berth, a sure sign he was not fit and only there to make up the numbers.

Despite the best efforts of 'King Willie', Hearts could not take advantage of the weakened Aberdeen outfit. A draw looked like being the likely outcome until, with time running out, Danny Paton swapped wings with Johnny Hamilton. The switch paid off with two minutes to go when Danny managed to break through on the right, only to shoot straight at Ogston. The ball ricocheted off the big keeper's legs and came back out to Danny, who was poised enough to control the ball before slipping it into the net.

Despite being second best for most of the game, the 'wee' Hearts had a one-goal advantage to take back to Edinburgh and were now firm favourites to add to the club's trophy tally for the season.

Hearts 'A': *Brown, Mackintosh, Lindores, Thomson, Milne, Higgins, Paton, Conn, Bauld, Smith and Hamilton*

There were only three days before the next leg at Tynecastle but that was enough time for Dave Mackay to have recovered fully from his toe injury and enable him to take part in his first game in over a month. With Bobby Blackwood also included, it was an experienced Hearts side that ran out in front of the 10,000 crowd.

Hearts started brightly and a great through-ball from Dave Mackay allowed Bobby Blackwood the chance to put the team into an early lead. The crowd could hardly believe it when he ballooned the ball over the bar with only the keeper to beat. However, the forwards were running the visitors ragged and it looked as if another trophy would end up in the Tynecastle boardroom. After eight minutes, they were awarded a penalty when Alfie Conn became the 'meat in the sandwich' between Willie Clydesdale and Ian Burns in the box. From the spot, Johnny Hamilton blasted the ball to 'Tubby' Ogston's right and the Maroons had a commanding 3–1 lead on aggregate.

Seven minutes after going in front, Bobby Blackwood had a chance to atone for his earlier miss when he neatly controlled a cross from Hamilton but, once again, he failed to trouble Ogston when his shot sailed over the bar. Minutes later, Alfie Conn got the better of left-back David Caldwell and was in on goal but the big Aberdeen keeper was quick off his line and managed to block Alfie's effort.

The Gorgie men were to rue these missed opportunities as Aberdeen fought their way back into the game. First, Norrie Davidson signalled his intentions when he pulled one back for the Dons. Despite the loss, Hearts continued to play with the conviction that the cup would be theirs. Thirty seconds into the second half, that conviction began to fade when great work by Bobby Wishart allowed Davidson to score his second of the game, thus putting Aberdeen ahead and level on aggregate.

In an effort to change the game, Bobby Blackwood switched places with Danny Paton and for a while it seemed to work. Willie Bauld forced Ogston into a magnificent stop after Blackwood had done all the spadework. Dave Mackay was showing real urgency and he was popping up all over the field; from his cross from the left wing, Alfie Conn rose majestically to head what looked to be a goal all the way until Ogston once again denied the home side. Davie was now playing as much at centre-forward as he was left-half and twice he went close to showing his forwards how it should be done. However, his enthusiasm for bursting forward in an attempt to win the game left gaps at the back and this was to be Hearts' undoing – six minutes from time, Norrie Davidson exploited it to the full when he completed his hat-trick to consign Hearts to defeat by Aberdeen in the final for the second season in a row.

Hearts 'A': *Brown, Thomson, Mackintosh, Mackay, Milne, Higgins, Paton, Blackwood, Bauld, Conn and Hamilton*

On the same day the reserves were playing their last game of the season, the last games of the season were being played in the senior league. Nearest rivals Rangers rounded off their campaign going down to a 1–0 home defeat against Dundee. Clyde, who'd pushed Hearts for so long during the season, fared little better and could only draw 1–1 at home to lowly Third Lanark. When the curtain came down on Hearts' greatest season *ever*, the league standings were as follows:

	Played	Won	Lost	Drawn	For	Against	Points
Hearts	34	29	1	4	132	29	62
Rangers	34	22	7	5	89	49	49
Celtic	34	19	7	8	84	47	46
Clyde	34	18	10	6	84	61	42
Kilmarnock	34	14	11	9	60	55	37
Partick Thistle	34	17	14	3	69	71	37
Raith Rovers	34	14	13	7	66	56	35
Motherwell	34	12	14	8	68	67	32
Hibs	34	13	16	5	59	60	31
Falkirk	34	11	14	9	64	82	31
Dundee	34	13	16	5	49	65	31
Aberdeen	34	14	18	2	68	76	30
St Mirren	34	11	15	8	59	66	30
Third Lanark	34	13	17	4	69	88	30
Queen of the South	34	12	17	5	61	72	29
Airdrie	34	13	19	2	71	92	28
East Fife	34	10	21	3	45	88	23
Queen's Park	34	4	29	1	41	114	9

10

THE GREATEST HEARTS TEAM EVER

In winning their first title in sixty-one years, Hearts created all sorts of records. Their tally of 132 goals beat Motherwell's then twenty-six-year-old record by thirteen. The point's tally of sixty-two from thirty-four games was a new post-war record, beating the fifty-five Rangers achieved the previous season, which had been a record in itself.

During the season, they completed fourteen 'doubles' and so became the first club to beat both Celtic and Rangers twice in one season. They had never been beaten at Tynecastle and had lost only once in total. They finished thirteen points ahead of second-placed Rangers, having scored forty-three goals more than them. They had conceded only twenty-nine times, twenty less than their nearest challengers.

During their forays in League and Scottish Cups, they added a further twenty-six goals for and fifteen against in the nine games played. This brings the totals to 158 for and forty-four against. If we include friendlies, the goals scored begins to look ridiculous. On this side of the Atlantic they scored twenty-one times, although their unusually poor record in these games saw them concede twenty-five. Things got better on the tour of Canada when in the nine games they played they managed to find the net on no fewer than sixty-four occasions (including scoring thirteen in a game *twice*) with the loss of nineteen. During the tour they lost only once, to Manchester City by an inexplicable 7–1 scoreline (but got their revenge in the next meeting with City, beating them 6–0). In total, then, if anyone had been fortunate to follow Hearts home and away that season, they would have seen the Gorgie men score nearly *250* times. (If those seven penalties had not missed during the season, it would have passed that mark.)

Hearts had beaten a Scotland side that was heading to the World Cup in Sweden. All right, I concede any decent team (and some not so decent ones) could beat Scotland, but they also did what even Adolf Hitler couldn't do, when they beat the British Army!

In winning the league, they became the first – and so far only – Edinburgh side to qualify for Europe's top competition. Let's not forget that, when Hibs played in the first year of the competition, they had been invited to represent Scotland. They had in actual fact only finished fifth in the league behind champions Aberdeen, Celtic, Rangers and *Hearts*.

With Hearts in 1957–58, there was strength in depth: the reserves won their league, scoring ninety-three times, and they would surely have broken the century barrier had they played slightly better towards the end of the season. They also reached the final of the Reserve League Cup, failing at the final hurdle for the second year in a row to Aberdeen.

There were, of course, disappointments and the failure to qualify for the knockout stages of the League Cup was one – but things were about to change there. Getting put out of the Scottish Cup by Hibs was another but maybe that was tempered by the fact that Hibs then went on to get beaten in the final (again).

In a season of many highs, perhaps the biggest low was the terrible injury that ended Tom Mackenzie's sixteen-year career at Tynecastle. 'Big Tam' had been a loyal servant to the club since joining from Haddington Athletic in 1942. But he was not the only injury victim through the season and Alfie Conn, Willie Bauld, Freddie Glidden, and John Cumming all missed games. However their replacements, George Thomson, Andy Bowman, Jimmy Murray and Alex Young all stepped up and became central to the success of the team.

I maintain that all of this adds up to the side of 1957–58 being the greatest Hearts team *ever*. I know that many will argue the team now affectionately known as 'McCrae's Battalion' is rightly acclaimed, but footballing-wise those brave lads tragically never got the chance to achieve their potential. As I said at the beginning of this book, my dad claims the 1954 side that brought the first trophy in forty-eight years back to Tynecastle was the best – a claim that has its merit. I am sure also that there are many who would contend that the 1956 cup-winning side were the best. However, I think there can be no doubt now that the class of '57–58 was indeed exactly that: *class*.

Their achievement has never been bettered and can only be compared in the modern era to that of the Arsenal team of 2003–04. The Gunners played some magnificent football when winning the Premiership and did go through the season undefeated – but then they only managed to score a miserly seventy-three goals in the process.

I started this book with a line from a famous old Hearts song and will end it with another:

> *. . . and it's Heart of Midlothian,*
> *Heart of Midlothian FC,*
> *They're by far the greatest team*
> *The world has ever seen.*

In 1957–58, they truly were.

11

THE MEN WHO DID IT –
AND THE SEASONS THAT FOLLOWED

THE PLAYERS

Gordon Marshall

Born: Farnham, 2 July 1939
Signed: 10 August 1956
Appearances: 31
Goals: 0

For the next five seasons Gordon continued to be the last line of
defence at Tynecastle. During that time he shared in the success of
the team, gaining three League Cup winner's medals in seasons
'58–59, '59–60 and '62–63. He had played in the drawn League Cup
final against Rangers in '61–62, but in the replay his place was taken
by Jim Cruickshank as he had sustained a 'dead leg' prior to the
game. Gordon's honours during his time at Hearts also included
another Championship winner's medal when he played in all but
one of the games during the '59–60 campaign.

He was not completely ignored at international level either and
was awarded Under-23 caps when he turned out for England against
both the British Army (when he saved a penalty) and France in 1959.
Perhaps his most memorable Under-23 appearance, though, was in
a remarkable 4–4 draw against Scotland at Ibrox in March 1961.
Despite the English side looking particularly strong with the likes of
George Cohen, Jimmy Greaves and Bobby Charlton, they couldn't
get the better of a resolute Scottish side that included Billy Higgins

at wing-half. Denis Law was in inspired form for the Scots who raced into a 4–1 lead shortly after half time. Gordon pulled off some terrific saves to keep England in the game and Jimmy Greaves went on to score a hat-trick to earn them the draw.

By 1963, though, Jim Cruickshank was coming more to prominence. Only a few days before he was to get married, Gordon was told that Hearts had accepted an offer of £18,000 from Newcastle United for his services. At that time Newcastle were managed by the legendary Joe Harvey and playing in the Second Division. Welsh international Dave Hollins was their regular no. 1, but on his arrival Gordon became the first-choice keeper. Following an indifferent first season, when United finished mid table, in season '64–65 Gordon added to his collection of medals as Newcastle won promotion to the First Division as champions.

For the next three seasons Newcastle, with Gordon in goals, future Hearts manager Bobby Moncur in defence and Bryan 'Pop' Robson and Wyn Davies up front, consolidated their position in the top flight. By 1968 Gordon was facing competition for the no. 1 jersey from a young Northern Irish lad called Iam McFaul, so when Nottingham Forest came in with an offer of £17,500 in October of that year, the bid was accepted and Gordon moved on to the City Ground.

With the likes of Joe Baker and Jim Baxter in the side, Forest were doing well in the First Division but injury to regular goalie Peter Grummitt set the alarm bells ringing. Forest manager Johnny Carey recognised the value of having someone of Gordon's experience but unfortunately things did not work out too well. He only managed seven games before Alan Hill was brought to the club from Rotherham United and took over in goals. It was fair to say that Gordon never really settled in the Nottingham area so, when old rivals Hibs made a move for him, he did not need too much persuasion to return to Scotland.

His arrival at Easter Road saw an instant improvement in Hibs' fortunes and, under the management of Bob Shankly, the Leith side became genuine title challengers. However, during the season the board wanted to cash in by selling players like Peter Marinello and Peter Cormack. It was a situation that Shankly could not go along with and he handed in his resignation. He was shortly followed out the door by the chairman, Bill Harrower. The club's bid for the title faltered and they eventually finished the season in third place, behind both Celtic and Rangers. After another season on the 'dark side' of town, Gordon was 'rewarded' with a free transfer – but he was soon snapped up by reigning champions Celtic.

Gordon's time at 'Darkhead' did not work out as he might have expected and he only managed one first-team appearance, in the European Cup against Boldklubben 1903 (later to become FC Copenhagen). Even then it was not a particularly happy experience, with the Glasgow club going down 2–1 in Denmark. Gordon left the Bhoys when Aberdeen manager Jimmy Bonthrone took him north to take over from regular keeper Bobby Clark, who was recovering from a cartilage operation. However, despite Gordon doing well during Clark's absence, it was always the Scotland international who was going to be first choice in goals at Pittodrie, so Clark's return to fitness left him looking for another club.

He then received an offer from Arbroath, but only on a part-time basis. With an eye to the future, he accepted the deal, which allowed him the time to open a newsagent's and hairdresser's business back in Edinburgh. For six years Gordon was the no. 1 for the Red Lichties, turning out on no fewer than 142 occasions. His service to the club was recognised when he was awarded a testimonial match with Alex Ferguson's Aberdeen providing the opposition.

After finally retiring from the game in 1978, Gordon concentrated on his business interests in Edinburgh. The shop in West Maitland Street operated very successfully and for a while Gordon Jnr managed the hairdressing side while Gordon Snr worked 'upstairs'. After 'young Gordon' went full time with his football career, he gave up his alternative profession and after a while his father decided to sell up and take life easier. Today Gordon is highly regarded at all his former clubs and regularly attends games at Easter Road, Gayfield Park and of course Tynecastle.

Thomas Wilson Brown

Born: Symington, 19 October 1934
Signed: 18 October 1952
Appearances: 3
Goals: 0

The following season, Wilson continued in his role as the back-up to Gordon Marshall, who remained in excellent form. He did manage three starts in the first team with two of them being against both halves of the 'Old Firm'. In the title-winning season of 1959–60, once again Gordon Marshall was the first choice in goal and Wilson's only first-team appearance was in the 3–1 win against Dunfermline on 19 September.

By the start of the 1960–61 season, Hearts had signed another keeper with potential called Jim Cruickshank. 'Crooky' became the regular second-team choice ahead of Wilson, who was then restricted to only thirteen league and cup games for the reserves. In April 1961 George Farm, the player/manager of Queen of the South, made an enquiry about the goalie and, hoping for regular football, Wilson agreed to move to Palmerston.

Although he had signed Wilson, it seemed George Farm was not prepared to end his own playing days (in goals for Queen of the South) and during season '61–62 Wilson played only nine first-team games in total. At the end of the season, Wilson was released by the Dumfries side and he returned to working on the family farm near Biggar. However, this did not signal the end of his professional playing days.

At the start of the 1965–66 season Andy Paton, the manager of newly promoted Hamilton Academicals, asked Wilson to come out of retirement and act as cover for regular keeper Billy Lamont. The temptation of £5 a week – plus a £1 bonus if the crowd was in excess of 3,000 – was hard to turn down, so Wilson signed for the Douglas Park outfit. There he linked up with his former Tynecastle team-mate Andy Bowman, who had arrived at the Accies after a spell with Newport County. During his spell with Hamilton, he turned out on seven occasions, his last competitive game being on 22 February 1966 against Dundee United.

Once again, Wilson returned to working on the family farm but he remained in the game by helping to train Symington Amateurs FC. During his time with the club, he helped them win the South of Scotland Cup in both 1969 and 1971.

In the mid 1970s, Wilson ended his association with the amateurs but kept up a sporting interest by starting to play carpet bowling with one of the local clubs. He soon showed that his sporting prowess was not confined to football and he became club champion. Inspired by his success indoors, he then moved on to green bowling at the Biggar Bowling Club. There he found more success and was twice the club champion.

In 1985 he decided to give up farming and move to Biggar where he bought the Townhead Café, which he ran for several years. During his time in Biggar, as well as maintaining his interest in bowling, Wilson also developed an interest in racing pigeons and it was through this sport that he met up with his former Gorgie team-mate George Thomson. George had been a keen pigeon fancier for several years and was well known within the 'doo' world in the Merseyside area. Wilson travelled down to Southport on several occasions to stay with George, with pigeons and the good old days at Tynecastle being the main subjects of conversation.

George was not the only former team-mate whom Wilson kept in touch with, as both John Cumming and Bobby Kirk had remained firm friends since his playing days. The three of them were often seen together at various Hearts supporters' functions, with the Craigmillar Hearts annual event being one of their favourites.

Tragically, aged only sixty-five, Wilson died suddenly from a brain haemorrhage on 18 June 2000.

Bobby Kirk

Born: Arniston, 12 August 1927
Signed: 31 May 1955
Appearances: 30
Goals: 2

Following the title success, Bobby was a mainstay of the team that narrowly missed out retaining the championship, playing in all bar the final game of the season. He did of course get some reward for his endeavours, picking up a League Cup winner's medal to complete the 'full set' of honours. When the title did return to Tynecastle in '59–60, Bobby went one better when, along with George Thomson, he played in every league and cup game.

By the time Hearts reached their next League Cup final in 1961, against Rangers, Bobby was being pushed for his place in the side by Danny Ferguson. However, he played in both games, unfortunately only gaining a runner's-up gong. It was to be his last season at Tynecastle, as Willie Polland was moved from centre-half to the right-back position.

He spent the whole of the '62–63 season with the reserves and was released by the club in April 1963. By this time, Bobby was a fully qualified masseur but still thought he had a few years left as a player. Berwick Rangers were the first to offer Bobby terms, in a player/coach role, but in the end he decided to return to junior football with Gala Fairydean.

He made a return to Tynecastle to help out with the colts for four years until 1971. He then moved on to Linlithgow Rose and during his time at Prestonfield he doubled up as club physio while running his own practice in Edinburgh. After a considerable number of years' service with the Rose, he ended his association with the club to concentrate on his own business. Now enjoying life in a care home in Dalkeith, Bobby enjoys nothing better than reminiscing about his days at Tynecastle.

Bobby Parker

Born: Riccarton, 16 February 1925
Signed: 3 April 1947
Appearances: 4
Goals: 0

After taking the decision to retire from the game in March 1958 due to injury, Bobby turned his attentions to his two newsagent shops, one in Gorgie Road and the other in the St Andrew Square bus station.

It was difficult for Bobby to end his association with the club and he eventually returned to Tynecastle as a scout and coach. Then, with a massive shareholding of eleven, he was appointed to the board of directors, taking over from Mr G. D. Fairbairn in 1970. He continued to serve the club in that capacity before taking over from Bill Lindsay as chairman in 1974.

He oversaw a time of fluctuating fortunes at Tynecastle, perhaps best illustrated in the '76–77 season when in September the team recorded a famous 5–1 victory over Locomotive Leipzig in the Cup Winners Cup. But by the end of April the following year, the team suffered the ignominy of being relegated from the top flight for the first time in the club's history.

With debt spiralling out of control, the club restructured their finances by way of a share issue. Bobby stepped down as chairman, to be replaced by Archie Martin, but still retained his place on the board. When Wallace Mercer bought into the club, Archie Martin resigned on 5 June 1981. As the Great Waldo went about changing the fortunes of the club he restructured the board, but although others departed, Bobby remained. He continued to serve as a director for a further ten years until he resigned on 16 August 1991.

After only five years of retirement, Bobby died on 1 March 1997.

Tom Mackenzie

Born: Edinburgh, 5 November 1922
Signed: 1 January 1942
Appearances: 8
Goals: 0

Although re-signed for the following season, Tam never regained his first-team place due to the fine form of George Thomson. After he'd served seventeen years with the club, Hearts announced on 29 March 1959 that Tom was to be released. His service to the club was recognised with the award of a third 'benefit' – something previously unheard of. With his £2,250 (minus tax) 'pay-off' and a thriving general store in Craigmillar, Tom might have been expected to retire from the game, so it was a surprise when he accepted an offer from English non-league outfit Wisbech Town.

The little club were showing great ambition and no Scottish side could match the terms of the Cambridgeshire set-up. Tom was also provided with both a job and a house; plus he found a couple of Scots were already there to welcome him to Wisbech. Aberdonian Jimmy Bowie, who had played for Chelsea, and Fife-born wing-half Jimmy McAdam were included in a side that could even boast an English international with veteran Jesse Pye playing at centre-forward.

After he had had a season with Wisbech, local rivals March Town made Tom an approach to become their player/manager. It was an offer that appealed to him so he made the short journey to take over the helm. He was there for two seasons before the financial practicalities of part-time football saw him seek employment outwith the game. This meant a move to nearby Peterborough where he began work with the Post Office. However, as he was still enjoying playing he signed for local amateur club Parsons Drove FC where his years of experience helped him stroll through games against younger opposition. His footballing services were in demand and he even found time to play in the occasional game for the Post Office.

Tragically, in November 1967 while driving home after playing in one of these games for his work team, Tom passed away after suffering a coronary thrombosis.

Willie Lindores
Born: Newcastleton, 3 May 1933
Signed: 16 July 1956
Appearances: 1
Goals: 0

After the championship-winning season and with Tam Mackenzie having moved down to Endland, Willie might have been looked upon to make the step-up to the first team during 1958–59. However, George Thomson had been outstanding after moving to the left-back berth and had made the position his own.

Willie then had the misfortune to break his ankle in a game, which effectively put an end to his season. Despite working hard to regain his fitness, John Lough had now established himself at left-back in the reserves and Willie found himself further down the pecking order at Tynecastle. At the end of the season Willie could see no future for himself at Tynecastle, so he left the club by mutual consent.

Shortly afterwards, he returned to his trade as a joiner and went south to work in the shipyard at Barrow where the local part-timers quickly signed him up. He joined a growing band of Scots that included Jackie Robertston (ex-Ayr United), Tommy McNab (ex-Partick Thistle), Charlie Kerr (ex-Morton), John Reid (ex-Airdrie), Willie Knox and Billy Munro (both ex-Kilmarnock). The previous season, Barrow had finished second bottom of the Fourth Division and had to be re-elected but with the help of the Scottish contingent they finished the '59–60 season well out of any danger.

Willie then returned north to take up a job as a site agent with Trentham the builders but he was not yet ready to hang up his boots. Gala Fairydean made an approach for his services and in 1961 Willie became player/manager of the Borders outfit. After two years he decided to end his playing days and, with his job with Trentham not allowing him enough time to carry out the manager's job at Netherdale, he retired from football.

Willie continued to work for the builders until he was sixty-three, when unfortunately he was made redundant. Most people would probably have used that as an excuse to retire a couple of years early but not the ever-active Willie Lindores. He then got a 'dream' job for most blokes when he went to work at the local brewery. He was there for the next two years until retiring in 1998.

Today, Willie still lives an active life in West Barns with his wife, Fiona. A fine all-round sportsman throughout his life, he still plays golf regularly at Winterfield, a pitching wedge away from his home. He is a previous captain of the club and although not now playing off the four handicap he once did, he is still a match for players half his age.

Willie enjoys the occasional visit back to Tynecastle as the guest of the Federation and recently attended his first Willie Bauld Memorial Club Dinner, which he hopes to be the first of many.

George Thomson

Born: Edinburgh, 19 October 1936
Signed: 3 September 1953
Appearances: 30
Goals: 2

The following season, George was the only 'ever-present' during the campaign, even turning out at inside-left for a few games after the regular forwards had made a stuttering start to the new year. He fancied himself to do a job up front and asked to be given a try, a request that, remarkably, was granted. His self-belief was justified when he scored the winner as Hearts beat Raith Rovers 2–1 in his first game in the no. 10 shirt. Better was to come when he hit the only 'hat-trick' of his career, against Third Lanark the following week. After a few weeks of the experiment he eventually dropped back to play right-half for the rest of the season.

THE MEN WHO DID IT – AND THE SEASONS THAT FOLLOWED

When the title was won in 1959–60, George was again an 'ever-present', playing all forty-six league and cup games that season. This time he only ever appeared at left-back but even then managed five goals, even although they were all from the penalty spot. It was also during this season that he picked up his first representative honour, playing for the Scottish League side against their Irish counterparts at Ibrox in October '59.

Given that he started 1960–61 as an automatic pick alongside Bobby Kirk at the back, it was a shock when the club announced in mid-November that they were willing to listen to offers for George. Even although Hearts had signed Davie Holt from Queen's Park, George was considered a mainstay of the side. Tommy Walker had decided it was time for change and George left Tynecastle in the deal that took both him and Alex Young to Everton.

Without reaching the celebrity status of Alex, he established himself as a firm favourite with the Goodison faithful and became a regular in the side. In his spell on Merseyside he turned out seventy-four times for the Toffees, but he was not quite as prolific goalwise as he had been at Tynecastle. His only strike for Everton came on 23 September 1961 against Burnley at Turf Moor. Regrettably, it was not enough to stop his side slip to a 2–1 defeat.

Almost exactly two years after joining Everton, George moved on to Brentford in November 1963. The Bees had been relegated to the Fourth Division the previous season and were looking for players to strengthen the team in their bid to bounce back up. Their manager at the time was ex-Celtic and Kilmarnock player Malky MacDonald (later to become Scotland's manager) and he knew that George could bring the necessary experience to Griffin Park. There he teamed up again with Chick Brodie who signed from Northampton on the same day, both of them having played in the same Scottish schoolboy team years earlier. With both gritty Scots in the side, Brentford were promoted as champions at the end of the season.

Brentford enjoyed a couple of seasons in Division Three before slipping back down to the Fourth. George continued to play until a knee injury forced him to end his playing days in 1968. He returned to Scotland for a while before moving back down south to live in Southport where he enjoyed nothing better than breeding champion racing pigeons.

Dave Mackay

Born: Edinburgh, 14 November 1934
Signed: 26 April 1952
Appearances: 28
Goals: 12

At the end of the season, Dave was one of the thirteen players who travelled to Sweden to represent Scotland for the World Cup finals. He played in the 2–1 defeat against France, taking over from Doug Cowie for the final game. From being a replacement in the side, he stepped up to become captain for the final two internationals during 1958 home championship games against Wales and Northern Ireland. Dave's performances that year were so outstanding that he was voted the 'Rex on Sunday' Player of the Year for 1958, the highest accolade for a player at the time.

When Hearts defeated Partick Thistle in the League Cup final the following season, it was Dave who led the team up the steps to pick up the trophy. Things could not have been better but his time at Tynecastle came to an abrupt end in March 1959. With Hearts challenging Rangers for the title, the board of directors accepted an offer of £32,000 from Tottenham Hotspur for Dave's services. It was a move that baffled both fans and player alike and arguably cost the club the championship, as by the end of the season they'd lost out to our friends from the west by two points.

Despite two leg breaks interrupting his career during his time in London, Dave went on to be a mainstay of the successful Spurs side of the '60s, winning the league and cup double as well as the FA Cup on a further two occasions. In 1969, Hearts made an approach to bring him back to Tynecastle as manager but the move was hijacked by a certain Brian Clough who persuaded him to join Second Division

Derby County. Under Dave's captaincy they went on to win the title, with Dave being voted the Football Writers' Player of the Year.

After a further season with Derby in the First Division, he joined Swindon Town from Division Two. There he took over as manager in November 1971 when Fred Ford resigned the post. And there he played his final competitive game in a 2–2 draw at Fratton Park on 1 April 1972.

Only eleven months into his managerial career, Dave was approached by Nottingham Forrest to become their manager. He took over a team there which contained the likes of Duncan McKenzie, Tony Woodcock, Viv Anderson and someone called Martin O'Neill. Dave helped the team make steady progress but a year later he was to return to Derby County as manager after Brian Clough had resigned the post. It was a big job to follow 'Old Big Head' but Dave managed it and Derby were crowned English champions in 1975. It was to be the highlight of his managerial career; but as can happen with all managers, Dave received his P45 from the directors in November 1976 after a series of indifferent results.

In March 1977, he accepted an offer to take the helm at Third Division Walsall where he stayed until he was asked to up sticks to Kuwait. There he managed Al-Arabi until 1986 when he moved to the Shabab Club of Dubai. After a season in the United Arab Emirates, Dave returned to England with Doncaster Rovers. It was not long before struggling Birmingham City asked him to turn their fortunes around. Unfortunately, Brummies are an impatient lot and after two seasons' steady progress but no promotion, Dave could see that his days in the Midlands were numbered and he resigned. It was not long before the Middle East called and Dave headed out to Egypt to manage Zamalek. After a season in charge there, his no-nonsense direct approach upset the directors and he once again found himself unemployed.

The old adage of 'you can't keep a good man down' was proved true when he was then asked to coach the Qatar national youth side. This he did successfully for the three years of his contract. He returned to England and it was there that he was diagnosed with cancer.

Thankfully, after treatment Dave returned to full health but he took it as a sign that he should bring to an end his managerial career. After forty-three years in the game, Dave had won championship and cup winners' medals in both Scotland and England, a Scottish League Cup medal, an English Division Two winner's medal and an English League Championship medal as a manager. He had represented Scotland on twenty-two occasions and, during his time at Hearts, he had played 185 games, scoring thirty-two times. On 9 November 2006, Dave rightfully became the first inductee to the Hearts Hall of Fame – he is not just a Hearts legend, though, but a true footballing legend.

Dave and his wife, Isobel, now live happily in the Nottingham area but they still return regularly to Whitecraig where he retains a home and he is a welcome visitor to Tynecastle and various Hearts functions.

Andy Bowman

Born: Pittenweem, 7 March 1934
Signed: 28 July 1955
Appearances: 18
Goals: 2

Although in the starting line-up for the League Cup campaign the following season, Andy was limited to a handful of league appearances. He was, however, part of the team that played for the first time in the European Cup against Standard Liège.

His lack of first-team games alerted a number of clubs, with Huddersfield Town making an enquiry about a possible transfer in April 1959. The interest was discouraged and by the '59–60 championship-winning season he was playing a more regular part in the back line, alternating with John Cumming, Jimmy Milne and Billy Higgins for a place. He picked up a League Cup winner's medal against Third Lanark but by the season end the half-back line had a settled look of Cumming, Milne and Higgins, with Andy spending most of his time in the reserves.

It was the same at the start of the following season until an injury to Billy Higgins saw Andy make his season debut against Clyde in the League Cup. He slotted in well and even managed to get his name on the scoresheet (along with the wonderfully named Boston Clegg) in an emphatic 6–2 victory. He kept his place in the side for the next few weeks and once again had the distinction of playing in the European Cup.

However, with two months of the season left, Cumming, Milne and Higgins became the regular selection again and with the arrival of Willie Polland from Raith Rovers, Andy's time at Tynecastle was all but over. On 28 April 1961 Tommy Walker handed him a free transfer but, despite interest from Morton, Andy decided to move down south to Newport County. There he teamed up with two notable Scots – ex-Celt Bobby Evans and former Hibee Jock Buchanan – but despite the best efforts of the trio, County were relegated when they finished bottom of the Third Division. Life in Division Four was tough and Andy only managed to play about half of County's games the following season. When they finished well down the league, narrowly avoiding seeking re-election, Andy decided to seek pastures new.

His first stop was at non-league Tonbridge before he made the move across the Atlantic to try out the burgeoning soccer league in the United States. After a spell there, he returned to Scotland and was signed up by Hamilton Academicals before moving on to Hawick Royal Albert. His time in the seniors was not over, however, as he had a spell with Stenhousemuir before eventually retiring from the game.

After his playing days were over, he took up employment with Scottish Brewers as a heating engineer before retiring. Now living in Pittenweem, Andy was delighted to return to Tynecastle at an event to celebrate the fiftieth anniversary of the 1956 Scottish Cup victory.

John Cumming

Born: Carluke, 17 March 1930
Signed: 6 January 1950
Appearances: 20
Goals: 5

After the '57–58 season, John went on to become the player to win the most medals in the famous maroon shirt. The championship triumph completed his 'set', as he was part of the League Cup-winning side in 1954 and the Scottish Cup winners in 1956. He added to that collection with a further three League Cup winner's medals ('58–59, '59–60 and '62–63) plus another championship medal in '59–60, playing thirty-two of the thirty-four games that season.

Scotland honours also continued to come his way and in 1960 after a five-year absence he was recalled to the international side for the Home Championship game against England at Hampden Park. John retained his international place for the next four Scotland internationals before making his ninth and final appearance in a 4–2 defeat against Turkey in Ankara.

Despite dropping out of the international picture, at the end of 1961 he became the second Hearts player to be named Rex Kingsley's Footballer of the Year, following Dave Mackay in 1958. Perhaps, though, the greatest honour bestowed on him was when everyone in his home town of Carluke contributed to a statuette that was presented to him at a ceremony in the local town hall.

John continued to be a mainstay at Tynecastle but it is hard to imagine that he did not play a single game in the fateful 1964–65 season. One can only imagine what might have been if the team had benefited from his defensive qualities against Dundee or Kilmarnock at Tynecastle.

John remained in Gorgie as a player but mainly in the reserves helping with the youngsters. It was his desire to remain in football as a coach when he finished playing and Johnny Harvey saw him as the ideal man to lead the second string. He played his final first team game against Dunfermline at Tynecastle on 12 November 1966.

By then he had made 612 appearances and had scored fifty-eight times for the club and, remarkably, had never once been booked.

After he finished playing he stepped into the role of club trainer and many of us will still remember the sight of John sprinting onto the field with his magic bag to tend to an injured player. His ability as a trainer led to him undertaking the position with the international side under Bobby Brown.

In 1977, after almost twenty-seven years at the club, John decided that he had had enough and left Tynecastle. He then got a job working in the steel industry and in his spare time he liked nothing better than to tend to his garden in Carluke; he also became a 'weel-kent' face on the bowling circuit. He regularly attended Tynecastle and was as proud as anyone in the ground when Hearts broke their barren spell of trophy wins at Parkhead in 1998.

John still stays in Carluke but recent ill health has curtailed visits to Tynecastle. His achievements with the club were rightly recognised when he was one of the first players to be elected to the Hearts Hall of Fame in 2006.

Freddie Glidden

Born: Newmains, 7 September 1927
Signed: 21 March 1946
Appearances: 13
Goals: 0

The following season, Freddie continued to vie with Jimmy Milne for the pivot's position at Tynecastle. Although Jimmy started in the first few League Cup games, Freddie made his season debut in a thrilling 5–4 win against Third Lanark at Cathkin Park. It was the start of an uninterrupted run in the team that included the League Cup final victory against Partick Thistle.

At end of November he injured his back playing against Kilmarnock, so Jimmy Milne took over for the next game. Jimmy's form was impressive as Hearts fought to retain the title and Freddie never got the opportunity to turn out for the first team again that season. On 18 March 1959 the club announced that, along with Tommy Mackenzie, he had been granted a free transfer. Dunfermline had attempted to sign him a few weeks earlier but Hearts had refused their offer. Now the transfer deadline had passed, the Fife club were slow to renew their interest and Dumbarton stepped in. The West of Scotland club had recently appointed former Hibs legend Bobby Combe as manager and he knew Freddie's qualities well from past rivalries.

It was no surprise that Freddie put in some outstanding performances in the lower division and he soon became the signing target of a First Division club – none other than Hibernian – but the Boghead board dismissed the offer out of hand. So Freddie continued to travel west for two seasons before deciding that it was time to hang up his boots in 1962.

He didn't give up a connection with the game entirely, as he spent the next two years training the juniors at Broxburn. It was also about this time that he decided on a career change and resigned from his post with West Lothian Water Board. He moved into Post Office management and ran the Post Office in Fountainbridge for over thirty years before retiring in 1994.

Today, Freddie is a keen golfer and plays regularly at Ratho Park where he has been a member for many years. He still attends Tynecastle frequently and is always a hugely popular figure at supporters functions throughout the country. Although he is fondly remembered by young and old alike as the captain of the 1956 Scottish Cup side, Freddie achieved much more in his time at Tynecastle. It was just a matter of time before he was given his rightful place alongside the other Hearts legends in the Hall of Fame and on 8th November 2007, Freddie was presented with another trophy to recognise his unique place in the club's history.

Jimmy Milne

Born: Arbroath, 30 June 1929
Signed: 8 August 1950
Appearances: 21
Goals: 3

Although 'Bim' went on to become the last captain of Hearts to lift the league trophy in 1960, in his eleven seasons at Tynecastle he had something of a 'cup hoodoo'. Hearts won the Scottish Cup once and the League Cup three times while he was with the club, but he did not manage to play in a side that lifted any of the trophies.

Jimmy was particularly unfortunate to miss the final in the 1959–60 season. This was due to picking up an ankle injury in a friendly match against Norwich City at Tynecastle twelve days before the final. John Cumming took over the no. 5 shirt, with Billy Higgins filling in for John as Hearts beat Third Lanark.

Jimmy started the following season well and was a first-team regular but a foot injury sustained against Kilmarnock at Tynecastle kept him out for eleven weeks. After he made his return in the Scottish Cup tie against Tarff Rovers, it was clear that the injury was still causing him trouble and he was in and out of the side until he eventually played his last game in maroon on 15 April 1961, against St Mirren (0–0) at Tynecastle. By this time, Hearts had signed Willie Polland from Raith Rovers and a few weeks later Jimmy was freed from Tynecastle.

Ex-Heart Alex McCrae was in charge at Falkirk and he saw Jimmy as the ideal man to strengthen the Brockville side's bid to remain in the First Division the following term. Unfortunately, during the '61–62 season, Jimmy was plagued by injury that saw him limited to eighteen appearances for the Bairns. Jimmy was released by the club at the end of the season but was quickly picked up by Forfar, for whom he played in the middle of defence for a further season before finally finishing his playing career in 1963.

After football he continued to work in Arbroath, with the engineering firm of Alexander Shanks & Sons. Later he moved to a job with the Post Office. But his love for his first club had not been diminished and soon he got involved with the Red Lichties once again. For many years he played an active part within the club as a director on the board. Dedicating a great deal of time and effort to the Gayfield outfit, he quickly became known throughout football circles as 'Mr Arbroath'.

He gained the respect of everyone in the game and Jimmy's loss was felt by the whole of Scottish football when he passed away on 2 March 2004.

Billy Higgins

Born: Edinburgh, 19 November 1939
Signed: 18 June 1957
Appearances: 1
Goals: 0

The following season, Billy continued to progress in the reserves and, surprisingly, never got a chance in the first team as they narrowly missed retaining the title. His opportunity finally came during the 1959–60 season on 3 October against Ayr United at Tynecastle. It turned out to be a pulsating game, with Hearts eventually winning 5–3. Despite the loss of three goals, Billy had acquitted himself well as a replacement for the injured John Cumming, but with John fit again by the following week Billy returned to the Second XI.

It was another injury, this time to Jimmy Milne, that allowed Billy to step up again two weeks later. With Milne struggling for fitness, Billy continued in the team and the following week picked up his second medal when he played against Third Lanark in the League Cup final.

His solid displays did not go unnoticed at international level and he was rewarded with an Under-23 cap against Wales on 25 November at Wrexham. Played in torrential rain, the game ended 1–1 with Tynecastle team-mate Alex Young grabbing the goal that earned the draw.

The next few seasons continued to be a period of change at Tynecastle and Billy took the opportunity to establish himself in the side alongside Willie Polland and John Cumming in the half-back line. It was during this time that, along with three further Under-23 caps, he gained another two League Cup medals – first as a runner-up to Rangers and then as a winner again on 27 October 1962, against Kilmarnock.

The disappointment of the runners-up medal in the League Cup final replay was nothing to the disaster that happened during 1964–65. It had started so well with Billy even getting the first goal of the season, against Kilmarnock in the League Cup. He played in all bar two of the league games that ended so cruelly on the last day of the season. Oh, if only he could have swapped that League Cup goal for one against Killie on 24 April.

Billy continued to play in an ever-changing side as Tommy Walker strove to find the 'magic' of the previous years. Alan Anderson, Roy Barry, George Miller and big Arthur Thomson were all staking a claim in the side, so when a local journalist raised the possibility of a move to South Africa, Billy packed his bags to try his luck in Durban. At the time, football in South Africa was a mixture of talent but didn't lack crowd appeal, with Durban City regularly playing in front of 25,000 plus. Billy was not the only one from the UK who had been attracted by the lifestyle and by the end of the decade he had been joined by ex-Hearts men Danny Ferguson and Alan Gordon as well as the likes of Johnny Byrne, George Eastham and Johnny Haynes to name but a few.

In his two-year spell with Durban City, Billy helped the club win three trophies, most notably the National Cup. His performances in midfield did not go unnoticed back home and Dundee United asked him to return to Scotland. However, after a three-month trial period the lure of the South African sunshine was enough to see Billy leave Scotland and sign for East London United. After two years there, he moved on to Rhodesia (now Zimbabwe) as player/coach of Salisbury (now Harare) where he experienced more success, winning a further three trophies.

It was during his time in Rhodesia that Billy came up against a young goalkeeper by the name of Bruce Grobbelaar. Billy recognised then what British fans would witness during Bruce's English career in the 1980s – a huge talent without discipline, but a great entertainer nevertheless.

After three years, Billy decided to call it quits and concentrate on a career in brewing back in South Africa. He returned to the greater Johannesburg area where he still lives. He now concentrates his sporting interest on squash, which helps him maintain his fitness levels though he did manage to gain provincial recognition in his days in Durban, East London and Salisbury.

Nearly forty years on, Billy loves to travel inside South Africa and beyond for both business and pleasure. He enjoys the occasional trip back to the UK, takes a keen interest in European football and is looking forward to 2010, when he will be able to share in the excitement when South Africa host the World Cup.

Johnny Hamilton

Born: Larkhall, 22 January 1935
Signed: 28 April 1955
Appearances: 4
Goals: 4

The following season, 'Hammy' established himself in the first team, alternating between either wing. The highlight of the season was obviously the League Cup win against Partick Thistle, with Johnny being one of the three scorers that day. His excellent form attracted attention from other clubs but interest from both Blackpool (to take over from Stanley Matthews) and Bristol City was not entertained by the board.

During 1959–60, with Gordon Smith now at the club, Johnny settled into the outside-left berth and again he scored in a League Cup final, pulling Hearts level after they had fallen behind to Third Lanark. When Alex Young netted the second, Johnny had gained his second League Cup medal in two years. By the end of the season, he had played twenty-seven times and scored seven goals as Hearts took the title for the second time in three years.

Although the following season was disappointing in comparison to what had gone before, Johnny's form was attracting the attention of other clubs. Both West Brom and Fulham made enquiries about his availability, with Fulham going as far as to table a rumoured £15,000 bid. The offer was immediately turned down by the board and Johnny stayed at Tynecastle to help the club reach yet another League Cup final. Regrettably this time it was as a runner-up, with Hearts losing out to Rangers after a replay. His success in the League Cup returned in '62–63 when he was part of the side that won the cup, beating Kilmarnock in the final.

Johnny continued to swap wings to accommodate the likes of Tommy Traynor and Roald Jensen and even had the 'distinction' of becoming Hearts' first-ever substitute, when he replaced the injured Chris Shevlane against Clyde on 20 August 1966. At the end of the '66–67 season, Johnny Harvey replaced Tommy Walker as manager and, although not exactly a 'new broom', he did 'sweep clean' and players such as Billy Higgins, Danny Ferguson, Alan Gordon and Hammy were all allowed to leave the club. Even at thirty-two a player of Johnny Hamilton's ability was in demand and Watford (then in the English Third Division) called upon his services.

Johnny spent a season at Vicarage Road, alongside ex-Falkirk keeper Bert Slater and the mercurial Tony Currie, before returning to Scotland (well, almost) when he joined Berwick Rangers on a part-time basis. He played at Shielfield Park for three years until, like Bobby Parker and Willie Bauld before him, he bought a newsagent's. Though now thirty-eight, he was still in tip-top condition and probably could have had a few more years in the game but with the commitment of his shop he decided to bring his playing career to an end.

Fortunately he was not lost to the game completely, as he accepted an offer from Hearts to return to Tynecastle as youth coach. Johnny passed on his knowledge to the youngsters for almost six years before he had to give up the job, once again to concentrate on running his newsagent business full time. He was a familiar face behind the counter in his shop on Slateford Road for many years before retiring.

John still stays in Edinburgh and stays as fit as ever, playing golf at least twice a week. Although he has not been back to Tynecastle for some time, he is well remembered by many as a true Hearts great.

Alex Young

Born: Loanhead, 3 February 1937
Signed: 16 August 1954
Appearances: 34
Goals: 24

The following season, Alex made twenty-seven league starts but the back of the net was harder to find. He scored seven times but, with Willie Bauld back to fitness, he was continually playing in different positions in the forward line and injury prevented him being part of the side when Hearts lifted the League Cup against Partick Thistle.

The 1959–60 season proved to be a busy one for Alex when despite being in the Army on national service duty, he re-found his goal touch. He was the top scorer, with twenty-three league goals, in what turned out to be Hearts' next championship-winning season. (His tally probably should be one better, as he was only credited with a hat-trick when Hearts hammered Hibs 5–1 on 1 January, but maintains to this day that it was he and not Hibs' Jackie Plenderleith who got the final touch on Hearts' final goal.) Also, not only did he make the starting line-up in the League Cup final against Third Lanark, but he notched the second goal in the 2–1 triumph.

He continued to play at home and abroad for the Army and, in a remarkable period towards the end of the season, he played for Hearts against Clyde on Tuesday, 5 April. This game was followed a day later by a Kentish Cup tie for the British Army side against France. The next day, he was turning out in an international practice match at Somerset Park before gaining the first of his full international caps, against England at Hampden on Saturday, 9 April. He was not finished there, as he then played in the championship-clinching game against St Mirren the following Saturday (16th) before gaining more Scotland Under-23s honours against Belgium in Ghent on 20 April. Finally, he played for his fourth team when he turned out for his Army unit in the British Army Cup final on 27 April in Aldershot.

After he had gained a further three full international caps in May and started the next season in his usual fine form, Hearts fans were shocked to see the headline 'BIDS EXPECTED FOR YOUNG' in the Edinburgh *Evening News* on 16 November. The word was that Alex had approached the management to see if there had been interest for him from other clubs in England. At a board meeting it was decided that they would be willing to listen to offers and now three English clubs were in the hunt.

Everton's manager, Johnnie Carey, tabled an offer for both Alex and George Thomson but it was not accepted immediately as Preston North End and Wolves had expressed a desire to have talks with Alex. After a few days of negotiations, both Alex and George travelled down to Liverpool with director Alec Irvine (Tommy Walker was in London, receiving his OBE) to conclude the deal. So on Wednesday, 23 November, Hearts lost two of the stalwarts of the '57–58 side for a combined fee of £55,000. Despite being injured and still doing his national service, £42,000 of the fee was for Alex. This made him the fourth most expensive player in the UK at the time; only Denis Law (Manchester City), George Eastham (Arsenal) and Albert Quixall (Manchester United) had cost more.

Because of the knee injury picked up playing for the British Army against Aberdeen, it was over two months before Alex made his Everton debut against Spurs – who had a certain Dave Mackay playing for them. He didn't manage to get his name on the scoresheet that day, as Everton went down 3–1, and it took a little while before he eventually did find the net. But on 31 March 1961 he broke his goal drought with two in a 3–1 win against Blackburn Rovers. It was the start of a very successful period on Merseyside and in the 1962–63 season, Alex repeated the feat he had achieved at Tynecastle five years earlier and was an 'ever-present' in the side that took the English league championship. His partnership with Roy Vernon made the Everton team one of the best in the country, so perhaps it was surprising that they had to wait until 1966 for the next honour when they lifted the FA Cup.

During his time at Goodison, Alex endeared himself to the Everton faithful, gaining the nickname of 'The Golden Vision'. (It is alleged that it was Spurs' forward Danny Blanchflower who originally coined the name: in a book by Neville Smith entitled *Three Sides of the Mersey*, Blanchflower was quoted by the author as saying, '. . . the view every Saturday that we have of a more perfect world, a world that has got a pattern and is finite. And that's Alex – the Golden Vision.')

Just how well thought of he was no better illustrated than when he could not play after being injured in training. Brian Labone (something of an Everton legend himself) was roundly booed by the crowd on the following Saturday, as he was the man who had caused the injury. It is also a little-known fact that Alex 'starred' in a BBC *Play of the Week*. In the play, appropriately entitled 'The Golden Vision', an Evertonian fan gets a call to play when the Blues go a man down. Our hero naturally scores the winning goal from a cross from the Golden Vision himself.

Alex turned out on 227 occasions, scoring eighty-seven goals in the process during his time in Liverpool. At international level, though, he only gained a further two caps, the first being in a World Cup qualifier against the Republic of Ireland in 1961. Though he scored twice in the 3–0 victory, it was not until 18 June 1966 when he won his eighth and final cap in a friendly international against Portugal at Hampden.

During 1967 and 1968, Alex suffered from a series of injuries that kept him out of the first team. Then, with the emergence of sixteen-year-old Joe Royle, he found it more and more difficult to regain his place. Frustrated by the lack of opportunities at Goodison, Alex was prompted to make the move into management, going to Glentoran in Northern Ireland. It is fair to say that the move was not quite as Alex had expected and a few months later, despite a lucrative offer from the New York Generals in the North American Soccer League, he was back in England with Stockport County.

At his spell with the Hatters, he played twenty-three times (five goals) before his career was cut short by a knee injury sustained in a pre-season friendly against Port Vale, at the early age of thirty-one. On 24 August 1969, football had lost one of its finest exponents.

Alex then returned to Scotland and was mine host at the Linton Hotel in West Linton before managing the family upholstery business in Stockbridge. He was never forgotten in Liverpool and, in August 2001, he was given a testimonial match by Everton with Spanish side Espanyol providing the opposition. As a more permanent tribute, the club also named a hospitality suite at Goodison in his honour.

Alex only played two more games for Everton than he did for Hearts but at Tynecastle he scored 119 times as opposed to 87 at Goodison. He won every trophy possible yet it seemed for a while he was held in higher regard on Merseyside than Gorgie. The balance was at last redressed on 8th November 2007 when Alex was selected to join other Hearts legends in the club's Hall of Fame. After a couple of recent scares, Alex is now in fine health and, despite being poorly treated in the past by the club, he now is a very popular visitor to Tynecastle on match days. He lives in Penicuik with his wife, Nancy.

Bobby Blackwood

Born: Edinburgh, 20 August 1934
Signed: 26 October 1950
Appearances: 23
Goals: 4

The following season Bobby turned out twenty-three times in all competitions but he was unfortunate to miss out on the club's highlight of the season, the League Cup final victory against Partick Thistle. He did have the distinction, however, of earlier in the season playing in the historic first European Cup tie against Standard Leige, both home and away.

When the title returned to Tynecastle in 1960, Bobby had made a telling contribution, regularly turning out in the no. 10 shirt and ending the season as the second highest scorer in the league (with twelve goals). It was perhaps his goals in the League Cup, though, for which he is best remembered: he netted five times as Hearts went on to lift the famous old trophy again. His performances during the season were rewarded when he was selected to play for the Scottish Football League against their English counterparts at Highbury. The game ended in a 1–0 defeat for the Scottish XI, but his partnership with Ian St John was a feature of the game.

The next two seasons were a transitional period for Hearts, but Bobby remained a regular in the team. However, with Alan Gordon and Willie Wallace beginning to emerge, Tommy Walker decided to place him on the 'open to transfer' list at the end of the '61–62 season. In June, the club accepted an offer of £10,000 from Alf Ramsay's Ipswich Town. It was an easy decision for Bobby, as the Tractor Boys had just become First Division champions after being promoted as champions from the Second Division the year before.

During his first season at Portman Road, Bobby played in the European Cup once again. He even scored the winner when Ipswich recorded a historic 2–1 victory over AC Milan. Unfortunately, the Italian side – containing such famous names as Trapattoni, Maldini and Rivera – had triumphed 3–0 in the other leg in Milan and the East Anglian side fell at the first hurdle. Just like Hearts.

During the season, Alf Ramsey left the club to become England manager and Jackie Milburn took over the reins. The magic of the past two seasons could not be repeated as they finished the season in the lower reaches of the division, Bobby scoring nine goals in his thirty appearances for the club. Worse was to follow for Bobby and Ipswich the following season when he could do nothing to prevent the club from taking the drop back down into the Second Division.

After a disastrous start to the season, Jackie Milburn's spell at the club came to a halt and he was replaced by Bill McGarry. The new manager had his own ideas and Bobby lost his place in the Ipswich forward line. But he was too experienced a player to be left out of the side and he took the step back to make most of his appearances that season in the half-back line. At the end of the season, Ipswich missed out on promotion and when Colchester United manager Roy Bentley came in with an offer of £15,000 for Bobby, it was accepted by the club and he made the short trip along the A12 to Layer Road.

Colchester had finished the season second bottom of Division Three and had been relegated, and ex-Chelsea and England Bentley saw Bobby as a man with the necessary experience to help the club regain their place in the higher league. With his help they accomplished the task, but only just. The 'U's clinched promotion, finishing in fourth place on fifty-six points, the same total as both Tranmere Rovers and Luton Town. Unlike Hearts the season before, goal average worked in their favour and by a margin of 0.08 they went back up to Division Three. With Bobby a regular in the no. 6 shirt, they stayed there the following season but they were relegated along with Grimsby Town and Scunthorpe United at the end of the '67–68 season.

It was during his time at Colchester that Bobby sustained an unfortunate injury when he broke his jaw in a clash with Reading's Dennis Allen. In a bizarre twist of fate, he suffered another broken jaw the following season, while playing against Reading and again in a collision with Dennis Allen. With so many of the Allen dynasty playing in the English divisions, perhaps it was with this in mind that Bobby decided to call a halt to his time in England.

Returning home, he became manager of Hawick Royal Albert in the East of Scotland League. The previous season, Hawick had won both that league and the Scottish Qualifying Cup but this turned out to be the peak of their success. After a couple of seasons with the Albert Park club, Bobby was approached by then Hearts manager Willie Ormond with a view to assisting with the reserves. It was a move that he readily accepted and for the next few years he was happy to be part of the Tynecastle set-up.

After his time back in Gorgie, Bobby was asked by his brother-in-law, Pilmar Smith, to manage one of his bookmaker's shops. So for a number of years Bobby was well known with the punters of Balerno. During his spare time, he by now had turned his sporting attentions to bowling and showed off his skills firstly at Balerno and then at Carrick Knowe Bowling Clubs.

After a long battle against cancer, Bobby died on 25 June 1997, aged only sixty-two. On the same day, the marine explorer Jacques Cousteau passed away and the report of his death took up a full page in the Edinburgh *Evening News*; shamefully, the death of Hearts great Bobby Blackwood was not reported. However, his achievements with the club will never be forgotten.

Robert 'Danny' Paton

Born: Breich, 27 January 1936
Signed: 23 May 1957
Appearances: 3
Goals: 1

The following season, Danny played a total of seven league and cup games. His appearances were limited due to the competition for the no. 7 shirt, with Johnny Hamilton, Bobby Blackwood and occasionally Alex Young all ahead of him in the pecking order. However, he was selected to play in the friendly against a South Africa XI and, given the responsibility when Hearts were awarded a penalty, he made no mistake as the game finished in a 3–3 draw.

After '58–59, he started his two years' national service in the Army. Stationed in England, he turned out for Yeovil Town who were at that time playing in the Southern League. Strangely enough, in one game he found himself up against former Hearts hero Tam Mackenzie, who then was playing for Wisbech Town. Also during his Army years, he was a regular in the same Army team as Alex Young, so he was kept up to date with the fine form of Gordon Smith in the outside-right position. But by the time Danny returned to Tynecastle at the start of the 1961–62 season, Gordon had left for Dundee and Hearts were in something of a 'transitional' phase. Danny was an instant hit and played twenty-two league and cup games, sharing right-wing duties with the likes of Bobby Ross and

Danny Ferguson. He was also selected at centre-forward on the odd occasion, no mean feat, considering that Willies Wallace and Bauld were at the club.

The next season, Danny gained a League Cup winner's medal as part of the side that beat Kilmarnock. However, probably his greatest moment in a Hearts jersey came on 8 September 1962 when he notched a hat-trick at Easter Road in a comfortable 4–0 win against the 'wee team'.

Cartilage trouble brought an end to his Tynecastle career in 1964 and he asked to be released by the Hearts. Despite the bother with his knee, he continued to play, moving to England and joining Oxford United. With Ron Atkinson in the side, United were in the English Fourth Division but won promotion in 1965 – Dannys's one goal in the two games he played being the telling contribution! After Oxford, he moved into non-league football with Bedford Town and Cambridge City. In 1971 he received a lucrative offer to play in the North American Soccer League and, for a couple of seasons, was a regular in the Atlanta Chiefs line-up before they were renamed the Atlanta Apollos. The change of name did not revive interest in the game in Atlanta, however, and the franchise eventually folded in 1973. Danny then returned to Scotland but having experienced the American lifestyle, he found it difficult to settle and it was not long before he headed back across the Atlantic. He had been given the opportunity to organise 'soccer camps' set up to promote the game in the States. For the next ten years he worked with various colleges, developing talent at grass roots level.

With his persistent knee problem giving him more difficulty, Danny packed his bags and returned to Scotland in 1983. Although he did have a couple of jobs on his return, the problem with his knee made it difficult for him to work and he took the decision to retire. Today Danny lives in Breich, West Lothian and still takes a keen interest in events at Tynecastle.

Alfie Conn

Born: Prestonpans, 2 October 1926
Signed: 17 June 1944
Appearances: 5
Goals: 4

Alfie began the following season in the reserves, as did Willie Bauld, with Jimmy Murray and Alex Young being preferred in the first team. Although Willie was promoted to the first team the following week, Alfie continued in the second string. In September, Raith Rovers manager Bert Herdman made an offer of £3,000 which was accepted by the Hearts board and Alfie became the first of the 'Terrible Trio' to leave Tynecastle.

There was a 'weel-kent' face to welcome Alfie to Stark's Park, as ex-Heart Johnny Urquart had been there for a few seasons. Ironically, Alfie's first game for Raith was due to be against Hibs but Alfie went down with the flu and missed the match. It was the start of an unlucky spell for him, as this was quickly followed by a bout of jaundice that kept him out of the side for a while longer. Having recovered, he then picked up an ankle injury, thus limiting his appearances even further. With that injury cleared up, his misery continued when he damaged his knee. He did recover in time to make a welcome return visit to Tynecastle in February 1959 and he scored for Raith as they went down 2–1.

Alfie saw out the rest of the season at Stark's Park before being released by the Fifers. Although Morton made him an offer, he decided to opt for a short spell in South Africa with Johannesburg Ramblers before returning to Scotland and signing for Gala Fairydean.

His time playing at the 'San Siro of the Borders' saw an upturn in the fortunes of the Netherdale club – something that did not go unnoticed with senior clubs. Eventually Raith Rovers asked him to return to Stark's Park, not as a player, but as their manager, but his time there was short and he then retired from football for good.

Alfie became a rep with the Harris paintbrush company and, like in his playing days, he was in demand, so after a number of years he moved to a job with Manders Paints. A popular figure within the industry, he finally moved to Joseph Mason Automotive Paints in Kirkcaldy as the company regional manager for the East of Scotland before retiring to Glenrothes, where he still lives. Although he does not make the journey across the water to Tynecastle these days, Alfie is rightly held in the highest esteem at the club and will always be remembered as a true Hearts legend.

Jimmy Wardhaugh

Born: Marshall Meadows, 21 March 1929
Signed: 21 March 1946
Appearances: 30
Goals: 28

Jimmy was another member of the League Cup-winning side in the '58–59 season, but after what was arguably his best season with the Hearts he only made fourteen league appearances. Despite this, his strike rate was remarkable, as he grabbed eleven goals on these outings.

The next season, after fourteen years and becoming the club's all-time record overall goal scorer with 376 in 517 appearances, Jimmy was transferred to Dunfermline for £2,000 in November 1959. His last formal appearance for Hearts had been made at Fir Park a couple of months earlier when he played at centre-forward in a 1–1 draw in a League Cup quarter-final tie.

However, his move over the Forth had caught many a Hearts fan on the hop, so to make sure Jimmy received the proper send-off he deserved, Tommy Walker reunited the 'Terrible Trio' one last time. The occasion was a testimonial match against Raith Rovers for ex-Hearts player George Dobbie. In his time with Hearts, Dobbie had been kept out of action after having a cartilage operation. He recovered well but was subsequently transferred to Raith Rovers where he had the misfortune to break his leg and put an end to his career. Ironically, the leg break happened in a game at Tynecastle.

So on 31 October 1960, Jimmy Wardhaugh took a final bow in his rightful place alongside Willie Bauld and Alfie Conn (who by now was playing for Gala Fairydean). The trio had last played together in Canada in 1958, so the game was a special occasion for all concerned. The game ended in a 2–2 draw with none of the trio getting on the scoresheet, but at least the Edinburgh public had at last had the chance to see them in action one final time.

After two years with Dunfermline, Jimmy finally hung up his boots for good and made the decision to emigrate with his family to Australia. Although the weather there was far better than back in Scotland, the family missed Auld Reekie and, after a year away, the Wardhaughs returned to Scotland. Jimmy became a full-time sports writer with the *Evening News*. He had begun to do this job on a part-time basis during his time at Tynecastle. From the *News* he moved to the *Scottish Daily Express* and then on to the BBC where he worked as a public relations officer. He never lost his love of the Hearts and it was Jimmy who edited the programme (or match-day magazine, as it is now called) in the mid '70s.

Then suddenly, on 2 January 1978, after he had returned home from watching Hearts beat East Fife 2–1 at Methil, Jimmy collapsed and died. His death stunned everyone and the football community mourned the loss of another legend. After a requiem mass in St John the Baptist Church, Corstorphine, Jimmy was laid to rest in Mount Vernon Cemetery on 5 January. On Saturday the 7th there was a minute's silence in Jimmy's honour at Tynecastle before Hearts played Dundee. Poignantly, his eldest daughter, Frances and Willie Bauld junior, whose own father had passed away a few months earlier, occupied his two seats in the stand.

Recently, Jimmy's widow Anne accepted an invitation to represent Jimmy at an evening to mark the fiftieth anniversary of Hearts' Scottish Cup win in 1956. More recently she attended Prestonfield House to be presented with a trophy recognising her husband's enrolment in the Hearts Hall of Fame. She has loaned the many medals Jimmy won to the National Museum of Scotland where they remain on display as a reminder of the genius of 'Twinkletoes'.

Jimmy Murray

Born: Edinburgh, 4 February 1933
Signed: 27 September 1950
Appearances: 33
Goals: 27

As the club embarked on the end-of-season tour to Canada and New York, Jimmy went in the other direction with Scotland to the World Cup in Sweden. He had played in Scotland's two 'warm-up' internationals against Hungary and Poland, so it was no surprise when he was picked to line up against Yugoslavia in the opening game of the section. It didn't take long for Scotland to fall behind, though, to a goal by Aleksandar Petakovic – he had hit the headlines a month earlier, scoring a hat-trick as Yugoslavia drubbed England 5–0 in a pre-World Cup friendly. The early setback didn't deter the Scots and they hit back after half an hour when Jimmy swept the ball past Vladimir Beara – Scotland's first-ever goal in the World Cup final stages.

The draw was the highlight of the tournament for Scotland and Jimmy, as he didn't play in the following game, a 3–2 defeat against Paraguay. He was back for the last game against France but another loss, this time by 2–1, meant that he was on the flight back home by mid June. With him he brought back a piece of Swedish crystal presented by the Swedish FA and a pair of 'revolutionary' new boots presented by Adidas, but, perhaps unsurprisingly, nothing from the SFA to mark not only his participation in the World Cup but his unique goal-scoring achievement.

Back at Tynecastle, and having made the no. 8 jersey his own, Jimmy carried his fine form into the following season and was a mainstay in the side that was pipped for the title by Rangers. The 1958–59 season did see him play in what he describes as the most memorable game of his career, the League Cup final against Partick Thistle. Jimmy's two goals helped Hearts thrash Partick 5–1 to ensure there was at least one trophy at Tynecastle.

With the arrival of Gordon Smith at the start of the '59–60 season, the Hearts forward line went through a few changes, but Jimmy played his part with an impressive strike rate of eleven goals in eighteen league appearances as the championship returned to Gorgie.

The following season was to be Jimmy's last for Hearts and he played his final game in a maroon shirt in a 1–0 victory against Third Lanark (who went on to finish third in the league) on 8 April 1961. For that game at Tynecastle, he turned out in the unfamiliar role of right-half as a disappointing season drew to a close. At that time, Tommy Walker announced that the club were 'willing to listen to offers' for Jimmy.

Alex McRae, the manager of newly promoted Falkirk, saw Jimmy as the ideal man to strengthen the Brockville defence and Jimmy began the 1961–62 season a Bairn. It was not a particularly happy time for Jimmy as he battled away to prevent Falkirk from going straight back down to the Second Division. In the end, the Bairns finished in a respectable position in the league but when Clyde manager John Prentice made an approach in December 1962, Jimmy was happy accept his offer.

Like Falkirk the season earlier, Clyde had been promoted to the top flight but were finding life a bit difficult, so Jimmy was drafted in to help fight the relegation battle. Unfortunately, it was not one they were to win and they went down an agonising two points behind third-bottom Hibernian! Clyde were in the main a part-time outfit and Jimmy had now taken a job as a representative selling domestic appliances, but this did not prevent him helping Clyde make an instant return to Division One. In the following seasons, Clyde consolidated their position in the top league and even finished the '66–67 season in third place behind the Old Firm.

When John Prentice moved from Shawfield to Falkirk, he asked Jimmy to join him as his assistant but although he did go back to Brockville, Jimmy found it difficult to sustain the dual role of playing and managing along with his job with Radiation. So when Raith Rovers manager George Farm invited him to join the club in a playing capacity only, he was happy to accept. However, after a season Jimmy decided to call an end to his playing days.

Back at Tynecastle, though, Bobby Seith saw him as the ideal man to help out with the third team and for a couple of years Jimmy was glad to oblige. Meanwhile, he had also advanced within the sales world and it was with this in mind that he gave up the post with the colts. Jimmy then continued to work with the company (which eventually became known as Creda) and after thirty years was their Scottish manager by the time he decided to retire at sixty.

Today, Jimmy lives in the Corstorphine area (in a house he helped build, incidentally) and is an honorary member of Baberton Golf Club. He enjoys frequent visits to Tynecastle and is a welcome face at many Hearts-related functions.

Willie Bauld

Born: Newcraighall, 24 January 1928
Signed: 1 May 1946
Appearances: 9
Goals: 5

It would seem almost pointless to document what happened to 'The King' after '57–58, as any self-respecting Hearts supporter should already know his story. However, perhaps for the younger readers . . .

Like so many others of the championship-winning side, Willie was part of the League Cup-winning team the following season. He put in an immaculate display and scored two of the five goals that day. In the league, though, he was limited to twenty appearances but he was still prolific in front of goal, scoring fifteen times. In the championship-winning season of 1959–60 he was reduced to seventeen outings, but kept up his impressive scoring average by grabbing ten goals.

The next two seasons saw Willie fall more and more out of the picture at Tynecastle and his appearances in the first team became fewer. Eventually, two weeks before the end of the season, he was told he was being released, so it turned out that he had made his final appearance in a maroon jersey against St Johnstone at Tynecastle six weeks earlier on 3 March 1962. Despite offers to continue his foot-balling career with Queen of the South and teams in Canada and Ireland, Willie had made the decision to hang up his boots forever and concentrated on running his newsagent's shop just a stone's throw from the ground.

The Gorgie faithful did get the opportunity to honour Willie prop-erly a few months later, as he was awarded a testimonial match against Sheffield United on 5 November 1962. A crowd of 18,000 turned out on a miserable Monday evening to see Willie kick his last ball for Hearts when he took to the field, smartly dressed in a suit and trilby hat, to get the game under way.

The game was an entertaining 2–2 draw but Hearts, being the club they were, could not help but spoil the occasion. The gate money was just under £3,000 and, from that, half went to Sheffield United for providing the opposition. To make matters worse, Willie received even less than the visiting club, for in their wisdom the Hearts board of directors deducted the cost of the match ball (£8) from Willie's share. Willie was understandably disappointed at the way he had been treated, having been a 'one-club man' during his whole career, so began a twelve-year spell when he was never seen at Tynecastle. The only opportunity anyone got to see Willie was in his shop on Gorgie Road: many a youngster (your author included) would go in before a game on a Saturday to get their sweets for the match and Willie always had time for them all.

Eventually, in 1975, he was persuaded to come from behind his counter and return to Tynecastle. The game was a Scottish Cup tie against Kilmarnock on 29 January 1975 and his nephew had been chosen as the mascot. Willie's appearance in the directors' box just before kick-off was the signal for Tynecastle to reverberate with the sort of sound that was last heard in Willie's heyday.

Alan Anderson recalls being in the dressing-room that day and hearing the sort of noise he had never heard before. When he emerged from the tunnel, he realised the cause of the furore was Willie still receiving a standing ovation.

In March 1977, Willie attended a function at the Longstone Hearts

Supporters' Club. He took ill, however, and the alarm was raised when newspapers still lay outside his shop at 9 o'clock the following morning. Tragically, William Russell Logan Bauld had passed away in his Slateford Road home on 11 March 1977 at the age of forty-nine.

Thousands stood in silent tribute on the route of the cortege on the way to Warriston Crematorium where over five hundred people waited to pay their last respects. So many people had turned up that the service was relayed by loudspeaker to those unable to get into the main chapel.

Willie was a true Hearts legend and he was among the first to be included in the Hearts Hall of Fame in 2006. Perhaps the most fitting words to complete Willie's profile is the poem entitled 'The Final Tribute' that was printed on the back of the programme for Willie's testimonial match:

> *Our thanks for a' the happy years,*
> *Frae fans baith young and auld,*
> *For a' your skills which earned our cheers,*
> *We thank you, WILLIE BAULD.*

Ian Crawford

Born: Edinburgh, 14 July 1934
Signed: 5 August 1954
Appearances: 25
Goals: 10

Further honours came Ian's way with the League Cup successes in 1958 and 1959 (after he had scored four times in the semi-final against Cowdenbeath) as well as another championship in 1960 when Ian contributed an impressive twelve goals from his eighteen outings.

However, he had become unsettled at Tynecastle and had handed in a couple of transfer requests – but on each occasion he was turned down by the board. However, in November 1960, when the headlines were all about the departure of George Thomson and Alex Young to Everton, the directors decided to grant Ian his wish. This immediately alerted clubs both north and south of the border, with Celtic, Partick Thistle and Ipswich Town all expressing a desire to get Ian to put pen to paper. In the end, nothing materialised and he continued to play his part in what turned out to be a rather disappointing season for the club.

At the end of April and with only one week left in the season, Morton made an offer for both Ian and Andy Bowman but, once again, Ian opted against moving from Tynecastle. Before the start of the following season, though, Hearts accepted a £10,000 offer from West Ham United and with the personal terms being acceptable, Ian moved to London to play alongside the likes of Bobby Moore, Geoff Hurst and Martin Peters.

With Ian on the right wing, the Hammers finished in a respectable eighth place but, despite the fact that he started the following season, he lost his place to Peter Brabrook, who was brought in from a Chelsea side that had been relegated to Division Two the previous season. By February '63, Ian saw his future elsewhere. So when Second Division Scunthorpe United came in for him, he accepted the offer to move to Glanford Park. There he teamed up with soon-to-be Hearts hero Alan Anderson, as Scunthorpe played out the last two months of the season.

His first full season with the Iron was something of a disaster, for they finished rock bottom of the division and were relegated. It was a natural disappointment to Ian and, when he received an offer from recently appointed Peterborough United manager Gordon Clark, he was happy to accept. Here there was yet another Hearts connection, as the Peterborough keeper was none other than his Scottish Cup-winning team mate Willie Duff. Up front, the Posh had a youngster by the name of Derek Dougan and Ian relished the opportunity to supply the crosses for the big centre. The combination was good, but not quite good enough to win promotion, as they just missed out.

By the beginning of the '65–66 season Ian was playing at left-back for the club and it was during this time that they recorded one of their best-ever cup runs. They reached the semi-final of the League

Cup after impressive victories over Newcastle United (4–3), Charlton (4–3), Millwall (4–1) and Burnley (4–0). In the semi they met West Brom but lost 2–1 at the Hawthorns and 4–2 at home.

It was another cup tie the following season that was to cause real problems for the club. Drawn against Sunderland in the fourth round of the FA Cup and with Ian at left-back as usual, Peterborough suffered a 7–1 drubbing. Bad enough – but worse was to follow, as during the next season the FA began an investigation into 'financial irregularities' at the club. By the end of the season, despite finishing in ninth place, they were demoted to Division Four with the game at Sunderland being cited as one in which 'illegal bonuses' were offered to certain players – it was perhaps a harsh punishment considering the scoreline!

After a season in the lower league, Ian decided that he was ready to retire from playing and duly hung up his boots for the final time. The Peterborough manager, Gordon Clark, introduced Ian to Arsenal boss Bertie Mee, who offered him a coaching role with the youth and reserve sides at Highbury. During his spell with the Gunners, Ian helped develop the talents of the likes of Liam Brady, Frank Stapleton and Graham Rix before they broke into the first team.

He ended his time in north London when he received an offer to manage in Norway where he stayed for almost nine years. Like his former colleague Dave Mackay, Ian then moved to the Middle East where he took on various coaching roles in Oman, Kuwait and Saudi Arabia. After six years in the sunshine, the lure of Scandinavia saw him move to Finland where he took over the reins at the club now known as Tampere United. The highlight of his time there was when he managed to take the club into Europe where they were a little unfortunate to be drawn against AS Roma, but did gain a creditable 1–1 draw at home before going down in Rome.

After almost eight years in the land of the midnight sun, Ian decided to retire from the game. He never lost his affection for Finland and divided his retirement years between his homes there and in Peterborough. He also made regular trips back 'home' to Edinburgh and it was on one of these visits that he attended the Hall of Fame dinner in early November 2007. At the event he presented an award to Jimmy Wardhaugh's widow Anne, and announced his intentions to move back to Edinburgh on a permanent basis. Tragically, Ian never got to realise his ambition as he passed away in his sleep on the 30th November. However, he did get to return *home* when on 18th July 2008, after a moving ceremony attended by family and friends, Ian's ashes were scattered over the pitch at Tynecastle Park.

Ian will always be remembered with the Hearts community – not least for his two goals against Celtic in the '56 cup final.

THE MANAGEMENT

Tommy Walker OBE

Tommy continued his managerial role for a period that saw the club narrowly fail to retain the championship, losing out to Rangers by only two points the following season. Compensation did come in the shape of another League Cup victory, of course.

Despite the loss of 'greats' such as Dave Mackay, Freddie Glidden, Alfie Conn and Jimmy Wardhaugh, by the end of the '59–60 season the club had retained the League Cup and the league flag once again flew over Tynecastle. Gordon Smith had been recruited from across the city and, with Billy Higgins settling into the half-back line, it looked as if once again Tommy Walker had moulded the next generation of great Hearts teams.

However, season '60–61 saw further changes to the side, both George Thomson and Alex Young surprisingly being allowed by the board to leave for Everton. Their loss was a blow, as the results showed: eighth place in the league, failure to qualify from the group stages of the League Cup and a quarter-final exit from the Scottish Cup were not what Hearts fans had come to expect.

The following season was not much better as Tommy continued with the changes to the team. Only a defeat to Rangers after a replay in the League Cup final could be called a 'highlight'. Hearts meanwhile trailed champions Dundee (and Gordon Smith) in sixth place in the League. During the '62–63 campaign, Tommy masterminded another League Cup triumph but the results in the league were mixed and the club finished in fifth place, fourteen points behind champions Rangers. The indifferent league form was continued into the next season, but this time there was no cup triumph to compensate (Motherwell ended Hearts' interest in both the League and Scottish Cups).

It was beginning to look as if Tommy had lost the 'magic' when Hearts again failed to qualify from their League Cup section in 1964. However, a thrilling 5–3 win over Hibs on the opening day of the league campaign raised everyone's hopes. They remained unbeaten for fourteen games before going down 3–1 to fellow title challengers Kilmarnock at Rugby Park. The new year started badly, with defeats to Hibs (1–0) and Dunfermline (3–2), but manager Walker got the team back on track as the team opened up a three-point advantage over second-place Kilmarnock. A thumping 7–1 loss to Dundee at Tynecastle saw the wheels come off the barrow a bit but by the last day of the season Hearts were still two points ahead of Killie and had home advantage over the Ayrshire side as the top two clashed. When Kilmarnock secured the required 2–0 win to pip Hearts to the title in the cruellest of manners, it proved to be the beginning of the end for Tommy Walker as Hearts manager.

He oversaw the next season but there was 'significant unrest' amongst the players, with the club having to deal with transfer requests from the likes of Jim Cruickshank, Willie Wallace, Billy Higgins and Alan Gordon. Hearts had finished in their worst league position for years and the start to the '66–67 season was not promising. On 28 September, Tommy Walker announced that he had resigned as manager, the truth of the matter being that the then chairman Bill Lindsay had told him the board were going to consider ending his time as manager 'in the best interests of the club'. Tommy took the dignified way out and ended his long association with Heart of Midlothian.

Dunfermline were not slow to utilise Tommy's vast experience and offered him an administrative role. But he was not there for long before near neighbours Raith Rovers appointed him as their manager in 1967, George Farm having vacated the post to travel in the opposite direction to take over at East End Park.

Tommy's reign at Stark's Park got off to the worst possible of starts when Raith suffered at the hands of Notts County in a pre-season friendly. The 5–1 scoreline was bad enough but perhaps the biggest loss was key player Willie Polland, who broke his leg in the game. Without the influential Polland, Raith struggled in the league and by Christmas they were real relegation candidates. The following month, in a move that mirrored the sale of Dave Mackay by Hearts years earlier, the club accepted an offer of £45,000 from Sunderland for Iain Porterfield, who had been the one success story of the season so far.

Despite the loss of Porterfield, Tommy managed to turn around the club's fortunes. Willie Polland had recovered from his injury and Gordon Wallace started to emulate the scoring feats of another Wallace who'd played for Raith a few years earlier, the Hearts hero, Willie. With both players at the top of their form, Raith eventually amassed twenty-five points – avoiding relegation by six points and finishing only five points behind Hearts!

The Rovers started their '68–69 campaign in reasonable form but the turning-point to their season came when, leading 4–0 at Rugby Park, they were left holding on for a 4–4 draw. Results started to go against them after that and, when they made a first-round Scottish Cup exit to local rivals Dunfermline, Tommy resigned his managerial duties to be replaced by ex-Rangers man Jimmy Millar. It didn't mean the end of Tommy's association with Raith, though, as he was offered – and more than happy to accept – a place on the board plus the role of club secretary.

By 1974, he was also working with the Scottish Education Examination Board when Hearts invited him to join the board at Tynecastle. The opportunity had arisen following the resignation of Bob Taylor, due to ill health. Bobby Parker was the chairman at the time so was well aware of Tommy's qualities and, with it being the club's centenary year, he appeared to be the obvious candidate.

However, all was not well at all levels of the club, so when Hearts were relegated for the first time in their history in 1977, the directors all came in for severe criticism. Although it could not have been the happiest of times for Tommy, he continued to work tirelessly for the club. By 1980 he was considering retirement and the following year he ended his time at Hearts for the final time when he resigned from the board on 23 May.

In the years that followed, Tommy spent the time quietly with his family and took an active part in the work of the St George's West church. He only made the occasional visit back to Tynecastle before passing away on 11 January 1993. Tommy's contribution to the rich history of the club both as a player and manager were rightly recognised in November 2007 when his name joined other legends in the club's Hall of Fame.

Johnny Harvey

Johnny continued to coach the first team with great success during the next eight seasons, before being appointed as manager following Tommy Walker's resignation in 1966. It is fair to say that he was something of a reluctant team manager, preferring a more hands-on coaching role. His first few seasons in charge did not produce any success, with Hearts finishing in the mid to lower half of the table. However, he did manage to guide the side to the Scottish Cup final in 1968 – only to be thwarted by Dunfermline.

Jock Wallace was brought in from Berwick Rangers as an assistant to Johnny and Hearts' form showed signs of improving over the next two seasons. It looked like Jock would become the natural successor to John in the not-too-distant future but before the move could take place, Rangers stepped in to appoint him as chief coach under Willie Waddell.

Despite wanting to step down, Johnny remained in charge at the start of the 1970–71 campaign. Unfortunately, the team got off to the worst possible start and finished bottom below Celtic, Dundee United and Clyde in their League Cup section. Things were no better in the league and in December, with his health causing him problems, John gladly passed the reins to Bobby Seith. It was not the end of his association with the club, though, as he reverted back to his favoured role of coach with the club's youngsters.

Later, Johnny moved from the coaching role to take up the post of chief scout, which suited him better as he lived quietly with his wife, Bunty, in Musselburgh. In January 1977 Johnny's health deteriorated and he was taken into the Eastern General hospital where he tragically passed away two months later on 16 March, only four days after the death of Willie Bauld.

Inside a week the Hearts community had lost two massive figures from the glory years of the '50s. Although 'King Willie' had played only a small part in the league success in 1957–58, the influence of Johnny Harvey had been integral and he should be remembered accordingly.

APPENDIX

STATISTICS OF THE GREATEST SEASON EVER

A. HEARTS' RESULTS, SEASON 1957–58

Date	Venue	Opponents	Competition	Score	Scorers
10/08/57	a	Kilmarnock	LC	1–2	Wardhaugh
14/08/57	h	Queen's Park	LC	9–2	Wardhaugh (3), Bauld (2), Crawford (2), Conn, Hamilton
17/08/57	a	Dundee*	LC	0–0	–
20/08/57	a	Dundee	LC	2–2	Wardhaugh Bauld
24/08/57	h	Kilmarnock	LC	1–1	Wardhaugh
28/08/57	a	Queen's Park	LC	0–0	–
31/08/57	h	Dundee	LC	4–2	Bauld (2), Kirk (pen), Wardhaugh
07/09/57	h	Dundee	L	6–0	Murray, Bauld, Crawford (2), Kirk (pen), Wardhaugh
14/09/57	a	Airdrieonians	L	7–2	Murray, Wardhaugh (3), Crawford (2), Kirk (pen)

21/09/57	h	Hibernian	L	3–1	Wardhaugh, Crawford, Murray
05/10/57	h	East Fife	L	9–0	Bauld (2), Mackay, Wardhaugh (3), Cumming, Young, Murray
07/10/57	h	Hibernian	F	2–4	Bauld, Wardhaugh
12/10/57	a	Third Lanark	L	0–0	–
14/10/57	a	Bolton Wanderers	F	1–1	Wardhaugh
19/10/57	h	Aberdeen	L	4–0	Murray (2), Young, Blackwood
26/10/57	a	Rangers	L	3–2	Wardhaugh, Bauld, Young
30/10/57	a	Norwich City	F	4–3	Wardhaugh (2), Murray, Young
02/11/57	h	Motherwell	L	2–2	Wardhaugh (2)
04/11/57	h	Manchester City	F	3–5	Murray (2), Bauld
09/11/57	a	Queen of the South	L	4–1	Murray (2), Cumming, Young
11/11/57	a	Partick Thistle	L	3–1	Young, Cumming, Wardhaugh
16/11/57	h	Queen's Park	L	8–0	Young (3), Mackay, Wardhaugh, Cumming (2), Paton

20/11/57	h	Newcastle United	F	2–2	Cumming, Wardhaugh
23/11/57	a	Clyde	L	1–2	Bauld
27/11/57	a	Newcastle United	F	0–2	–
30/11/57	h	Falkirk ·	L	9–1	Mackay (3 [1 pen]), Wardhaugh, Young (4), Murray
02/12/57	h	British Army	F	3–5	Conn, Mackay, Wardhaugh
07/12/57	a	Raith Rovers	L	3–0	Wardhaugh (2), Murray
14/12/57	h	Kilmarnock	L	2–1	Mackay, Wardhaugh
21/12/57	h	St Mirren	L	5–1	Murray (2), Young, Wardhaugh, Mackay
28/12/57	a	Celtic	L	2–0	Wardhaugh, Young
01/01/58	a	Hibernian	L	2–0	Young, Mackay
02/01/58	h	Airdrieonians	L	4–0	Murray (3), Mackay (pen)
04/01/58	a	Dundee	L	5–0	Wardhaugh (3 [1 pen]), Murray, Mackay
11/01/58	h	Partick Thistle	L	3–1	Murray, Mackay, Wardhaugh, Blackwood
18/01/58	a	East Fife	L	3–0	Young, Hamilton (2)

265

25/01/58	h	Third Lanark	L	7–2	Young, Blackwood, Murray (2), Hamilton (2), Milne (pen)
01/02/58	a	East Fife	SC	2–1	Murray, Blackwood
15/02/58	h	Albion Rovers	SC	4–1	Young (2), Blackwood, Wardhaugh
22/02/58	a	Motherwell	L	4–0	Conn (2), Milne (pen), Murray
01/03/58	h	Hibernian	SC	3–4	Hamilton, Wardhaugh, Murray
03/03/58	h	Scotland	F	3–2	Young, Hamilton, Mackay
08/03/58	a	Queen's Park	L	4–1	Conn (2), Young, Mackay
10/03/58	h	Queen of the South	L	3–1	Murray, OG, Milne (pen)
14/03/58	h	Celtic	L	5–3	Crawford (2), Blackwood, Murray (2)
19/03/58	h	Clyde	L	2–2	Crawford, Young
22/03/58	a	Falkirk	L	4–0	Murray (2), Crawford, Young
29/03/58	h	Raith Rovers	L	4–1	Murray (2), Wardhaugh, Young

05/04/58	a	Kilmarnock	L	1–1	Bowman
12/04/58	a	St Mirren	L	3–2	Young (2), Wardhaugh
16/04/58	a	Aberdeen	L	4–0	Crawford, Wardhaugh, Young, Bowman
23/04/58	h	British Army	F	3–1	Crawford (pen), Murray, Young
30/04/58	h	Rangers	L	2–1	Wardhaugh (2)

* *game abandoned*

B. MISSED PENALTIES

Bauld, v Dundee, 20/08/57
Crawford, v Kilmarnock, 24/08/57
Kirk, v Rangers, 28/10/57
Mackay, v Queen's Park, 16/11/57
Mackay, v Partick, 11/01/58
Milne, v Queen of the South, 10/03/58
Milne, v Celtic, 14/03/58

C. 0–9 LEAGUE GOALS

9   East Fife, Falkirk
8   Queen's Park
7   Airdrie, Third Lanark
6   Dundee
5   St Mirren, Dundee, Celtic
4   Aberdeen (twice), Queen of the South, Airdrie, Partick Thistle, Motherwell, Queen's Park, Falkirk, Raith Rovers
3   Hibs, Rangers, Partick Thistle, Raith Rovers, East Fife, Queen of the South, St Mirren

2   Motherwell, Kilmarnock, Celtic, Hibs, Clyde, Rangers
1   Clyde, Kilmarnock
0   Third Lanark

D. HEARTS 'A' TEAM RESULTS, SEASON 1957–58

Date	Venue	Opponents	Competition	Score	Scorers
10/08/57	h	Kilmarnock	LC	1–0	Young
14/08/57	a	Queen's Park	LC	3–1	McFadzean (2), Dobbie
17/08/57	h	Dundee	LC	5–0	Young (4), Murray
24/08/57	a	Kilmarnock	LC	4–2	Murray (2), Howieson, Finlay
28/08/57	h	Queen's Park	LC	2–0	Paton, Goldie
31/08/57	a	Dundee	LC	1–1	OG
07/09/57	a	Dundee 2nd XI	SC	2–1	Goldie, Paton
09/09/57	a	Dunbar United	F	1–2	Blackwood
14/09/57	h	Airdrie	L	7–1	Paton, Blackwood (3), Campbell (2), Goldie
23/09/57	a	Hibs	L	2–0	Hamilton, Thomson G.
28/09/57	h	Partick Thistle	L	4–0	Paton, Finlay, Blackwood, Thomson G.
12/10/57	h	Third Lanark	L	9–2	Campbell (3), Paton, OG, Milne (pen), Conn (2), Finlay

19/10/57	a	Aberdeen	L	0–0	–
25/10/57	h	Rangers	L	2–1	Goldie, Conn
02/11/57	a	Motherwell	L	4–2	Paton, Hamilton, Goldie (2)
09/11/57	h	Queen of the South	L	1–1	Goldie
16/11/57	a	Queen's Park	L	4–0	Goldie (2), Milne (pen), Finlay
18/11/57	a	Motherwell 2nd XI	SC	1–1	Crawford
22/11/57	h	Clyde	L	0–0	–
30/11/57	a	Falkirk	L	1–2	Howieson
06/12/57	h	Raith Rovers	L	4–3	Dobbie, Hamilton (pen), Howieson (2)
14/12/57	a	Kilmarnock	L	2–0	McFadzean, Conn
21/12/57	a	St Mirren	L	1–0	Dobbie
27/12/57	h	Celtic	L	3–3	Paton, Hamilton (pen), Conn
30/12/57	h	Hibs	L	3–2	Hamilton, McFadzean, Paton
04/01/58	h	Dundee	L	2–1	Howieson (2)
14/01/58	a	Partick Thistle	L	4–1	Hamilton, Conn, Campbell, Howieson
18/01/58	h	East Fife	L	6–3	Howieson (2), Smith (2), Conn (2)
27/01/58	h	Motherwell 2nd XI	SC (R)	1–2	Crawford
15/02/58	a	Rangers	L	1–4	Goldie

22/02/58	h	Motherwell	L	4–1	Crawford (3), McFadzean
01/03/58	a	Queen of the South	L	4–2	Smith (2), Campbell, Finlay
08/03/58	h	Queen's Park	L	5–0	Smith (2), Wardhaugh (2), Bauld
17/03/58	a	Airdrie	L	1–1	Paton
19/03/58	a	Clyde	L	1–6	Goldie
22/03/58	h	Falkirk	L	4–1	Bauld (2), Finlay, Paton
29/03/58	a	Raith Rovers	L	4–2	Hamilton, Conn, Bauld (2)
02/04/58	a	Rangers 2nd XI	LC	3–3	Higgins, Paton, Hamilton
07/04/58	h	Kilmarnock	L	1–0	Paton
12/04/58	h	St Mirren	L	5–2	Smith (2), Conn, Bauld (2)
14/04/58	h	Rangers 2nd XI	LC	1–0	Smith
16/04/58	h	Aberdeen	L	2–2	Bauld, Goldie
18/04/58	a	Dundee	L	1–1	Paton
25/04/58	a	Celtic	L	1–1	Smith
28/04/58	a	Third Lanark	L	0–5	–
30/04/58	a	East Fife	L	0–1	–
07/05/58	a	Aberdeen 2nd XI	LC	2–1	Bauld, Paton
10/05/58	h	Aberdeen 2nd XI	LC	1–3	Hamilton

E. RESERVE LEAGUE FINAL PLACINGS

	Played	Won	Lost	Drawn	For	Against	Points
Hearts	**34**	**21**	**5**	**8**	**93**	**51**	**50**
Aberdeen	34	19	8	7	73	46	45
Kilmarnock	34	18	8	8	86	53	44
Rangers	34	17	10	7	76	53	41
Celtic	34	17	10	7	54	41	41
Hibs	34	17	11	6	76	63	40
Clyde	34	16	10	8	65	38	40
Partick Thistle	34	16	12	6	71	53	38
Dundee	34	15	12	7	65	49	37
East Fife	34	13	13	8	50	65	34
Third Lanark	34	12	17	5	64	75	29
Motherwell	34	13	19	2	67	67	28
Falkirk	34	11	19	4	54	83	26
St Mirren	34	11	19	4	55	84	26
Queen of the South	34	11	20	3	46	81	25
Airdrie	34	9	21	4	52	85	22
Raith Rovers	34	5	20	9	43	71	19
Queen's Park	34	5	25	4	41	91	14